ASIA BOND MONITOR
NOVEMBER 2020

ASIAN DEVELOPMENT BANK

ADB

© 2020 Asian Development Bank
6 ADB Avenue, Mandaluyong City, 1550 Metro Manila, Philippines
Tel +63 2 8632 4444; Fax +63 2 8636 2444
www.adb.org

Some rights reserved. Published in 2020.
Printed in the Philippines.

ISBN 978-92-9262-501-6 (print), 978-92-9262-502-3 (electronic), 978-92-9262-503-0 (ebook)
ISSN 2219-1518 (print), 2219-1526 (electronic)
Publication Stock No. SPR200321-2
DOI: http://dx.doi.org/10.22617/SPR200321-2

The views expressed in this publication are those of the authors and do not necessarily reflect the views and policies of the Asian Development Bank (ADB) or its Board of Governors or the governments they represent.

ADB does not guarantee the accuracy of the data included in this publication and accepts no responsibility for any consequence of their use. The mention of specific companies or products of manufacturers does not imply that they are endorsed or recommended by ADB in preference to others of a similar nature that are not mentioned.

By making any designation of or reference to a particular territory or geographic area, or by using the term "country" in this document, ADB does not intend to make any judgments as to the legal or other status of any territory or area.

Corrigenda to ADB publications may be found at http://www.adb.org/publications/corrigenda.

Note:
ADB recognizes "Hong Kong" and "Hongkong" as Hong Kong, China; "China" as the People's Republic of China; "Korea" as the Republic of Korea; "Siam" as Thailand; "Vietnam" as Viet Nam; and "Saigon" as Ho Chi Minh City.

Cover design by Erickson Mercado.

Contents

Emerging East Asian Local Currency Bond Markets: A Regional Update

Highlights

Key Trends

- Financial conditions recovered in emerging East Asian markets from 31 August to 6 November.[1] Investor sentiment improved during the review period amid economic recovery in major advanced economies in the third quarter. However, risks remained tilted to the downside amid a resurgence of the coronavirus disease (COVID-19) in major advanced economies and uncertainty about the trajectory of the global economic recovery.
- Between 31 August and 6 November, 2-year local currency (LCY) government bond yields fell in most emerging East Asian markets as central banks maintained an accommodative monetary stance in response to weak economic outlooks. Meanwhile, 10-year bond yields showed a mixed pattern, tracking market-specific conditions.
- Most regional equity markets rose and regional currencies strengthened during the review period. Credit default swap spreads also narrowed. Regional LCY bond markets experienced net foreign fund inflows in the third quarter of 2020. Net inflows were also observed in equities markets in early November.
- Emerging East Asia's LCY bond market expanded to USD18.7 trillion at the end of September on growth of 4.8% quarter-on-quarter and 17.4% year-on-year in the third quarter of 2020. Growth was largely driven by the increased financing needs of both the public and private sectors due to the pandemic. Government bonds comprised 61.6% of the region's total LCY bonds outstanding at the end of September.

Risks to Financial Stability

- Risks remain tilted to the downside. The overriding risk is the ongoing COVID-19 pandemic, which may last longer than initially forecast.
- Other risks include ongoing tensions between the People's Republic of China and the United States, and heightened social unrest resulting from the economic impact of COVID-19.

Special Section: Financing a Sustainable Recovery

- This issue of the *Asia Bond Monitor* includes a special section with discussion boxes on how green and social finance can contribute to a sustainable economic recovery from the COVID-19 pandemic.
- The first discussion box reviews existing knowledge on how various environmental and social challenges hamper economic growth.
- Another box reviews the development of green and social finance during the COVID-19 pandemic.
- A third box outlines why externalities matter for the financial sector, covering topics such as reduced systematic and idiosyncratic risks, client demands and fund flow concerns, hedging for climate-related risks, and social pressure.
- A fourth box discusses the economic effects of green and social finance.

---

[1] Emerging East Asia comprises the People's Republic of China; Hong Kong, China; Indonesia; the Republic of Korea; Malaysia; the Philippines; Singapore; Thailand; and Viet Nam.

Theme Chapter: Bank Efficiency and Bond Markets—Evidence from Asia and the Pacific

- The theme chapter investigates the link between bond market development and the profit and cost efficiencies of banks. The bond market is relevant for different aspects of banking sector operations. On the one hand, government bonds offer alternative risk-free assets for depositors and thus compete with bank deposits, while corporate bonds serve as an alternative direct financing instrument to bank loans for high-quality clients. On the other hand, government bonds serve as a liquidity management instrument to shorten the maturity profile of asset portfolios, while corporate bonds serve as a financing instrument that allow banks to tap longer-term funding.
- This study finds that banks consistently become more profit-efficient but less cost-efficient in economies with relatively more developed bond markets. Results also show that the structure of the bond market has an impact on bank efficiency.
- The study highlights the important role of well-functioning and balanced bond markets in financing economic development.

Executive Summary

Financial conditions in emerging East Asia strengthened from 31 August to 6 November.[1] Global investment sentiment showed improvement on the back of economic recoveries in major advanced economies in the third quarter (Q3) of 2020. However, risks remain tilted to the downside amid a recent spike in coronavirus disease (COVID-19) cases in advanced economies and lingering uncertainty about the trajectory of the global economic recovery.

Between 31 August and 6 November, local currency (LCY) government bond yields in most emerging East Asian markets fell at the shorter-end of the curve, while 10-year yields showed a mixed pattern across the region.

Improved investment sentiment was evident in the gains in most regional equities markets, strengthening of regional currencies, and declines in risk premiums. The positive sentiment was also visible in foreign portfolio inflows into regional bond markets in Q3 2020 and into some equity markets in early November.

Due to uncertainty over the trajectory of the pandemic, downside risks weigh heavily on the global economic outlook. Above all, COVID-19 remains the overriding downside risk for the world and the region. Other downside risks include ongoing tensions between the People's Republic of China and the United States, and domestic political and social instability in some economies.

Local currency bonds outstanding in emerging East Asia expanded to USD18.7 trillion at the end of September.

The size of emerging East Asia's LCY bond market climbed to USD18.7 trillion at the end of September. Growth moderated to 4.8% quarter-on-quarter (q-o-q) in Q3 2020 from 5.0% q-o-q in the second quarter. On a year-on-year (y-o-y) basis, growth accelerated to 17.4% in Q3 2020 from 15.5% in the prior quarter.

Government bonds outstanding continued to dominate the region's LCY bond market, totaling USD11.5 trillion at the end of September and representing a 61.6% share of the total bond stock. Corporate bonds summed to USD7.2 trillion and accounted for the remaining 38.4% share.

The People's Republic of China led the region in terms of LCY bond market size, representing a 77.5% share of the region's aggregate bond stock at the end of September. The Republic of Korea accounted for an 11.9% share, and member economies of the Association of Southeast Asian Nations (ASEAN) had a combined 9.0% share.[2]

Emerging East Asia's LCY bond market as a share of the region's gross domestic product increased to 95.6% at the end of September from 91.6% at the end of June. The rising share of bonds outstanding to gross domestic product was due to regional governments' increased financing needs to combat the adverse effect of the COVID-19 pandemic.

In Q3 2020, LCY bond issuance totaled USD2.2 trillion on growth of 6.4% q-o-q and 39.8% y-o-y. Growth was largely driven by government bonds, which rose 11.4% q-o-q and 51.8% y-o-y. On the other hand, issuance of corporate bonds marginally contracted by 0.6% on a q-o-q basis but was up 24.3% y-o-y.

The November issue of the *Asia Bond Monitor* includes four special discussion boxes. Three boxes analyze the impact of COVID-19 on the regional economy and its financial markets, and one box reviews the role of LCY bond financing amid exchange rate volatility. Also included in this issue is a special section on financing sustainable development, which presents four boxes on how sustainable finance can contribute to green and inclusive development in the post-COVID-19 era and a theme chapter on bank efficiency and bond market development.

---

[1] Emerging East Asia comprises the People's Republic of China; Hong Kong, China; Indonesia; the Republic of Korea; Malaysia; the Philippines; Singapore; Thailand; and Viet Nam.
[2] LCY bond statistics for the Association of Southeast Asian Nations include the markets of Indonesia, Malaysia, the Philippines, Singapore, Thailand, and Viet Nam.

Box 1: Global Financial Markets and Capital Flows: COVID-19 Impacts and Policy Responses

This box examines the impact of COVID-19 on global financial markets and capital flow dynamics. Data show that the pandemic has had a big impact on sovereign bond yields in both advanced economies and emerging market economies (EMEs). The impact was more pronounced across financial markets in EMEs. Fiscal stimulus and monetary policy easing had a bigger effect on sovereign bond yields and stock prices in advanced economies, with spillover effects in EMEs. Despite capital outflows from EMEs in the initial stages of the pandemic, policy measures were effective in restoring confidence, which led to net inflows into EME equities and bond markets in Q3 2020. This points to the need for EMEs to strengthen policy measures to address financial market volatility and manage capital flows.

Box 2: The Effect of COVID-19 on Financial Stability in ASEAN

ASEAN's relatively high level of globalization and financial openness suggests that COVID-19 will adversely affect the region's economic growth and financial stability. The region suffered during the 1997/98 Asian financial crisis and, to a limited extent, during the 2007–2009 global financial crisis. In 2020, expansionary monetary policies and fiscal stimulus packages have contributed to the restoration of financial stability in ASEAN. In addition to domestic policy measures, regional financial safety nets such as the Chiang Mai Initiative Multilateralization and the ASEAN Disaster Risk Financing and Insurance scheme can also mitigate financial turbulence. Policy recommendations in the context of regional cooperation that can reduce the negative economic impact of the pandemic include (i) establishing an ASEAN task force on pandemics to facilitate the coordination and alignment of policy responses among member economies, (ii) building-up an ASEAN pandemic network to share information and knowledge on health care, and (iii) strengthening regional financial safety nets.

Box 3: Local Currency Bond Markets and Exchange Rate Risks

The 1997/98 Asian financial crisis underlined the importance of developing LCY bond markets to boost financial resilience. LCY bond markets mobilize private sector savings and channel them into long-term investments. They also mitigate currency and maturity mismatches on the balance sheets of public and private institutions. This discussion box shows that LCY bond markets serve as useful financing instruments in emerging markets during periods of exchange rate volatility by lowering possible exchange rate risk exposure among financing entities. The impact of COVID-19 has demonstrated the importance of developing deep and balanced LCY bond markets to boost financial sector resilience.

Box 4: The Duration of Recoveries from Economic Shocks Like COVID-19

It will take some time before the global economy recovers from the COVID-19 pandemic. Analysis of past economic downturns finds that it takes about 4 years for economic output and 3 years for employment to recover from such an impactful event. The severity of the recession, presence of a financial crisis, and depth of supply and demand shocks are all significant factors that affect the time to recovery. In addition, trade openness contributes to a faster recovery.

Special Section: Financing a Sustainable Recovery

Box 5: Environmental and Social Externalities and Economic Growth and Development

The 2016 Paris Agreement reflected the international community's recognition of the disastrous effects of climate change and environmental destruction, and the global commitment to take action to achieve the United Nations Sustainable Development Goals. Rapid environmental pollution has been linked to climate change; hence, a virtuous or a vicious cycle can ensue between a country's environmental state and its economic growth. Social development can also contribute to sustainable economic growth. Investment in areas such as education, sanitation, health care, gender equality, and affordable housing fosters social development, which in turn promotes economic development and inclusive growth that reaches vulnerable groups. Economy-level evidence points to a significant and positive impact of improved environmental, social, and governance policies on economic growth when adopting sustainable and socially responsible practices. The nexus between environmental and social factors on one hand and economic growth on the other is the blueprint for sustainable development in the future.

Box 6: Development of Green and Social Finance in Developing Asia amid the COVID-19 Pandemic

The economies of Asia and the Pacific need to invest USD1.5 trillion annually from 2016 to 2030 to achieve the United Nations Sustainable Development Goals.[3] The COVID-19 pandemic has heightened awareness of the need to support vulnerable groups and improve public health and sanitation. Amid declining tax revenue and increased spending to fight the pandemic, the public sector is facing greater constraints to financing such huge demands. Thus, the region needs to leverage and mobilize more resources from the private sector to finance investment and promote sustainable development that reduces poverty, benefits vulnerable groups, and decreases inequality. Around the world, a growing awareness of social finance has been observed in 2020, as evident in the rapid growth in social bond issuance and large-scale COVID-19 bond financing. Developing Asia is actively utilizing financial markets to finance social investments, with its social bond issuance ranked second among different regions of the world.[4] Social and green finance will support environmentally sound and inclusive post-COVID-19 growth in developing Asia.

Box 7: Why Environmental and Social Externalities Matter for Financial Markets

This box reviews extant knowledge on why environmental and social externalities matter for the financial sector and investors. Practicing social responsibility provides social capital to hedge against systematic and idiosyncratic risks, and against environmental and social shocks as well as related regulatory risks. Delivering positive social and environmental impacts can also match stakeholder preferences and contribute to meeting funding needs.

Box 8: Economic Consequences of Green and Social Finance

Green and social finance mobilizes funding resources for investments with environmental and social impacts. Besides generating positive externalities, green and social finance also delivers economic benefits. This box reviews the economic benefits of green and social finance such as reduced financing costs, a broadened investor base, higher company valuations, and greater innovation. There is also evidence showing that a shift to green operation creates more jobs.

Theme Chapter: Bank Efficiency and Bond Markets—Evidence from Asia and the Pacific

The theme chapter investigates the link between bond market development and the profit and cost efficiencies of banks. The bond market is relevant for different aspects of banking sector operations. On the one hand, government bonds offer alternative risk-free assets for depositors and thus compete with bank deposits, while corporate bonds serve as an alternative direct financing instrument to bank loans for high-quality clients. On the other hand, government bonds serve as a liquidity management instrument to shorten the maturity profile of asset portfolios, while corporate bonds serve as a financing instrument that allow banks to tap longer-term funding. This study finds that banks consistently become more profit-efficient but less cost-efficient in economies with relatively more developed bond markets. Results also show that the structure of the bond market has an impact on bank efficiency. The study highlights the important role of well-functioning and balanced bond markets in financing economic development.

---

[3]   Based on estimates of the United Nations Economic and Social Commission for Asia and the Pacific.
[4]   Developing Asia refers to the 36 developing member economies of the Asian Development Bank.

Global and Regional Market Developments

Yields for 2-year local currency (LCY) government bonds declined in most emerging East Asian economies between 31 August and 6 November, while 10-year bond yield movements were mixed due to individual market differences.[1] Global financial conditions improved during the review period as investment sentiment was boosted by the enhanced performance of key advanced economies in the third quarter (Q3) of 2020. However, some caution remained as confirmed coronavirus disease (COVID-19) cases rose in many advanced economies and uncertainty about the global economic recovery lingered.

Between 31 August and 6 November, 2-year and 10-year bond yields rose in the United States (US) and declined in other developed economies (**Figure A**). In the US, 2-year and 10-year government bond yields rose by 2 basis points (bps) and 11 bps, respectively. The uptick in yields was largely due to expectations of a new phase of spending on pandemic relief despite uncertainty regarding the timing and size of the stimulus package following the US election.

While the Federal Reserve noted that the US economy showed signs of recovery during Q3 2020 and left monetary policy unchanged at its September meeting, it also acknowledged uncertainty regarding the impact of COVID-19. US economic data have been mixed. Retail sales growth contracted to 0.6% month-on-month in October from 1.6% month-on-month in September, and the unemployment rate fell to 6.9% in October from 7.9% in September. Gains in nonfarm payrolls, however, declined to 672,000 in September and 638,000 in October from 1.5 million in August.

The Federal Reserve also upgraded its 2020 gross domestic product (GDP) growth forecast to –3.7% in September from –6.5% in June, and it revised downward the GDP growth forecasts for 2021 and 2022 from 5.0% and 3.5%, respectively, to 4.0% and 3.0%.

At the press conference following the Federal Reserve meeting, Chairman Jerome Powell indicated that it

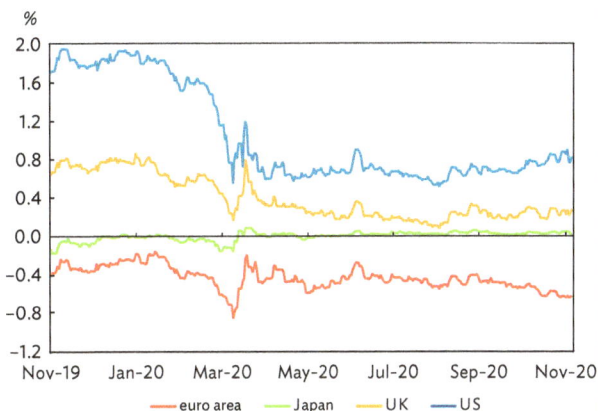

Figure A: 10-Year Government Bond Yields in Major Advanced Economies (% per annum)

UK = United Kingdom, US = United States.
Note: Data as of 6 November 2020.
Source: Bloomberg LP.

would take time for the US economy to return to its pre-COVID-19 output level and that additional fiscal support would be required. The Federal Reserve subsequently also left its monetary policy stance unchanged during its 4–5 November meeting.

In line with the Federal Reserve, the European Central Bank (ECB) left its monetary policy unchanged at its monetary policy meeting on 10 September. The ECB also noted some improvement in economic performance in the euro area, but remained cautious over uncertainty associated with COVID-19. The ECB's forecast for 2020 GDP growth was revised upward to –8.0% in September from –8.7% in June, while the 2021 and 2022 GDP forecasts were lowered slightly to 5.0% and 3.2%, respectively, from 5.2% and 3.3%. The euro area's economic recovery remained weak, as industrial production declined 6.8% year-on-year (y-o-y) in September and fell 6.7% y-o-y in August. The recent rise in COVID-19 cases in the euro area also heightened uncertainty over the economic recovery, while expectations of further monetary easing pulled bond yields down in the euro area.

---

[1] Emerging East Asia comprises the People's Republic of China; Hong Kong, China; Indonesia; the Republic of Korea; Malaysia; the Philippines; Singapore; Thailand; and Viet Nam.

In line with the ECB's forecasts, the euro area's GDP growth improved in Q3 2020, with GDP expanding 12.6% quarter-on-quarter (q-o-q) in Q3 2020 after declining 11.8% q-o-q in the prior quarter. However, on a y-o-y basis, GDP growth was negative at –4.4% in Q3 2020, which was still an improvement from a decline of –14.8% posted in the second quarter (Q2) of 2020.

During its 29 October monetary policy meeting, the ECB again left its monetary policy unchanged. However, the ECB noted that rising COVID-19 cases were dampening growth and initial data suggested that fourth quarter growth would be weaker. The ECB also hinted that it might ease monetary policy in December when its economic forecasts are updated.

The Bank of Japan (BOJ) also left its monetary policy unchanged at its monetary policy meeting on 17 September. While the BOJ noted some gains in the domestic economy's performance, the recovery is considered to be delicate. Japan's 2-year and 10-year yields marginally fell 1 bp each, despite expectations of expanded stimulus that could increase the debt supply to fund spending. The BOJ again left its monetary policy unchanged on 29 October. Updated economic forecasts from the BOJ showed a downgrade in 2020 GDP growth to –5.8% from –4.7% in July. The GDP forecast for 2021 was adjusted upward to 3.6% from 3.3%. However, the

BOJ noted that the forecasts were highly uncertain given the impact of COVID-19. Japan posted an annualized quarterly GDP growth of 21.4% in Q3 2020 from –28.8% in Q2 2020. However, concerns that the gains may not be sustained led to Prime Minister Yoshihide Suga to call for a third extra budget.

Between 31 August and 6 November, yields on 2-year government bonds fell in most emerging East Asian markets, while 10-year bond yield movements were mixed (**Table A**). The declining short-term bond yields reflected the accommodative monetary policies of most central banks in the region.

All emerging East Asian markets except the People's Republic of China (PRC) and Viet Nam recorded contractions in Q3 2020 GDP. However, while all other emerging East Asian economies recorded GDP contractions in Q3 2020, the pace of decline moderated compared with Q2 2020. The most significant improvement was noted in Malaysia as GDP declined to –2.7% y-o-y in Q3 2020 from –17.1% y-o-y in Q2 2020 buoyed by the easing of quarantine restrictions. In Singapore, advance estimates showed that GDP contraction slowed to –7.0% y-o-y in Q3 2020 from –13.3% y-o-y in Q2 2020, fuelled by the recovery in the manufacturing sector. Other markets with y-o-y GDP contractions in Q3 2020 include Hong Kong, China

Table A: Changes in Global Financial Conditions

	2-Year Government Bond (bps)	10-Year Government Bond (bps)	5-Year Credit Default Swap Spread (bps)	Equity Index (%)	FX Rate (%)
Major Advanced Economies					
United States	2	11	–	0.3	–
United Kingdom	2	(4)	(0.05)	(0.9)	(1.6)
Japan	(3)	(3)	(0.6)	2.6	2.5
Germany	(13)	(22)	0.1	(3.6)	(0.5)
Emerging East Asia					
China, People's Rep. of	38	18	(1)	(2.5)	3.6
Hong Kong, China	(13)	(4)	–	2.1	(0.04)
Indonesia	(20)	(57)	(10)	1.9	2.5
Korea, Rep. of	(2)	4	0.8	3.9	6.0
Malaysia	(0.7)	8	(6)	(0.4)	0.8
Philippines	(6)	19	(5)	13.6	0.3
Singapore	2	(23)	–	1.8	0.9
Thailand	3	(11)	5	(3.9)	1.5
Viet Nam	(9)	(32)	(14)	6.4	(0.004)

( ) = negative, – = not available, bps = basis points, FX = foreign exchange.
Notes:
1. Data reflect changes between 31 August and 6 November 2020.
2. A positive (negative) value for the FX rate indicates the appreciation (depreciation) of the local currency against the United States dollar.
Sources: Bloomberg LP and Institute of International Finance.

(–3.5% from –9.0% in Q2 2020), Indonesia (–3.5% from –5.3% in Q2 2020), the Republic of Korea (–1.3% from –2.7% in Q2 2020), the Philippines (–11.5% from –16.9% in Q2 2020), and Thailand (–6.4% from –12.1% in Q2 2020). In contrast, Viet Nam experienced an economic recovery in Q3 2020, with GDP growth rising to 2.6% y-o-y from 0.4% y-o-y in Q2 2020, buoyed by strong exports. The PRC's GDP expanded 3.2% y-o-y in Q2 2020, and accelerated to 4.9% y-o-y in Q3 2020, the fastest growth rate among all regional markets.

To support economic recovery, regional central banks are expected to maintain their accommodative monetary stances. During the review period, all regional central banks held their policy rates steady, while the State Bank of Vietnam (SBV) further reduced its refinancing rate by 50 bps to 4.00% on 1 October to support the economy. On 19 November, both Bangko Sentral ng Pilipinas and Bank Indonesia (BI) reduced their respective policy rates by 25 bps each. From January through 20 November, emerging East Asia's central banks lowered policy rates, with a few central banks cumulatively cutting policy rates by 100 bps or more, including Bangko Sentral ng Pilipinas (200 bps), SBV (200 bps), BI (125 bps), and Bank Negara Malaysia (125 bps) (**Table B**).

The movement of 10-year bond yields depended largely on market-specific factors as well as individual government responses to the COVID-19 pandemic. The weak economic outlook and subdued inflation were reflected in long-term bond yields across the region. In Indonesia, 10-year government bond yields fell by 57 bps during the review period amid efforts by BI to boost liquidity through macroprudential measures that included lowering banks' reserve requirement ratios and increasing central bank bond purchases, among others. Foreign bond inflows in October also helped push down rates. Viet Nam posted a decline of 32 bps between 31 August and 6 November, as SBV reduced policy rates on 1 October to support the economy. In Singapore and Thailand, 10-year yields fell 23 bps and 11 bps, respectively.

The PRC's bond market continued to buck the regional trend on the back of the domestic economic recovery, with the 2-year government bond yield gaining 38 bps between 31 August and 6 November, and the 10-year yield rising 18 bps. In the Philippines, the 10-year yield rose 19 bps due to an expected higher budget deficit in 2021 as well as increased government borrowing. In Malaysia, the 10-year yield rose 8 bps. A few markets witnessed a marginal change in the 10-year government bond yield, including the Republic of Korea (4 bps) and Hong Kong, China (–4 bps).

Economic Outlook

COVID-19 continues to cast a dark cloud over global economic prospects. The growth of confirmed cases and deaths has been exponential, with the worldwide numbers of cases and deaths surpassing 40 million and 1 million, respectively, as of 20 October 2020. The global nature of the pandemic is evident in the dispersed

Table B: Policy Rate Changes

Economies	Policy Rate 31-Dec-2019 (%)	Rate Changes (%)											Policy Rate 20-Nov-2020 (%)	Year-to-Date Change in Policy Rates (basis points)
		Jan-2020	Feb-2020	Mar-2020	Apr-2020	May-2020	Jun-2020	Jul-2020	Aug-2020	Sep-2020	Oct-2020	Nov-2020		
United States	1.75			↓ 1.50									0.25	↓ 150
Euro Area	(0.50)												(0.50)	
Japan	(0.10)												(0.10)	
China, People's Rep. of	3.25		↓ 0.10		↓ 0.20								2.95	↓ 30
Indonesia	5.00		↓ 0.25	↓ 0.25			↓ 0.25	↓ 0.25				↓ 0.25	3.75	↓ 125
Korea, Rep. of	1.25			↓ 0.50		↓ 0.25							0.50	↓ 75
Malaysia	3.00	↓ 0.25		↓ 0.25		↓ 0.50		↓ 0.25					1.75	↓ 125
Philippines	4.00		↓ 0.25	↓ 0.50	↓ 0.50		↓ 0.50					↓ 0.25	2.00	↓ 200
Thailand	1.25		↓ 0.25	↓ 0.25		↓ 0.25							0.50	↓ 75
Viet Nam	6.00			↓ 1.00		↓ 0.50					↓ 0.50		4.00	↓ 200

( ) = negative.
Notes:
1. Data as of 20 November 2020.
2. For the People's Republic of China, data used in the chart is the 1-year medium-term lending facility rate. While the 1-year benchmark lending rate is the official policy rate of the People's Bank of China, market players use the 1-year medium-term lending facility rate as a guide for the monetary policy direction of the People's Bank of China.
Sources: Various central bank websites.

locations of the top 10 countries in terms of numbers of infections—the US, India, Brazil, the Russian Federation, Spain, Argentina, Colombia, France, Peru, and Mexico. The US, which also leads the world in the number of deaths, accounts for around 20% of both confirmed cases and deaths despite having only 4% of the global population. While there has been some progress in the development of treatments and vaccines, there is still a lot of uncertainty about when safe and effective treatments, and especially vaccines, will become widely available.

The bottom line is that the world is not out of the woods on the health front, which largely explains why a full-fledged global recovery is nowhere in sight yet. The unprecedented restrictions on the movement of individuals due to lockdowns, community quarantines, stay-at-home orders, and travel bans is crimping economic activity. Even when authorities relax restrictions, plenty of anecdotal evidence—such as Google community mobile data—indicates that individuals are often reluctant to venture outside over concerns that they may become infected. Furthermore, authorities have sometimes been forced to reintroduce stringent restrictions in response to a second wave—that is, a large increase in confirmed cases after a period of stabilization and decline. While the reintroduction is necessary to safeguard public health, it inevitably has a negative impact on economic activity in the short term.

Both the US and Europe have recently begun to experience a second wave of COVID-19. Europe, in particular, is experiencing a spike in new infections despite having tackled the first wave much more effectively than the US. In response, the governments of many European countries, including big economies—such as Germany, France, the United Kingdom, Italy, and Spain—have reintroduced various restrictions. There are growing concerns that Europe may experience a double-dip recession as the restrictions will hinder mobility and economic activity, causing a second recession just when the region had been recovering from the prior one. Europe's economy may contract in the fourth quarter of 2020 instead of growing at a healthy pace, as was widely expected before the second wave. Until a safe and effective COVID-19 vaccine is developed and distributed widely, the viral cloud of fear and uncertainty will limit global mobility and growth.

Despite the gloomy and uncertain economic outlook, the International Monetary Fund (IMF) has slightly upgraded its short-term global growth forecast. In its *World Economic Outlook*, released in October 2020, the IMF forecast that the world economy would contract by 4.4% in 2020, whereas in June it had forecast a larger contraction of 5.2%. According to projections, the world economy will grow by 5.2% in 2021, slightly down from its June forecast of 5.4%. The improvement in the forecast for the global economy's contraction in 2020 was driven by substantially upgraded growth projections for advanced economies. The IMF is now forecasting a contraction of 5.8% for this group of countries in 2020, compared to a significantly bigger contraction of 8.1% in its June forecast. On the other hand, for emerging markets and developing economies, the IMF's 2020 growth forecast was −3.3% in October versus −3.1% in June. For 2021, the IMF's October growth forecast for advanced economies was 3.9%, down from its 4.8% forecast in June. Its October forecast for growth of 6.0% in 2021 for emerging markets and developing economies was slightly up from the 5.8% forecast in June. It remains to be seen whether the second wave of COVID-19 and the reintroduction of restrictions in advanced economies, especially Europe, will perceptibly affect global growth outcomes in 2020 and 2021.

Developing Asia is not immune to the negative economic impact of COVID-19, but the impact is noticeably smaller than in the rest of the world. Partly, this is due to the fact that the region has done a relatively good job of containing the pandemic. Although some Asian countries, most notably India, have suffered major outbreaks, Asia has mostly weathered the COVID-19 storm better than other regions. This is especially true in East Asia, particularly the PRC, where everyday life is returning to a semblance of normalcy as a result of the remarkable success in containing the disease. In fact, the PRC is the lone bright spot in an otherwise gloomy global economic landscape. Its economy grew by a healthy 4.9% y-o-y in Q3 2020 after an expansion of 3.2% in Q2 2020 and a historic contraction in the first quarter.

According to the Asian Development Bank's *Asian Development Outlook Update*, released in September 2020, the PRC's economy is expected to grow by 1.8% in 2020 and 7.7% in 2021. The corresponding figures for the Association of Southeast Asian Nations (ASEAN) are −3.8% and 5.5%; for the Republic of Korea, the expected growth rates are −1.0% and 3.3%; and for Hong Kong, China, the respective figures are −6.5% and 5.1%. Output in developing Asia as a whole is projected to shrink by 0.7% in 2020 before expanding by 6.8% in 2021. The PRC's recovery is contributing to the resilience of other ASEAN+3 economies that trade heavily with the PRC, especially since the PRC's growth appears to be increasingly broad-based.[2] In particular, retail sales, a good bellwether of domestic demand, have risen since August after contracting during the first 7 months of the year.

Notwithstanding some positive trends, including the gathering momentum of the PRC's recovery, the overall economic outlook for ASEAN+3 remains subject to a great deal of uncertainty. The fundamental reason is that the global economic outlook will remain uncertain and negative until there is some clarity on when and if COVID-19 will recede. The second wave of new cases, which is forcing European governments to reintroduce restrictions that restrict mobility and hamper economic activity, is a stark reminder that the virus can derail economic recovery at any time until it is firmly brought under control. Until then, economic recovery is more likely to be an intermittent and fitful stop-and-go process rather than a smooth continuous one. Furthermore, many negative effects of the pandemic—such as large-scale unemployment and business closures—are likely

to persist for some time.

As economic performance in major advanced economies strengthened and the results of the US election became more clear, investor sentiment improved on expectations of an additional stimulus package in the US. Most equity markets in emerging East Asia posted gains during the review period (**Figure B.1**). Among regional equity markets, the Philippines gained the most with a 13.6% increase, as the economy showed signs of recovery with the easing of social restrictions. In Viet Nam, the equity market rose 6.4% as the government was successful in gradually lifting restrictions put in place in response to the COVID-19 outbreak. In contrast, declines in equity markets were noted in Thailand (−3.9%), which was driven by rising political concerns, and in the PRC (−2.5%) (**Figure B.2**)

From August through October, investment sentiment was subdued amid rising COVID-19 cases in Europe and uncertainty related to the US election, which led to capital outflows from the region's equities markets. Inflows, however, were noted in early November, buoyed by strong inflows in the markets of the PRC and the Republic of Korea (**Figure C**). The COVID-19 pandemic has significantly shaped global capital flows. **Box 1** examines the effectiveness of COVID-19-related policy

Figure B.1: Equity Indexes in Emerging East Asia

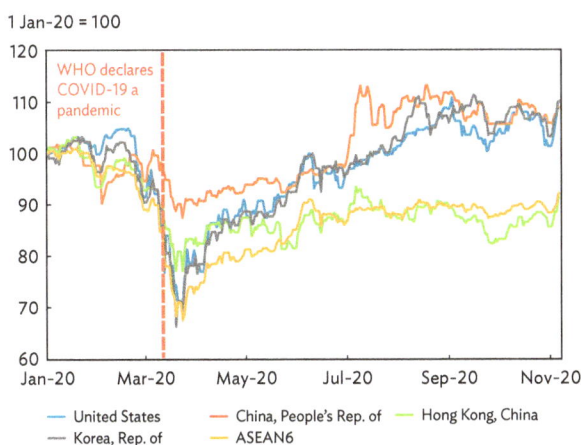

ASEAN = Association of Southeast Asian Nations, COVID-19 = coronavirus disease, WHO = World Health Organization.
Notes:
1. Data as of 6 November 2020.
2. ASEAN6 comprises Indonesia, Malaysia, the Philippines, Singapore, Thailand, and Viet Nam.
3. The World Health Organization declared COVID-19 a pandemic on 11 March.
Source: Bloomberg LP.

Figure B.2: Changes in Equity Indexes in Emerging East Asia

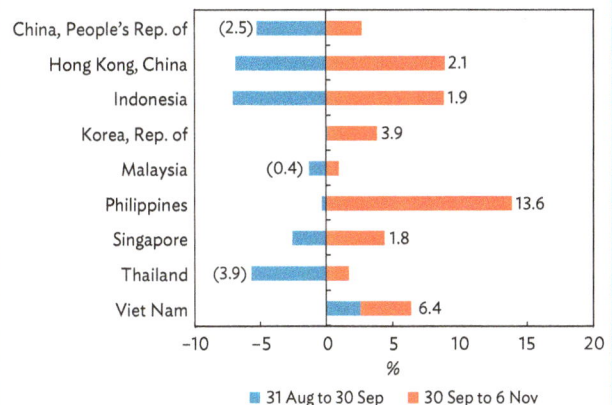

( ) = negative.
Notes:
1. Changes from 31 August to 30 September 2020, and from 30 September to 6 November 2020.
2. Figures on the chart refer to the net change between the two periods.
Source: *AsianBondsOnline* computations based on Bloomberg LP data.

---

[2] ASEAN+3 comprises the 10 members of ASEAN plus the PRC, Japan, and the Republic of Korea.

Box 1: Global Financial Markets and Capital Flows: COVID-19 Impacts and Policy Responses

The coronavirus disease (COVID-19) pandemic and the resulting lockdowns have led to an unprecedented economic contraction and turbulence in financial markets, which initially caused the largest ever outflows of portfolio capital from emerging market economies (EMEs).[a] Globally, governments have responded to the crisis with substantial fiscal stimulus packages. In addition, central banks around the world have eased monetary policies, with many EME central banks implementing quantitative easing (QE) measures for the first time. Recent Asian Development Bank Institute research examined the impact of COVID-19 on bond yields, stock prices, and exchange rates for a sample of 38 advanced and emerging markets (Beirne et al. 2020). In addition, the effect of the pandemic on EME equity and bond flows across 14 EMEs was assessed. This research also estimated the effectiveness of COVID-19-related policy responses on financial markets and capital flow dynamics.

Figure B1 demonstrates that COVID-19 has had the greatest relative effect on sovereign bond markets across both advanced and emerging economies. In addition, based on an empirical analysis over the period from 4 January 2010 to 30 April 2020, Beirne et al. (2020) show that the magnitude of the effect of COVID-19 on financial markets is notably higher for emerging rather than advanced economies by a factor of around two across bond, stock, and exchange rate markets. In particular, bond yields in European and Asian EMEs are estimated to have declined by 24 basis points (bps) and 14 bps over the sample period, respectively, due to COVID-19. While EME bond yields rose sharply at the onset of COVID-19, coupled with substantial net capital outflows, it is striking that the overall effect on bond yields was negative, which may seem counterintuitive since an increase in COVID-19 cases might be expected to worsen financial market turmoil and increase sovereign bond yields. There are two explanations for why the overall effect on bond yields was negative. First, government bonds were perceived as safer assets than corporate bonds given that the corporate sector, with few exceptions, was very heavily affected by COVID-19 lockdowns. With many businesses fighting for survival, sovereign bonds were seen as the better alternative, even if the crisis also cast questions on the sustainability of public debt. Second, the crisis gave way to extremely accommodative central bank policies in most economies, with slashes in interest rates and new rounds of QE policies in all major advanced economies. Turning to the impact on stock markets, the greatest relative impact of COVID-19 is estimated to have been in advanced Asian economies and Latin America, whose markets plunged sharply.

Figure B1: Relative Impact of COVID-19 on Financial Markets and Capital Flows

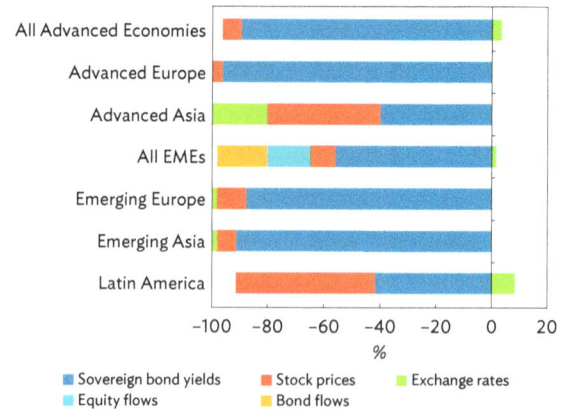

COVID-19 = coronavirus disease, EMEs = emerging market economies.
Note: The estimation period runs from 4 January 2010 to 30 April 2020, with COVID-19 defined as the number of daily new confirmed COVID-19 cases per one million population. The statistically significant coefficients for the COVID-19 variable are reported via a panel regression that uses each of the asset markets and capital flows as dependent variables, expressed as a percentage relative to the total. These results are consistent with an updated estimation by the authors over the period from 4 January 2010 to 31 August 2020.
Source: J. Beirne, N. Renzhi, E. Sugandi, and U. Volz. 2020. Financial Market and Capital Flow Dynamics During the COVID-19 Pandemic. *Asian Development Bank Institute Working Paper.* No. 1158. Tokyo: Asian Development Bank Institute.

On exchange rates, advanced Asian economies were most affected in relative terms, experiencing currency depreciations due to COVID-19, although the magnitude of these effects was not as large overall when compared to the effects on stock and bond markets. With regard to EME capital flows, COVID-19 has led to significant outflows of both equities and bonds, reflecting investors' flight to safety.

While there has been substantial heterogeneity across regions in the magnitude of the effects of COVID-19 on markets, the results in Beirne et al. (2020) show that this has also been the case in relation to the effectiveness of policy responses. Compared to EMEs, fiscal stimulus packages in advanced economies have had around twice the impact in terms of compressing sovereign bond yields. On monetary policy, while interest rate reductions passed through along the yield curve with similar magnitudes in both advanced and emerging economies, the impact on bond yields due to QE was statistically significant for advanced economies only. However, the advanced economy QE measures spilled over to EMEs, reducing EME bond yields by around 27 bps.

---

[a] This box was written by John Beirne (Research Fellow) of the Asian Development Bank Institute and Ulrich Volz (Director of the SOAS Centre for Sustainable Finance) of the SOAS University of London.

continued on next page

Box 1: Global Financial Markets and Capital Flows: COVID-19 Impacts and Policy Responses
continued

As regards stock markets, interest rate reductions were more effective in advanced compared to emerging economies by a factor of around two. In addition, QE measures in advanced economies, as well as spillovers to EMEs, helped to boost domestic stock prices by around 12% and 16%, respectively. Moreover, QE by central banks in emerging Asia helped to increase stock prices by around 6%. The impact of fiscal policy on stock markets was confined to European advanced economies and EMEs overall, increasing stock prices by an average of around 8%. At the global level, while the magnitude of the effect of policy responses on exchange rates was much lower than in other markets, QE measures in EMEs led to a rise in net capital inflows by around 14% in the case of equities and around 16% in the case of bonds. Moreover, fiscal stimulus packages in EMEs increased net equity inflows by around 9%.

Overall, although heightened uncertainty due to the COVID-19 pandemic has affected the financial markets of EMEs more detrimentally than advanced economies, it appears that most EMEs have performed well in their policy responses to the pandemic. Whereas fiscal stimulus packages have contributed to restoring confidence in domestic financial markets, QE policy measures and interest rate reductions have also been effective in Asian economies by supporting stock prices. Notably, these measures also

helped to stabilize capital flows. The scale of bond and equity capital outflows from EMEs highlights the importance of strengthening the domestic investor base to be less reliant on international portfolio investment. The COVID-19 crisis has illustrated the need for concerted efforts at bolstering domestic financial resource mobilization in EMEs and for reducing exposure to international portfolio capital and financial contagion. The extent of capital outflows also strengthens the case for reviving discussions around the management of capital flows and the development of a global financial safety net. It is important for EMEs to develop further their overall policy toolkits to respond to spikes in financial market volatility and crisis episodes, notably with the use of QE measures. With conventional monetary policy having easing limits and fiscal policy space constrained by excessive public debt, using QE policies can be a potent stimulator in domestic markets, particularly where inflation expectations are contained and exchange rates are flexible.

References

J. Beirne, N. Renzhi, E. Sugandi, and U. Volz. 2020. Financial Market and Capital Flow Dynamics During the COVID-19 Pandemic. *Asian Development Bank Institute Working Paper*. No. 1158. Tokyo: Asian Development Bank Institute.

Figure C: Capital Flows into Equity Markets in Emerging East Asia

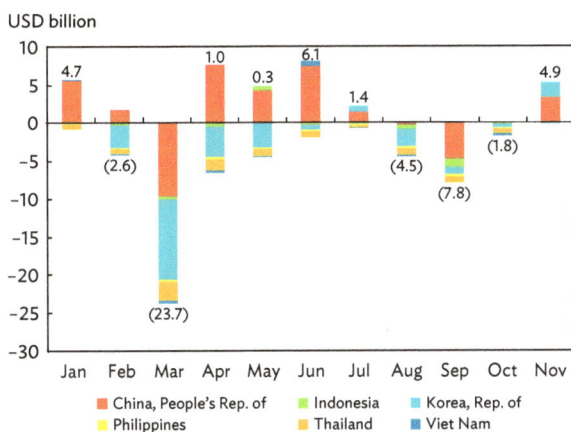

USD billion

( ) = outflows, USD = United States dollar.
Notes:
1. Data as of 6 November 2020.
2. Figures refer to net inflows (net outflows) for each month.
Source: Institute of International Finance.

responses with regard to financial markets and capital flow dynamics.

Foreign holdings of LCY government bonds showed mixed patterns in Q3 2020 (**Figure D.1**). The foreign holdings share declined in Indonesia, the Philippines, and Thailand between the end of June and the end of September. In Indonesia, the foreign holdings share fell from 30.2% to 27.0% during the review period. Foreign investors dumped Indonesian bonds on concerns over debt monetization and a wide budget deficit in the 2021 state budget. The foreign holding shares in the Philippines and Thailand declined from 1.9% and 14.4% at the end of June, respectively, to 1.5% and 14.0% at the end of September.

The PRC and Malaysia witnessed slight increases in their respective shares of foreign holdings in the LCY government bond market. In Malaysia, the foreign holdings share climbed to 23.6% at the end of September from 22.7% at the end of June on expectations that

Figure D.1: Foreign Holdings of Local Currency Government Bonds in Select Asian Markets (% of total)

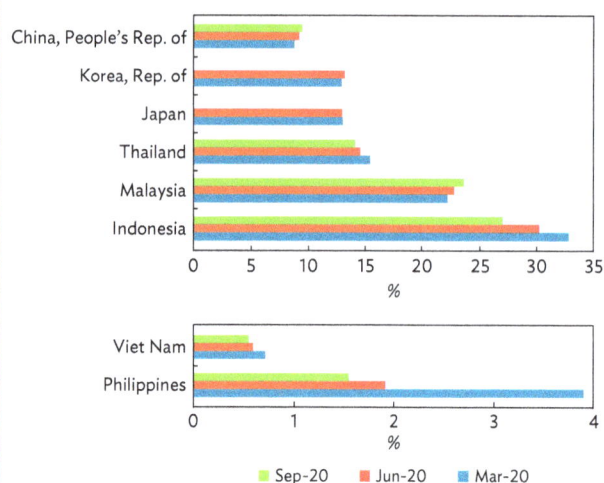

Note: Data for Japan and the Republic of Korea as of 30 June 2020.
Source: *AsianBondsOnline*.

Figure D.2: Foreign Bond Flows in Select Emerging East Asian Economies

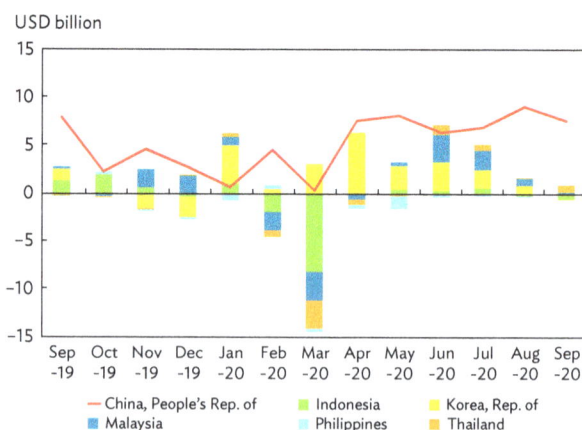

USD = United States dollar.
Notes:
1. The Republic of Korea and Thailand provided data on bond flows. For the People's Republic of China, Indonesia, Malaysia, and the Philippines, month-on-month changes in foreign holdings of local currency government bonds were used as a proxy for bond flows.
2. Data as of 30 September 2020.
3. Figures were computed based on 30 September 2020 exchange rates to avoid currency effects.
Sources: People's Republic of China (*Wind Information*); Indonesia (Directorate General of Budget Financing and Risk Management, Ministry of Finance); Republic of Korea (Financial Supervisory Service); Malaysia (Bank Negara Malaysia); Philippines (Bureau of the Treasury); and Thailand (Thai Bond Market Association).

Malaysia would be kept in FTSE Russell's World Global Bond Index (WGBI). (On 24 September, FTSE Russell kept Malaysia's sovereign bonds in the WGBI; however, Malaysia remains on the negative watch list.) In the PRC, the foreign holdings share inched up to 9.4% at the end of September from 9.1% at the end of June as it continued to liberalize its bond markets. On 26 September, the PRC announced that it would streamline regulations for its Renminbi Qualified Foreign Institutional Investor and Qualified Foreign Institutional Investor programs into a single set of rules. Also, on 24 September, the FTSE Russell announced the inclusion of PRC government bonds in its WGBI starting in October 2021.

Foreign bond inflows into the region's LCY bond markets totaled USD29.8 billion in Q3 2020, slightly down from inflows of USD35.1 billion in the previous quarter (**Figure D.2**). All markets for which data are available posted positive quarterly inflows except for Indonesia and the Philippines. The PRC and the Republic of Korea are the only bond markets in emerging East Asia that have consistently posted positive quarterly foreign flows in 2020.

Most regional currencies gained vis-à-vis the US dollar between 31 August and 6 November (**Figure E.1**). The Korean won appreciated the most of all currencies in the region, gaining 6.0% on capital inflows into its financial market and improved economic conditions. The Chinese yuan also strengthened, rising 3.6% as its economic

growth continued to gain traction. The Indonesian rupiah gained 2.5% and the Thai baht gained 1.5% (**Figure E.2**).

Improved investment sentiment also led to a decline in credit default swap spreads in most emerging East Asian markets between 31 August and 6 November. During the review period, a spike was noted from the middle of September through early October when the Federal Reserve indicated that more fiscal support would be needed to support the economy and the US President tested positive for COVID-19, heightening risk uncertainty. Credit default swap spreads trended downward during the first half of October before rising toward the end of the month on the back of uncertainty over US stimulus negotiations, increased COVID-19 cases in European economies and the subsequent return of lockdown measures, and the US election. Credit default swap spreads subsequently declined again in the first week of November (**Figure F**). The sovereign stripped spreads showed a similar trend (**Figure G**).

While financial conditions improved during the review period, uncertainty over COVID-19 and its impact on economic recovery weighed on global investment sentiment despite accommodative monetary stances

Figure E.1: Changes in Spot Exchange Rates vs. the United States Dollar

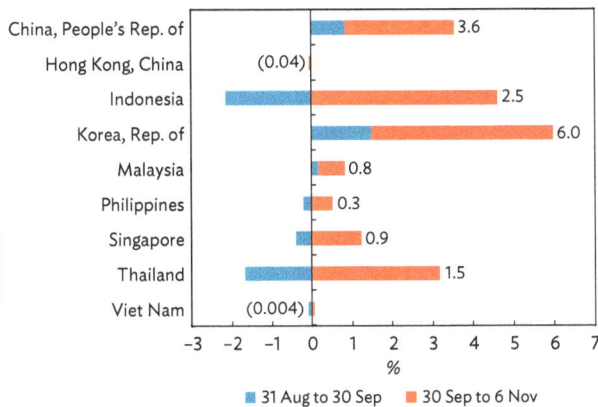

China, People's Rep. of — 3.6
Hong Kong, China — (0.04)
Indonesia — 2.5
Korea, Rep. of — 6.0
Malaysia — 0.8
Philippines — 0.3
Singapore — 0.9
Thailand — 1.5
Viet Nam — (0.004)

%

■ 31 Aug to 30 Sep   ■ 30 Sep to 6 Nov

Notes:
1. Changes from 31 August to 30 September 2020, and from 30 September to 6 November 2020.
2. Numbers on the chart refer to the net change between the two periods.
3. A positive (negative) value for the foreign exchange rate indicates the appreciation (depreciation) of the local currency against the United States dollar.
Source: Bloomberg LP.

Figure E.2: Currency Indexes in Emerging East Asia

1-Jan-20 = 100

— China, People's Rep. of   — Korea, Rep. of
— ASEAN6   — USD Index

ASEAN = Association of Southeast Asian Nations, USD = United States dollar.
Notes:
1. Data as of 6 November 2020.
2. ASEAN6 comprises Indonesia, Malaysia, the Philippines, Singapore, Thailand, and Viet Nam.
Source: *AsianBondsOnline* computations based on Bloomberg LP data.

Figure F: Credit Default Swap Spreads in Select Asian Markets (senior 5-year)

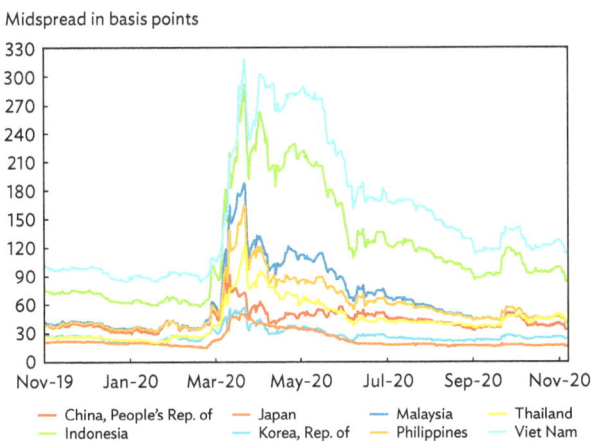

Midspread in basis points

— China, People's Rep. of   — Japan   — Malaysia   — Thailand
— Indonesia   — Korea, Rep. of   — Philippines   — Viet Nam

USD = United States dollar.
Notes:
1. Based on USD-denominated sovereign bonds.
2. Data as of 6 November 2020.
Source: Bloomberg LP.

Figure G: JP Morgan Emerging Markets Bond Index Sovereign Stripped Spreads

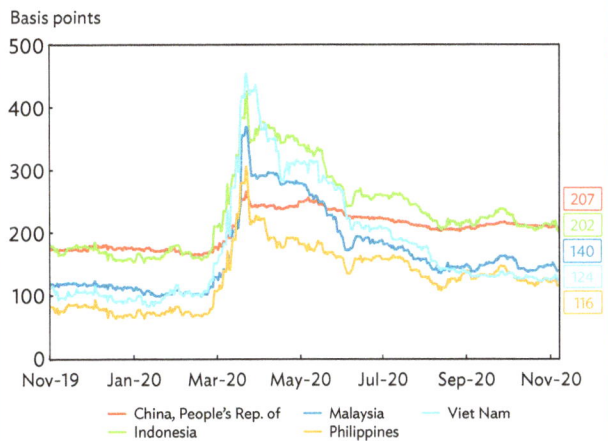

Basis points

207
202
140
124
116

— China, People's Rep. of   — Malaysia   — Viet Nam
— Indonesia   — Philippines

USD = United States dollar.
Notes:
1. Based on USD-denominated sovereign bonds.
2. Data as of 6 November 2020.
Source: Bloomberg LP.

and fiscal stimulus. Fragile investment sentiment and an uncertain economic outlook will challenge financial stability across the region. **Box 2** discusses the effect of COVID-19 on financial stability in ASEAN markets. During periods when exchange rates witness increased volatility, public and private sector borrowers tend to tap LCY bond markets to reduce their exposure to

currency risks (**Box 3**), underscoring the importance of the bond market as a channel to mobilize LCY funding resources for development. Currently, the largest risk to global economies remains the course and duration of the COVID-19 pandemic. **Box 4** examines previous COVID-19-like shocks to determine the average duration of recovery from such events.

Box 2: The Effect of COVID-19 on Financial Stability in ASEAN

The coronavirus disease (COVID-19) pandemic is a once-in-a-century global public health and economic crisis.[a] Member countries of the Association of Southeast Asian Nations (ASEAN) have been profoundly affected by COVID-19's impact.[b] Like the rest of the world, ASEAN has seen a significant number of confirmed cases and fatalities. Although the region has been spared huge outbreaks such as those in the United States, India, the Russian Federation, and Brazil, the numbers are far from trivial. As of 7 October, ASEAN as a whole had suffered over 500,000 confirmed cases and over 10,000 deaths. To contain the pandemic, the region's governments imposed various restrictions—lockdowns, community quarantines, and travel bans—which limited the mobility of people within and across countries. As a result, the region was hit hard economically. According to the forecast of the *Asian Development Outlook 2020 Update*, which was released in September 2020, the 10 economies of ASEAN will collectively shrink by 3.8% in 2020, although they will bounce back into positive territory with growth of 5.5% in 2021. In addition to the COVID-19-related restrictions, the dire global outlook is another major factor in the region's severe economic downturn.

ASEAN's relatively high level of economic globalization, in terms of both trade and capital flows, suggests that COVID-19 may adversely affect not only the region's economic growth but also its financial stability. The region suffered a devastating blow during the 1997/98 Asian financial crisis as a result of a sudden and sharp reversal of capital flows. Since then, ASEAN economies have strengthened fundamentals to protect themselves from another financial crisis. These robust fundamentals served ASEAN well during the 2007–2009 global financial crisis, which had only a limited impact on the region's financial stability. Nevertheless, the unprecedented scale and global nature of the COVID-19 shock, in conjunction with the region's relative financial openness, poses a clear and present danger to financial stability. The global financial market turmoil of March 2020 also affected ASEAN economies, as evident in the tangible depreciation of their currencies (**Figure B2.1**). Financial conditions have subsequently turned more benign in ASEAN and the rest of the world. Nevertheless, if the pandemic persists, instability may return to financial markets.

A major contribution to the restoration of financial stability in ASEAN in 2020 has been the concerted implementation

Figure B2.1: Depreciation of Select ASEAN Currencies vs. the United States Dollar, 1 January–23 March 2020 (%)

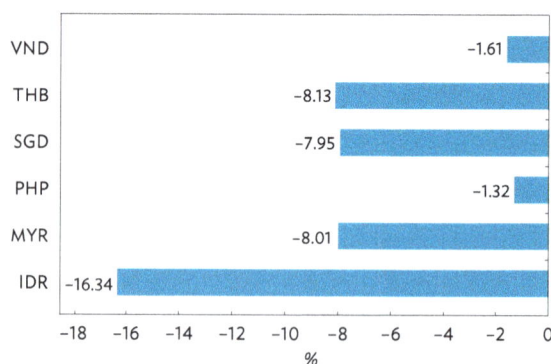

ASEAN = Association of Southeast Asian Nations, IDR = Indonesian rupiah, MYR = Malaysian ringgit, PHP = Philippine peso, SGD = Singapore dollar, THB = Thai baht, VND = Vietnamese dong.
Source: Bloomberg LP.

of expansionary monetary policy. Like their counterparts elsewhere, the central banks of ASEAN have cut benchmark interest rates decisively (**Figure B2.2**). They have also taken other measures to inject additional liquidity into their financial systems. These include reducing reserve requirement ratios, creating funds for lending to firms, implementing temporary suspensions of interest repayments, and relaxing payment conditions for loans related to COVID-19. In addition, ASEAN governments have launched fiscal stimulus packages to support growth and protect vulnerable groups. Such fiscal stimulus indirectly supports financial stability by boosting growth and thus preventing a rise in business closures and nonperforming loans. At the same time, stimulus expands fiscal deficits and public debt, which can eventually pose a risk to financial stability. While these strong domestic policy measures are the primary defense against financial turbulence, regional financial safety nets can also make a significant contribution.

Regional financial safety nets matter because there can be significant spillovers across the region from major shocks. This was painfully evident during the 1997/98 Asian financial crisis. In response to that crisis, ASEAN created the ASEAN+3 financial cooperation initiative.[c] The Chiang Mai Initiative Multilateralization (CMIM) process emerged in

---

[a] This box was written by Donghyun Park (Principal Economist) of the Asian Development Bank (ADB), Pitchaya Sirivunnabood (Capacity Building and Training Economist) of the ADB Institute, and Santi Setiawati (Intern) of the ADB Institute.
[b] Unless otherwise stated, data for ASEAN in this box include the markets of Indonesia, Malaysia, the Philippines, Singapore, Thailand, and Viet Nam.
[c] ASEAN+3 refers to the 10 members of ASEAN plus the People's Republic of China, Japan, and the Republic of Korea.

continued on next page

Box 2: The Effect of COVID-19 on Financial Stability in ASEAN   *continued*

Figure B2.2: Policy Rate Changes in Select ASEAN Economies, 31 December 2019–7 October 2020 (bps)

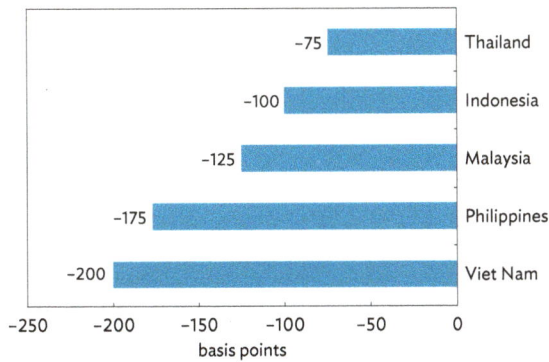

ASEAN = Association of Southeast Asian Nations, bps = basis points.
Note: Negative value denotes reduction of policy rate.
Source: Various central bank websites.

in both the CMIM and ADRFI initiatives for dealing with transnational disease outbreaks includes the lack of technical and financial capacity building and public health sector cooperation among ASEAN countries. This includes funding hospitals and medical clinics; health care training for lower-income countries; and the stockpiling of medicines, alcohol, surgical masks, vaccines, and other emergency equipment to quickly tackle the spread of a transnational disease. At the global and regional levels, international financial institutions have also supported countries affected by the COVID-19 outbreak. The International Monetary Fund uses the Catastrophe Containment and Relief Trust to support its member countries, while multilateral development banks like the Asian Development Bank are supporting countries—including Thailand, the Philippines, and Indonesia—through grants and loans. Although this financial support is helpful, it is nowhere near enough to respond to a systemic financial crisis.

March 2010 under the ASEAN+3 initiative as a network of bilateral swap arrangements amounting to USD120 billion. CMIM's implementation and surveillance processes are being strengthened to improve its effectiveness and speed in tackling financial crisis.

Separately, the ASEAN Disaster Risk Financing and Insurance (ADRFI) scheme is being developed to strengthen regional financial resilience in the context of climate change and natural hazards. The comprehensive framework is designed to equip ASEAN member countries with risk management and risk transfer capabilities. ADFRI will enable them to overcome the financial burden caused by extreme events through both ex-ante and ex-post arrangements.

ASEAN has yet to develop a regional mechanism for the COVID-19 pandemic crisis or similar shocks. The policy gap

Appropriate and timely policies supported by regional cooperation can reduce the negative economic impacts of the pandemic. We propose three policy recommendations. First, the establishment of an ASEAN task force on pandemics would facilitate the coordination and alignment of policy responses among member countries. A regional framework for policy responses can create public trust and promote transparency. Second, the building-up of an ASEAN pandemic network—consisting of hospitals, healthcare workers, pharmaceutical companies, and research institutions—is needed to share information and knowledge on healthcare resources for mitigating pandemic-related shocks and preparing financing schemes. Third, regional financial safety nets must be strengthened, including their role in mitigating the impact of COVID-19 and other similar shocks to financial stability.

Box 3: Local Currency Bond Markets and Exchange Rate Risks

The 1997/98 Asian financial crisis underlined the importance of developing local currency (LCY) bond markets to boost financial resilience.[a] LCY bond markets mobilize private sector savings into long-term investments, while also mitigating currency and maturity mismatches in the balance sheets of public and private institutions. LCY bond markets absorb capital inflows, thereby contributing to financial stability.[b] Park, Shin, and Tian (2018) showed that LCY bond markets also play a significant role in stabilizing currencies against external shocks.[c]

In recent decades, LCY bond markets in emerging Asian economies have expanded rapidly, catching up to European LCY markets in size. Since the Asian Bond Markets Initiative was launched in 2002 by the Association of Southeast Asian Nations (ASEAN) and the People's Republic of China, Japan, and the Republic of Korea—a grouping collectively known as ASEAN+3—regional LCY bond markets have experienced rapid growth. As of June 2020, LCY bonds outstanding in emerging East Asia had reached USD17.2 trillion, a more than 14-fold increase since 2002. Furthermore, LCY bonds outstanding as a share of the region's gross domestic product reached 91.6% in 2020. The rapid development of regional LCY bond markets has reduced financial vulnerability to sudden capital flow reversals, as evidenced by the resilience of the region's financial systems and economies during the 2007–2009 global financial crisis and the "taper tantrum" in 2013.

Well-developed LCY bond markets allow domestic borrowers to tap LCY funding when exchange rates are volatile, thus mitigating currency risk in investments and project implementation. **Figure B3.1** confirms that demand for LCY financing in Asia rose in recent years when exchange rates were more volatile.

Currency depreciation adversely affects balance sheets in both the public and private sectors, especially when exposure to foreign currency financing is large. When a domestic currency weakens, it becomes more costly to repay foreign currency debt. LCY bonds thus offer a financing solution that is cheaper and free of exchange-rate risk for LCY investment and spending. **Figure B3.2** reveals that when emerging market currencies depreciate, the demand for LCY financing tends to increase, as evidenced by greater LCY bond issuance in

Figure B3.1: Currency Volatility and Local Currency Bond Issuance

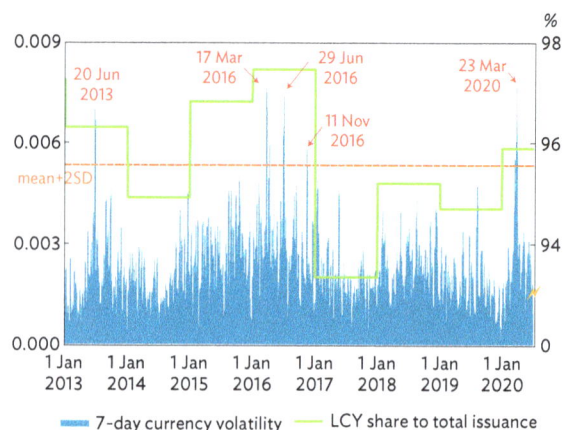

LCY = local currency, SD = standard deviation.
Notes:
1. Volatility is defined as the 7-day rolling standard deviation of the log difference of the MSCI Emerging Market Currency Index in United States dollars, which measures the total return of 25 emerging market currencies relative to the dollar where the weight of each currency is equal to its country weight in the MSCI Emerging Markets Index.
2. The share of LCY bonds as a percentage of total bond issuances in Armenia, Georgia, the People's Republic of China, India, Indonesia, Malaysia, Pakistan, the Philippines, the Republic of Korea, Singapore, Thailand, and Viet Nam.
Source: Authors' calculation based on Bloomberg LP data.

emerging Asia. This implies that better developed LCY bond markets serve as an important alternative funding source for local borrowers when the domestic currency weakens.

The outbreak of the coronavirus disease (COVID-19) soured global investment sentiment and caused turmoil in global financial markets in March and April 2020, putting emerging market currencies under pressure. A huge amount of financing will be needed to tackle COVID-19 and its economic effects. As evidenced by Figures B3.1 and B3.2, LCY bond issuance is an important funding mechanism for public and private sector borrowers in emerging markets, especially those facing significant uncertainty.

Larger LCY bond markets also offer central banks an additional tool for monitoring liquidity in the financial system. During market turmoil, major central banks trade LCY bonds to smooth liquidity conditions in the financial sector and

---

[a] This box was written by Donghyun Park (Principal Economist), Shu Tian (Economist), and Mai Lin Villaruel (Economics Officer) in the Economic Research and Regional Cooperation Department of the Asian Development Bank (ADB).
[b] ADB. 2019. *Good Practices for Developing A Local Currency Bond Market: Lessons from the ASEAN+3 Asian Bond Markets Initiative.* Manila.
[c] D. Park, K. Shin, and S. Tian. 2018. Do Local Currency Bond Markets Enhance Financial Stability? *ADB Economics Working Paper Series.* No. 563. Manila: ADB.

continued on next page

Box 3: Local Currency Bond Markets and Exchange Rate Risks   *continued*

Figure B3.2: Exchange Rate Performance and Issuance of Local Currency-Denominated Bonds in Select Asian Economies

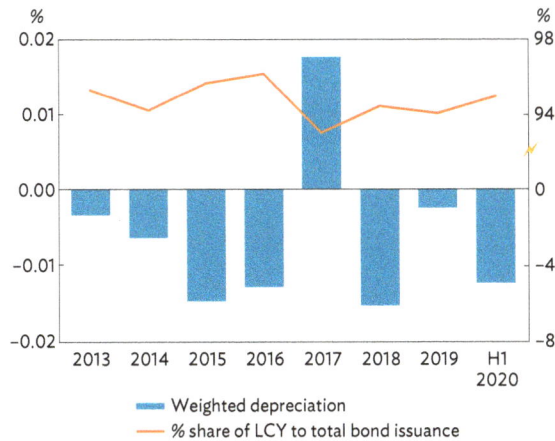

— Weighted depreciation
— % share of LCY to total bond issuance

Notes:
1. Weighted depreciation of the nominal exchange rate (%) is measured as annual mean depreciation (previous over current) of the daily nominal exchange rate of selected Asian economies (Armenia, Georgia, the People's Republic of China, India, Indonesia, Malaysia, Pakistan, the Philippines, the Republic of Korea, Singapore, Thailand, and Viet Nam) weighted using gross domestic product at current prices in United States dollars.
2. Share of LCY to total bond issuance of Armenia, Georgia, the People's Republic of China, India, Indonesia, Malaysia, Pakistan, the Philippines, the Republic of Korea, Singapore, Thailand, and Viet Nam
Source: Authors' calculation based on Bloomberg LP data.

support financial stability. Recent analysis shows that LCY bond yields fell significantly after central banks announced asset purchase programs in response to the COVID-19 pandemic, but exchange rates were largely unaffected.[d] Others argue that credible emerging market central banks could consider purchasing LCY government bonds to support COVID-19-related health and welfare expenditures, and fiscal stimulus.[e]

Overall, LCY bond markets serve as useful financing instruments for emerging markets during periods of volatility and weakening exchange rates. They not only mitigate the double mismatch problem but also offer a tool to smooth liquidity in the domestic financial system. The impact of COVID-19 has demonstrated the importance of developing deep and balanced LCY bond markets to boost financial sector resilience.

[d] Y. Arslan, M. Drehmann, and Boris Hofmann. 2020. Central Bank Bond Purchases in Emerging Market Economies. *BIS Bulletin*. No. 20. Basel: Bank for International Settlements.
[e] B. Gianluca, J. Hartley, A. García–Herrero, A. Rebucci, and E. Ribakova. 2020. Credible Emerging Market Central Banks Could Embrace Quantitative Easing to Fight COVID-19. *CEPR Policy Portal*. Washington, DC.

Box 4: The Duration of Recoveries from Economic Shocks Like COVID-19

Introduction

Attention is beginning to turn from the magnitude of the economic impact of the outbreak of the coronavirus disease (COVID-19) to the likely trajectory of recovery.[a] In this connection, Eichengreen, Park, and Shin (2020) seek to make headway on the question of what recovery from a COVID-19 recession may look like, focusing on the duration of the recovery; that is, how long will it take to re-attain the levels of output and employment reached at the prior business cycle peak?

We start by categorizing all post-1950 recessions in advanced economies and emerging markets into those that were induced by a supply shock, a demand shock, or both shocks. We measure recovery duration as the number of years required to re-attain prerecession levels of output and employment. We then rely on existing literature on business cycle dynamics to identify candidate variables that can help account for variations in recovery duration following different kinds of shocks. By asking which of these variables are operative in the COVID-19 recession, we can then draw inferences about the duration of the recovery under different scenarios.

Empirical findings

The main findings of the empirical analysis are as follows. For gross domestic product (GDP) per capita, both the amplitude of the recession and the presence of a double-dip increase recovery duration, as expected; that is, severe recessions and double-dip recessions lengthen the time it takes an economy to recover. Similarly, both global recessions and the presence of a financial crisis lengthen recovery durations. There is also some indication that experiencing both supply and demand shocks—as is during the current COVID-19 recession—lengthens recovery time. Recession amplitude, double-dip, financial crisis, and both shock variables remain significant when included simultaneously.

Additional analysis indicates that the results for the duration of employment recoveries are broadly similar with the results for GDP per capita recoveries. In addition, we find that economies with floating exchange rate regimes did better in general, albeit not in response to global recessions. This is likely because flexible exchange rates are not very useful if all economies are in trouble simultaneously. Also, there is evidence that trade openness is associated with faster recoveries. This is consistent with the idea that recovery

Data and Empirical Methodology

Our primary data are real gross domestic product (GDP) per capita in national accounts and employment. These were collected from the Penn World Table 9.1. Dates of financial crises were obtained from Reinhart and Rogoff (2009) and Laeven and Valencia (2018). De facto exchange rate regimes were taken from Ilzetzki, Reinhart, and Rogoff (2019). We considered 23 advanced economies and 21 major emerging markets. The sample period of GDP and employment for advanced economies is from 1950 to 2017. The sample period of GDP and employment for emerging markets varies. For some, it is also from 1950 to 2017, but for others the sample starts as late as 1990. The frequency is annual in all cases. The recovery duration of per capita GDP and employment is defined as how many years it takes for the two variables to recover to their levels at the preceding business cycle peak. For the entire sample, we find that it takes real GDP per capita and employment around 4 years and 3 years, respectively, to recover to their previous peak.

The business cycle chronology is calculated by applying the Bry and Boschan (1971) algorithm as coded by Jorda, Schularick, and Taylor (2013) for both advanced economies and emerging markets. Then we calculate the duration of recoveries, which is defined as number of years for GDP per capita from peak to recovery of prior peak. Then we investigate the determinants of the duration by employing a parametric survival model with a Weibull distribution. We estimate both pooled regressions and panel regressions with random effects. The coefficients estimated determine the hazard rate so that a positive sign on a coefficient means that it shortens the duration of the recovery.

The dependent variable is the duration of the GDP recovery, defined as number of years for GDP per capita from previous peak to recovery of prior peak. We estimate coefficients based on the panel survival model with a Weibull distribution. A negative sign on a coefficient means that it lengthens the time to recovery (i.e., it reduces the likelihood of the ongoing recovery spell ending in the current period).

---

[a] This box was written by Barry Eichengreen (Professor of Economics and Political Science) in the University of California at Berkeley, Donghyun Park (Principal Economist) in the Economic Research and Regional Cooperation Department of the Asian Development Bank, and Kwanho Shin (Professor of Economics) in Korea University.

continued on next page

Box 4: The Duration of Recoveries from Economic Shocks Like COVID-19   *continued*

is aided by the ability to substitute exports for domestic demand.

Some implications for developing Asia's post-COVID-19 recovery prospects

What are the implications of these findings for recovery from the COVID-19 recession in general and in developing Asian economies in particular? A number of our empirical results point in the direction of lengthy recoveries. The COVID-19 recession is unusually severe, which will make for extended recoveries if history is any guide. The fact that the COVID-19 recession is global points in the same direction. It means that economies, including a growing number of emerging markets in Asia and globally, that had been moving in the direction of more freely floating exchange rates will not be able to exploit that policy flexibility by depreciating their currencies and crowding-in exports since their export markets are also likely to slowly recover. It means that the tendency for economies

that are more open to trade to recover more quickly, something that normally works in developing Asia's favor, will be less potent this time.

Another troubling omen is that the COVID-19 recession involves both aggregate supply and aggregate demand shocks, as first supply was disrupted by lockdowns and then households and firms reduced their spending owing to the loss in incomes. Our results strongly suggest that these are the recessions from which recovery is slowest. The negative supply shock is unavoidable under the circumstances, but the negative demand shock can be mitigated by policy. Emerging markets, including those in Asia, have responded more aggressively than to previous recessions. Some of those with greater fiscal space than in previous recessions have used this advantage more aggressively. In addition, the rapid responses of multilaterals such as the International Monetary Fund and the Asian Development Bank have provided low-income economies with additional fiscal space.

Risks to Economic Outlook and Financial Stability

Downside risks continue to dominate upside risks to the global and regional economic outlook and to financial stability. The overriding downside risk remains the uncertain trajectory of the COVID-19 pandemic. Europe's recent experience suggests that economic performance will be inextricably linked to success in containing outbreaks. In February, the European Union (EU) suffered a major outbreak that began in Italy and soon spread to the rest of the continent. EU governments imposed lockdowns and other stringent restrictions that helped contain the disease but also took a heavy toll on the economy. Reduced mobility and economic activity sharply lowered the EU's GDP in Q2 2020 by more than 10.0% q-o-q. However, the restrictions helped to bring the pandemic under control, as evident in a sharp decline in cases and deaths. This allowed governments to ease restrictions, which immediately boosted demand and growth. Third quarter gross domestic growth reached almost 10.0% q-o-q, and there was growing optimism about a sustained recovery. However, a virulent second wave of COVID-19 cases struck Europe in October, and optimism quickly turned to pessimism. In response, governments across the continent have imposed a new round of restrictions. In

September, the ECB forecast that the euro area would grow at a healthy pace of more than 3% in the fourth quarter of 2020. However, some economists are now predicting an outright contraction.

Emerging East Asian economies have fared relatively well in terms of containing COVID-19. In particular, the PRC, which is a major engine of growth for the region, has seen normality return to everyday life after successfully containing COVID-19. As a result, its economic recovery is gathering momentum and becoming more broad-based. Most promisingly, whereas the recovery in Q2 2020 was driven by public infrastructure investment and exports, consumption began to show signs of life in the third quarter as the PRC's retail sales rose by 3.3% y-o-y in September.

The key takeaway for Asia from Europe's second wave is that economic performance is intimately linked to the state of public health. Furthermore, the European experience suggests that even an apparently robust recovery is powerless in the face of sudden and unexpected worsening of the COVID-19 situation. Therefore, if the PRC and other emerging East Asian economies suffer a sharp spike in cases and deaths that tests their public health capacity, it is likely that economic growth and financial stability will also be tested.

The main upside risk is the rapid development of a safe and effective COVID-19 vaccine. The mere news of a breakthrough vaccine would sharply lift business and consumer confidence. Overall, there is cause for optimism as several candidates have already reached Phase 3 clinical trials, which typically involve thousands of participants to confirm and evaluate the overall risks and benefits of a vaccine. At the same time, the temporary suspension of clinical trials by AstraZeneca and Johnson & Johnson due to sick participants suggests that there is still some work left.

While COVID-19 dominates all other risks, there are nevertheless some significant risks besides the pandemic. The conflict between the PRC and the US, which seems to be rooted in structural differences, shows no signs of abating. On a positive note, tensions between the two have not become noticeably worse in recent months. Emerging East Asian economies depend on close economic links with both the PRC and the US. As such, persistent conflict between the two economic giants represents a significant source of risk and uncertainty. Political and social instability due to various factors is another source of risk and uncertainty. In many countries, central governments are grappling with growing opposition from the general population and regional governments to lockdowns and other COVID-19 restrictions. In the US, there are widespread concerns about whether the government transition following the presidential election on 3 November can be completed smoothly and without major disruption. Any prolonged legal disputes over the election outcome could harm US and global financial stability. Other countries, such as Thailand, are experiencing political instability due to country-specific factors. Finally, as always, a number of geopolitical risks, including geopolitical tensions in the Middle East, loom on the horizon.

Bond Market Developments in the Third Quarter of 2020

Size and Composition

The outstanding amount of local currency bonds in emerging East Asia reached USD18.7 trillion at the end of September.

At the end of September, the size of emerging East Asia's local currency (LCY) bond market reached USD18.7 trillion.[3] The region's bond market growth moderated to 4.8% quarter-on-quarter (q-o-q) in the third quarter (Q3) of 2020 from 5.0% q-o-q in the second quarter (Q2) (**Figure 1a**). The slowdown in growth was primarily driven by a weaker expansion in corporate bonds. Governments continued to issue sovereign debt to finance economic relief measures amid the economic fallout brought about by the coronavirus disease (COVID-19). Meanwhile, risk-off sentiment amid the protracted economic slowdown led to weaker growth in the region's corporate bond markets.

All nine bond markets posted positive q-o-q growth in Q3 2020. The region's smaller bond markets—Viet Nam, Indonesia, and the Philippines—posted the highest growth rates, while Singapore; Malaysia; the Republic of Korea; and Hong Kong, China recorded the slowest expansions. Compared with Q2 2020, the q-o-q growth rate accelerated in six of the region's nine bond markets, including Hong Kong, China; Indonesia; Malaysia; the Philippines; Thailand; and Viet Nam. However, q-o-q growth dropped in three bond markets including the two largest—the People's Republic of China (PRC) and the Republic of Korea—leading to slower regional q-o-q growth.

On a year-on-year (y-o-y) basis, emerging East Asia's LCY bond market growth accelerated to 17.4% in Q3 2020 from 15.5% in Q2 2020 (**Figure 1b**). All markets in the region posted positive y-o-y growth in Q3 2020. Indonesia, the Philippines, and the PRC posted the fastest y-o-y growth rates, while the rest of the region posted moderate growth rates. Hong Kong, China recorded the weakest y-o-y expansion in Q3 2020. Except for

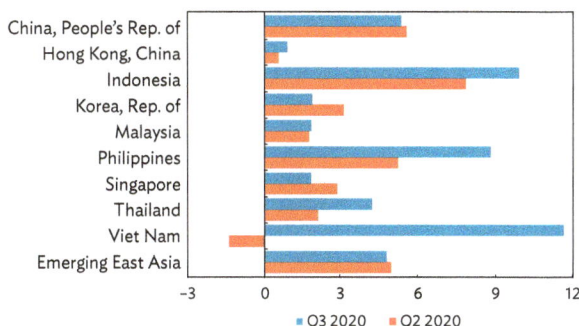

Figure 1a: Growth of Local Currency Bond Markets in the Second and Third Quarters of 2020 (q-o-q, %)

q-o-q = quarter-on-quarter, Q2 = second quarter, Q3 = third quarter.
Notes:
1. For Singapore, corporate bonds outstanding are based on *AsianBondsOnline* estimates.
2. Calculated using data from national sources.
3. Growth rates are calculated from local currency base and do not include currency effects.
4. Emerging East Asia growth figures are based on 30 September 2020 currency exchange rates and do not include currency effects.
Sources: People's Republic of China (CEIC); Hong Kong, China (Hong Kong Monetary Authority); Indonesia (Bank Indonesia; Directorate General of Budget Financing and Risk Management, Ministry of Finance; and Indonesia Stock Exchange); Republic of Korea (*EDAILY BondWeb* and The Bank of Korea); Malaysia (Bank Negara Malaysia); Philippines (Bureau of the Treasury and Bloomberg LP); Singapore (Monetary Authority of Singapore, Singapore Government Securities, and Bloomberg LP); Thailand (Bank of Thailand); and Viet Nam (Bloomberg LP and Vietnam Bond Market Association).

Singapore, all markets in the region posted higher y-o-y growth in Q3 2020 than in Q2 2020.

The PRC's LCY bond market remained the region's largest with an outstanding bond stock of USD14.5 trillion at the end of September. The PRC's share of the regional bond market increased to 77.5% in Q3 2020 from 77.1% in Q2 2020. Growth in the PRC's LCY bond market moderated to 5.4% q-o-q in Q3 2020 from 5.6% q-o-q in Q2 2020. The slower growth in Q3 2020 was driven by a deceleration in corporate bond market growth, as interest rates continued to rise. Growth in the government bond segment continued to accelerate, rising to 6.6% q-o-q in Q3 2020 from 5.4% q-o-q in the previous quarter. The continuing expansion of the LCY government bond market has been fueled by strong issuance of Treasury and other

---

[3] Emerging East Asia comprises the People's Republic of China; Hong Kong, China; Indonesia; the Republic of Korea; Malaysia; the Philippines; Singapore; Thailand; and Viet Nam.

Figure 1b: Growth of Local Currency Bond Markets in the Second and Third Quarters of 2020 (y-o-y, %)

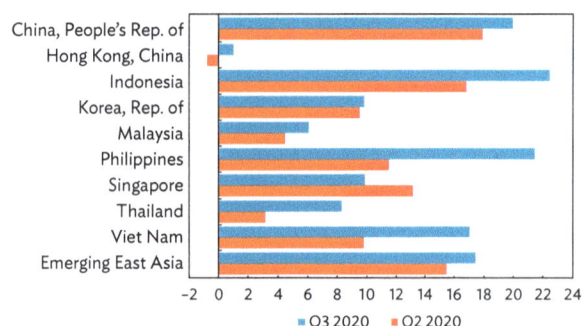

Q2 = second quarter, Q3 = third quarter, y-o-y = year-on-year.
Notes:
1. For Singapore, corporate bonds outstanding are based on *AsianBondsOnline* estimates.
2. Calculated using data from national sources.
3. Growth rates are calculated from local currency base and do not include currency effects.
4. Emerging East Asia growth figures are based on 30 September 2020 currency exchange rates and do not include currency effects.
Sources: People's Republic of China (CEIC); Hong Kong, China (Hong Kong Monetary Authority); Indonesia (Bank Indonesia; Directorate General of Budget Financing and Risk Management, Ministry of Finance; and Indonesia Stock Exchange); Republic of Korea (*EDAILY BondWeb* and The Bank of Korea); Malaysia (Bank Negara Malaysia); Philippines (Bureau of the Treasury and Bloomberg LP); Singapore (Monetary Authority of Singapore, Singapore Government Securities, and Bloomberg LP); Thailand (Bank of Thailand); and Viet Nam (Bloomberg LP and Vietnam Bond Market Association).

government bonds as the government continued to raise funds to support economic recovery amid the COVID-19 pandemic. Growth in the PRC's corporate bond stock dropped to 3.2% q-o-q in Q3 2020 from 5.9% q-o-q in Q2 2020. On a y-o-y basis, the PRC's LCY bond market growth picked up, rising to 19.9% in Q3 2020 from 17.9% in Q2 2020.

The Republic of Korea is home to the second-largest LCY bond market in emerging East Asia, with an outstanding bond stock of USD2.2 trillion at the end of September. However, its share of the regional total slipped to 11.9% in Q3 2020 from 12.3% in the previous quarter. Growth in the Republic of Korea's total bond stock dropped to 1.9% q-o-q in Q3 2020 from 3.1% q-o-q in Q2 2020, driven by weaker growth in both the government and corporate bond segments. Government bonds outstanding rose 3.0% q-o-q in Q3 2020, down from 4.6% q-o-q in Q2 2020. Growth in the corporate bond stock also slowed to 1.1% q-o-q in Q3 2020 from 2.1% q-o-q in the previous quarter. On a y-o-y basis, the Republic of Korea's LCY bond market growth inched up to 9.8% in Q3 2020 from 9.5% in Q2 2020.

Hong Kong, China's LCY bonds outstanding reached USD295.1 billion at the end of September. Growth in the total bond stock inched up to 0.9% q-o-q in Q3 2020 from 0.5% q-o-q in the prior quarter. The government bond segment posted marginal growth of 0.1% q-o-q in Q3 2020, a slight recovery from the 1.1% q-o-q decline in Q2 2020. The growth was driven largely by an expansion in the outstanding amount of Hong Kong Special Administrative Region bonds. Growth in the corporate bond segment moderated to 1.6% q-o-q in Q3 2020 from 2.3% q-o-q in Q2 2020. On an annual basis, Hong Kong, China's LCY bond market rose 1.0% in Q3 2020, reversing the 0.8% contraction in Q2 2020. Hong Kong, China's bond market posted the slowest pace of q-o-q and y-o-y growth among emerging East Asian markets in Q3 2020, as the deepening economic contraction brought about by political uncertainties and COVID-19 continued to impact its financial markets.

The total amount of LCY bonds outstanding of the member economies of the Association of Southeast Asian Nations (ASEAN) reached USD1.7 trillion in Q3 2020, up from USD1.6 trillion in Q2 2020.[4] Overall growth accelerated to 4.7% q-o-q in Q3 2020 from 3.2% q-o-q in Q2 2020. The total government bond stock amounted to USD1.2 trillion, while the total corporate bond stock reached USD0.5 trillion at the end of September. Thailand, Malaysia, and Singapore remained the three largest bond markets among all ASEAN members.

Thailand's LCY bonds outstanding amounted to USD443.7 billion at the end of September. Overall growth picked up in Q3 2020, rising to 4.2% q-o-q from 2.1% q-o-q in Q2 2020. The faster expansion stemmed from stronger growth in the government bond segment combined with a recovery in the corporate bond segment. Growth in outstanding government bonds accelerated to 5.4% q-o-q in Q3 2020 from 4.1% q-o-q in Q2 2020, as the government continued to issue sovereign debt to help fund stimulus measures. Corporate bonds outstanding increased 1.1% q-o-q in Q3 2020, reversing the 2.6% q-o-q decline in the prior quarter. On a y-o-y basis, Thailand's bond market growth jumped to 8.3% in Q3 2020 from 3.2% in Q2 2020.

The outstanding amount of Malaysia's LCY bonds reached USD381.0 billion at the end of September on

[4] LCY bond statistics for ASEAN include the markets of Indonesia, Malaysia, the Philippines, Singapore, Thailand, and Viet Nam.

growth of 1.9% q-o-q and 6.1% y-o-y. Growth in the outstanding government bond stock moderated to 2.3% q-o-q in Q3 2020 from 3.2% q-o-q in Q2 2020. The corporate bond segment rose 1.3% q-o-q in Q3 2020, up from 0.2% q-o-q in the previous quarter amid a slight recovery in investor sentiment.

Malaysia is home to the largest *sukuk* (Islamic bond) market in emerging East Asia, with a total of USD239.0 billion *sukuk* outstanding at the end of September. In Q3 2020, the stock of government *sukuk* totaled USD96.5 billion, or 47.3% of total government bonds. Outstanding corporate *sukuk* reached USD142.4 billion, or 80.5% of total corporate bonds.

The outstanding amount of Singapore's LCY bonds amounted to USD358.5 billion at the end of September. Growth in total outstanding bonds dropped to 1.8% q-o-q in Q3 2020 from 2.9% q-o-q in Q2 2020, driven by weaker growth in the government bond segment. Government bonds outstanding rose 2.0% q-o-q in Q3 2020, down from 4.4% q-o-q in the prior quarter. Meanwhile, growth in outstanding corporate bonds jumped to 1.6% q-o-q in Q3 2020 from tepid growth of 0.3% q-o-q in Q2 2020. On a y-o-y basis, Singapore's bond market expansion moderated to 9.8% in Q3 2020 from 13.2% in Q2 2020.

Indonesia's LCY bond market reached a size of USD264.8 billion at the end of September, with growth rising to 9.9% q-o-q in Q3 2020 from 7.8% q-o-q in Q2 2020. The faster growth in Q3 2020 was supported by a strong expansion in the government bond segment and a recovery in the corporate bond segment. Growth in the outstanding stock of LCY government bonds quickened to 10.9% q-o-q in Q3 2020 from 9.5% q-o-q in the previous quarter. Indonesia posted the fastest growth in its government bond stock in emerging East Asia in Q3 2020, bolstered by heightened issuance of government debt to finance economic relief measures. Corporate bonds outstanding rose 2.6% q-o-q in Q3 2020, reversing the 3.0% q-o-q drop in the prior quarter. On an annual basis, Indonesia's LCY bond market expanded 22.4% y-o-y in Q3 2020, up from 16.8% y-o-y in Q2 2020.

The outstanding amount of LCY bonds in the Philippines reached USD167.8 billion at the end of September. Overall growth quickened to 8.8% q-o-q in Q3 2020 from 5.2% q-o-q in Q2 2020, supported by faster growth

in the government bond segment and a recovery in the corporate bond segment. Outstanding government bonds rose 10.1% q-o-q in Q3 2020, up from 6.8% q-o-q in the prior quarter on increased issuance due to heightened financing needs for stimulus measures. The corporate bond market expanded 3.8% q-o-q in Q3 2020, recovering from a 0.4% q-o-q contraction in Q2 2020. On a y-o-y basis, overall LCY bond market growth almost doubled to 21.5% in Q3 2020 from 11.5% in Q2 2020.

Viet Nam's LCY bond market reached a size of USD65.3 billion at the end of September, with overall growth of 11.6% q-o-q in Q3 2020 reversing the 1.4% q-o-q contraction in Q2 2020. The recovery in q-o-q growth was driven by a resurgence in government bond market growth in Q3 2020. Government bonds outstanding rose 9.1% q-o-q in Q3 2020, a reversal of the 7.8% q-o-q drop in the previous quarter. Meanwhile, growth in outstanding corporate bonds slowed to 26.9% q-o-q in Q3 2020 from 68.9% q-o-q in Q2 2020. On an annual basis, Viet Nam's LCY bond market growth jumped to 17.0% y-o-y in Q3 2020 from 9.8% y-o-y in the prior quarter.

At the end of September, government bonds continued to account for the majority of emerging East Asia's LCY bond stock, representing a 61.6% share. In nominal terms, the outstanding stock of government bonds in the region reached USD11.5 trillion on growth of 6.1% q-o-q and 17.3% y-o-y (**Table 1**). The PRC and the Republic of Korea maintained their positions as the two largest government bond markets in the region with a combined share of 88.4% in Q3 2020.

ASEAN economies accounted for 10.3% of aggregate government bonds outstanding in emerging East Asia at the end of Q3 2020. Among ASEAN economies, Thailand had the largest stock of LCY government bonds at the end of September at USD324.7 billion. Indonesia, Singapore, and Malaysia followed with outstanding LCY government bonds of USD235.2 billion, USD228.3 billion, and USD204.1 billion, respectively. The Philippines and Viet Nam had the two smallest government bond stocks at USD134.1 billion and USD54.7 billion, respectively.

LCY corporate bonds outstanding in emerging East Asia totaled USD7.2 trillion at the end of September. The growth in the region's aggregate corporate bonds outstanding slowed to 2.7% q-o-q in Q3 2020 from 4.7% q-o-q in Q2 2020. The slower growth stemmed

Table 1: Size and Composition of Local Currency Bond Markets

	Q3 2019 Amount (USD billion)	Q3 2019 % share	Q2 2020 Amount (USD billion)	Q2 2020 % share	Q3 2020 Amount (USD billion)	Q3 2020 % share	Growth Rate (LCY-base %) Q3 2019 q-o-q	Q3 2019 y-o-y	Q3 2020 q-o-q	Q3 2020 y-o-y	Growth Rate (USD-base %) Q3 2019 q-o-q	Q3 2019 y-o-y	Q3 2020 q-o-q	Q3 2020 y-o-y
China, People's Rep. of														
Total	11,459	100.0	13,189	100.0	14,457	100.0	3.6	14.9	5.4	19.9	(0.5)	10.4	9.6	26.2
Government	7,402	64.6	8,332	63.2	9,240	63.9	3.5	12.9	6.6	18.6	(0.6)	8.5	10.9	24.8
Corporate	4,057	35.4	4,857	36.8	5,217	36.1	3.9	18.6	3.2	22.2	(0.2)	14.0	7.4	28.6
Hong Kong, China														
Total	289	100.0	293	100.0	295	100.0	(0.9)	4.2	0.9	1.0	(1.3)	4.1	0.9	2.2
Government	149	51.7	149	51.0	149	50.6	0.5	1.4	0.1	(1.1)	0.2	1.2	0.1	0.0
Corporate	140	48.3	143	49.0	146	49.4	(2.4)	7.4	1.6	3.2	(2.8)	7.3	1.6	4.4
Indonesia														
Total	227	100.0	251	100.0	265	100.0	4.8	16.4	9.9	22.4	4.3	22.2	5.4	16.8
Government	196	86.4	221	88.0	235	88.8	4.8	18.6	10.9	25.8	4.3	24.5	6.3	20.1
Corporate	31	13.6	30	12.0	30	11.2	4.9	4.4	2.6	0.7	4.4	9.6	(1.7)	(3.9)
Korea, Rep. of														
Total	1,982	100.0	2,123	100.0	2,224	100.0	1.7	6.6	1.9	9.8	(1.9)	(1.2)	4.7	12.2
Government	797	40.2	863	40.7	914	41.1	0.8	2.8	3.0	12.1	(2.7)	(4.7)	5.8	14.6
Corporate	1,184	59.8	1,260	59.3	1,310	58.9	2.3	9.4	1.1	8.2	(1.3)	1.4	4.0	10.6
Malaysia														
Total	357	100.0	363	100.0	381	100.0	0.3	8.3	1.9	6.1	(1.0)	7.0	5.0	6.9
Government	188	52.6	193	53.3	204	53.6	0.8	8.3	2.3	8.0	(0.5)	7.1	5.5	8.8
Corporate	169	47.4	169	46.7	177	46.4	(0.2)	8.3	1.3	3.9	(1.6)	7.0	4.5	4.7
Philippines														
Total	129	100.0	150	100.0	168	100.0	(0.1)	15.7	8.8	21.5	(1.2)	20.6	11.8	29.9
Government	101	78.4	119	79.0	134	79.9	(0.7)	14.4	10.1	23.8	(1.8)	19.2	13.2	32.4
Corporate	28	21.6	32	21.0	34	20.1	2.1	20.7	3.8	12.9	1.0	25.8	6.7	20.7
Singapore														
Total	322	100.0	345	100.0	358	100.0	4.9	11.9	1.8	9.8	2.7	10.7	3.9	11.2
Government	200	62.2	219	63.6	228	63.7	5.6	15.0	2.0	12.5	3.4	13.8	4.1	13.9
Corporate	122	37.8	126	36.4	130	36.3	3.8	7.2	1.6	5.4	1.7	6.1	3.7	6.7
Thailand														
Total	423	100.0	435	100.0	444	100.0	(0.7)	6.6	4.2	8.3	38.1	52.2	2.0	4.9
Government	301	71.2	315	72.4	325	73.2	(1.1)	6.0	5.4	11.3	33.3	44.9	3.1	7.8
Corporate	122	28.8	120	27.6	119	26.8	0.2	8.3	1.1	0.9	51.8	74.3	(1.1)	(2.3)
Viet Nam														
Total	56	100.0	58	100.0	65	100.0	4.7	3.1	11.6	17.0	5.2	3.6	11.7	17.1
Government	51	91.7	50	85.7	55	83.8	5.2	2.9	9.1	6.9	5.7	3.4	9.2	7.0
Corporate	5	8.3	8	14.3	11	16.2	(0.7)	5.1	26.9	129.1	(0.2)	5.6	26.9	129.3
Emerging East Asia														
Total	15,244	100.0	17,208	100.0	18,657	100.0	3.1	13.1	4.8	17.4	0.3	9.6	8.4	22.4
Government	9,386	61.6	10,462	60.8	11,484	61.6	3.0	11.6	6.1	17.3	0.3	8.4	9.8	22.3
Corporate	5,857	38.4	6,746	39.2	7,173	38.4	3.2	15.5	2.7	17.6	0.3	11.5	6.3	22.5
Japan														
Total	10,963	100.0	11,082	100.0	11,492	100.0	0.4	1.9	1.3	2.3	0.1	7.2	3.7	4.8
Government	10,187	92.9	10,288	92.8	10,664	92.8	0.2	1.5	1.3	2.2	(0.04)	6.8	3.7	4.7
Corporate	776	7.1	794	7.2	828	7.2	2.8	7.2	1.9	4.1	2.6	12.8	4.3	6.6

( ) = negative, LCY = local currency, q-o-q = quarter-on-quarter, Q2 = second quarter, Q3 = third quarter, USD = United States dollar, y-o-y = year-on-year.

Notes:
1. For Singapore, corporate bonds outstanding are based on *AsianBondsOnline* estimates.
2. Corporate bonds include issues by financial institutions.
3. Bloomberg LP end-of-period LCY–USD rates are used.
4. For LCY base, emerging East Asia growth figures are based on 30 September 2020 currency exchange rates and do not include currency effects.
5. Emerging East Asia comprises the People's Republic of China; Hong Kong, China; Indonesia; the Republic of Korea; Malaysia; the Philippines; Singapore; Thailand; and Viet Nam.

Sources: People's Republic of China (CEIC); Hong Kong, China (Hong Kong Monetary Authority); Indonesia (Bank Indonesia; Directorate General of Budget Financing and Risk Management, Ministry of Finance; and Indonesia Stock Exchange); Republic of Korea (*EDAILY BondWeb* and The Bank of Korea); Malaysia (Bank Negara Malaysia); Philippines (Bureau of the Treasury and Bloomberg LP); Singapore (Monetary Authority of Singapore, Singapore Government Securities, and Bloomberg LP); Thailand (Bank of Thailand); Viet Nam (Bloomberg LP and Vietnam Bond Market Association); and Japan (Japan Securities Dealers Association).

primarily from a growth slowdown in the PRC and the Republic of Korea, the region's two largest corporate bond markets. Corporate bond market growth also slowed in Viet Nam and Hong Kong, China in Q3 2020 compared with Q2 2020. The rest of the emerging East Asia's corporate bond markets posted faster growth in Q3 2020 than in Q2 2020, but the weaker growth in the PRC and the Republic of Korea curtailed the region's overall growth in Q3 2020.

ASEAN economies accounted for 7.0% of emerging East Asia's corporate bond market at the end of September. Among ASEAN economies, Malaysia, Singapore, and Thailand had the largest corporate bond markets with outstanding bond stocks of USD176.9 billion, USD130.2 billion, and USD118.9 billion, respectively. The Philippines and Indonesia followed, with outstanding bond stocks of USD33.7 billion and USD29.6 billion, respectively. Viet Nam remained home to the region's smallest corporate bond market, with an outstanding stock of USD10.6 billion at the end of September.

Emerging East Asia's total LCY bond market was equivalent to 95.6% of the region's gross domestic product (GDP) at the end of September, climbing from 91.6% at the end of June and 82.5% at the end of September 2019 (**Table 2**). The share of government bonds to GDP, expressed as a percentage, increased to 58.8% at the end of Q3 2020 from 55.7% at the end of Q2 2020, while the corporate bonds-to-GDP share increased to 36.8% from 35.9%. The rising bonds-to-GDP share in Q3 2020 is attributed to the expansion of all bond markets in the region during the quarter, largely due to governments raising funds for their COVID-19 responses, while economic output continued to experience moderate to negative growth due to the lingering adverse impact of the pandemic.

The bond markets of the Republic of Korea, Malaysia, and Singapore were the largest in the region, measured as a percentage of GDP, at the end of Q3 2020, with their GDP shares each exceeding 100%. The Republic of Korea's bond market had the highest GDP share in the region at 141.7%. Indonesia and Viet Nam accounted for the smallest bond market shares at 25.0% each. All economies saw increases in their bond-to-GDP shares between Q2 2020 and Q3 2020.

Table 2: Size and Composition of Local Currency Bond Markets (% of GDP)

	Q3 2019	Q2 2020	Q3 2020
China, People's Rep. of			
Total	84.3	94.4	98.1
Government	54.5	59.7	62.7
Corporate	29.8	34.8	35.4
Hong Kong, China			
Total	78.8	82.1	83.4
Government	40.7	41.8	42.2
Corporate	38.0	40.2	41.2
Indonesia			
Total	20.6	22.8	25.4
Government	17.8	20.1	22.5
Corporate	2.8	2.7	2.8
Korea, Rep. of			
Total	129.0	138.6	141.7
Government	51.9	56.3	58.2
Corporate	77.1	82.3	83.5
Malaysia			
Total	106.0	114.0	116.9
Government	55.8	60.8	62.6
Corporate	50.2	53.2	54.3
Philippines			
Total	35.0	39.7	44.4
Government	27.4	31.4	35.5
Corporate	7.6	8.4	8.9
Singapore			
Total	87.3	99.7	103.6
Government	54.3	63.4	66.0
Corporate	33.0	36.3	37.6
Thailand			
Total	77.1	82.9	88.1
Government	54.9	60.0	64.5
Corporate	22.2	22.9	23.6
Viet Nam			
Total	22.0	22.1	24.5
Government	20.2	19.0	20.5
Corporate	1.8	3.2	4.0
Emerging East Asia			
Total	82.5	91.6	95.6
Government	50.8	55.7	58.8
Corporate	31.7	35.9	36.8
Japan			
Total	214.3	221.4	227.1
Government	199.1	205.5	210.8
Corporate	15.2	15.9	16.4

GDP = gross domestic product, Q2 = second quarter, Q3 = third quarter.
Notes:
1. Data for GDP are from CEIC. Q3 2020 GDP figures carried over from Q2 2020 for Singapore.
2. For Singapore, corporate bonds outstanding are based on *AsianBondsOnline* estimates.
Sources: People's Republic of China (CEIC); Hong Kong, China (Hong Kong Monetary Authority); Indonesia (Bank Indonesia; Directorate General of Budget Financing and Risk Management, Ministry of Finance; and Indonesia Stock Exchange); Republic of Korea (*EDAILY BondWeb* and The Bank of Korea); Malaysia (Bank Negara Malaysia); Philippines (Bureau of the Treasury and Bloomberg LP); Singapore (Monetary Authority of Singapore, Singapore Government Securities, and Bloomberg LP); Thailand (Bank of Thailand); Viet Nam (Bloomberg LP and Vietnam Bond Market Association); and Japan (Japan Securities Dealers Association).

By segment, Singapore had the highest government bonds-to-GDP share in the region at 66.0%, while the Republic of Korea had the largest corporate bonds-to-GDP share at 83.5%. Viet Nam had the lowest government bonds-to-GDP share at 20.5%, while Indonesia had the lowest corporate bonds-to-GDP share at 2.8%.

Foreign Investor Holdings

The foreign holdings share of LCY government bonds declined in most markets in Q3 2020.

The foreign investor holdings share at the end of Q3 2020 was lower than at the end of Q2 2020 in Indonesia, Thailand, the Philippines, and Viet Nam, while it increased in the PRC and Malaysia (**Figure 2**). Lingering uncertainty and risk surrounding the COVID-19 pandemic weighed down foreign investor sentiment, negatively impacting investment in most markets in the region.

Foreign investors continued to increase their holdings of the PRC's government bonds. The share of foreign holdings increased to 9.4% at the end of September from 9.1% at the end of June. Government bonds in the PRC have higher returns compared to advanced economies such as the United States (US) and Japan, resulting in sustained foreign interest in the domestic bond market. The stability of the Chinese yuan is also a factor in the

increase in foreign holdings. Moreover, the PRC published new draft rules in September making foreign access to the LCY bond market easier to further boost the market's development. Foreign investor demand was also driven by news that PRC government bonds would be included in the FTSE Russell World Government Bond Index in October 2021.

Malaysian government securities continued to attract foreign participation in the bond market with the share of offshore holdings climbing to 23.6% at the end of September from 22.7% at the end of June. Favorable yields amid high global liquidity and signs of domestic economic recovery supported the bond market's appeal to foreign investors. The increase in Malaysian government bonds' weight in the Government Bond Index-Emerging Markets Global Diversified Index as well as the decision to keep Malaysia's bonds in the FTSE Russell World Government Bond Index, with another review to follow in March 2021, has also lent a boost to demand. Malaysia has the second-largest share of foreign-held government bonds in the region.

Foreign ownership of government bonds in Indonesia and in the Philippines further declined in Q3 2020. Indonesia reached a share of 27.0% at the end of September, a record low dating to June 2012, over concerns about Indonesia's debt monetization plan. The share of offshore holdings has fallen about 10 percentage points from the start of the year. Foreign investor sentiment toward the local bond market remained weak in Q3 2020 as evidenced by low to negative monthly fund flows. The massive borrowings by the government to fund its pandemic response were mainly absorbed by domestic investors, resulting in the slide in the share of foreign holdings. Despite the decline, Indonesia continued to have the highest foreign holdings share in the region. In the Philippines, foreign ownership of government bonds dropped to its lowest level since data are available, falling to 1.5% at the end of September from 1.9% at the end of June. While foreign funds returned to the government bond market in September, the inflow was merely enough to have a small offsetting impact on past outflows. Domestic investors are the main participants in the local government bond market expansion.

Foreign participation in Thailand's government bond market has not fully recovered from the initial impact of the COVID-19 pandemic. The decline in the share of debt paper held by foreign investors continued to decline in

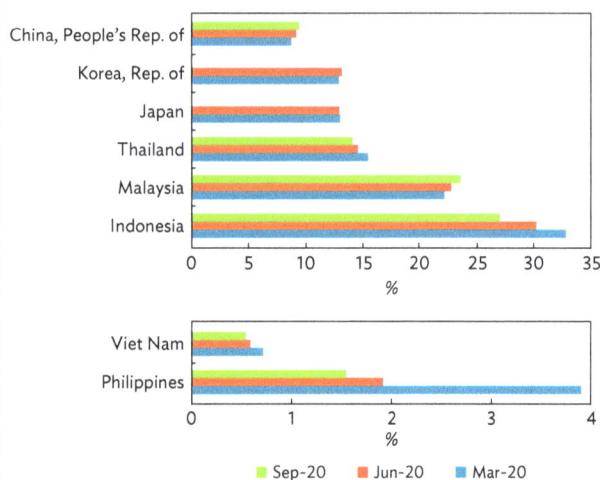

Figure 2: Foreign Holdings of Local Currency Government Bonds in Select Asian Markets (% of total)

Note: Data for Japan and the Republic of Korea as of 30 June 2020.
Source: AsianBondsOnline.

Q3 2020, as increases in debt were largely absorbed by domestic investors. The foreign holdings share was down to 14.0% at the end of September, its lowest level since December 2016, even as monthly fund flows have been positive since June.

In Viet Nam, the share of foreign ownership was practically unchanged in Q3 2020, remaining at 0.6% at the end of September. The foreign holdings share in Viet Nam is the smallest in the region.

The uptrend in the foreign holdings share in the Republic of Korea's government bond held through the end of June. Foreign investors held 13.0% of Korean government bonds, up from 12.8% at the end of March and the highest level of foreign ownership share since data are available. The appeal of government bonds is owed to high returns as well as sound fiscal and financial conditions in the economy.

Foreign Bond Flows

Foreign buying of government bonds was sustained in most emerging East Asian markets in Q3 2020.

Inflows of foreign funds into government bond markets continued in Q3 2020 in most emerging East Asian economies after rebounding in Q2 2020 (**Figure 3**). This resulted in total net inflows of USD29.9 billion in the region during the quarter. Ample global liquidity, high-yielding government debt, and some signs of recovery among emerging East Asian economies amid progress in COVID-19 containment measures were the key factors driving the positive flows. The highest monthly net inflows in the region during Q3 2020 were recorded in July, amounting to an aggregate of USD11.7 billion, with only the Philippines experiencing outflows. Foreign buying, however, decelerated in succeeding months, registering only USD7.9 billion in aggregate net inflows in September, with Indonesia and the Republic of Korea registering outflows.

The PRC attracted USD23.3 billion in foreign funds in Q3 2020, its highest quarterly inflow total to date. Its largest monthly inflows during the quarter occurred in August with USD9.0 billion. Attractive yields, initiatives to open up its financial markets to international investors, and the PRC bond market's inclusion in investing indexes

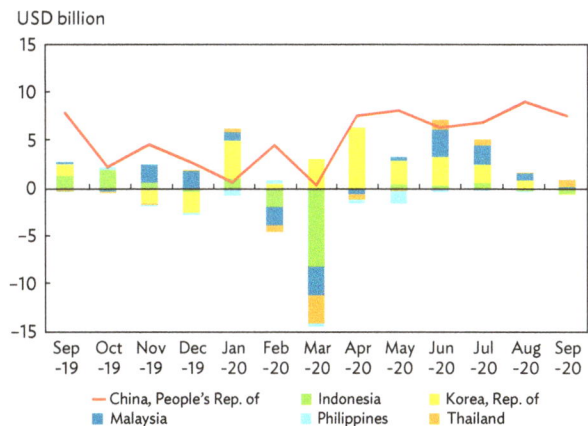

Figure 3: Foreign Bond Flows in Select Emerging East Asian Economies

USD = United States dollar.
Notes:
1. The Republic of Korea and Thailand provided data on bond flows. For the People's Republic of China, Indonesia, Malaysia, and the Philippines, month-on-month changes in foreign holdings of local currency government bonds were used as a proxy for bond flows.
2. Data as of 30 September 2020.
3. Figures were computed based on 30 September 2020 exchange rates to avoid currency effects.
Sources: People's Republic of China (*Wind Information*); Indonesia (Directorate General of Budget Financing and Risk Management, Ministry of Finance); Republic of Korea (Financial Supervisory Service); Malaysia (Bank Negara Malaysia); Philippines (Bureau of the Treasury); and Thailand (Thai Bond Market Association).

have fueled foreign participation in the LCY debt market. The PRC had the highest fund inflows among all emerging East Asian economies during the quarter.

In the Republic of Korea, cumulative net inflows amounted to USD2.7 billion in Q3 2020, which was partially offset by the foreign sell-off in September. The fund outflows in September, amounting to USD26.5 million, were the first since the start of the year. Profit-taking by investors, following 8 months of foreign buying, mainly caused the outflows.

Overseas investors continued to pour funds into the Malaysian and Thai government debt markets in Q3 2020. Malaysia received total inflows of USD2.9 billion during the quarter, with the bulk occurring in July before slowing in August and September. In Thailand, total inflows amounted to USD1.4 billion during the quarter with the highest monthly total occurring in September at USD0.8 billion. Relatively higher returns in these markets, especially as real interest rates were pushed higher by deflation, drove the continued foreign buying.

Indonesia saw foreign fund outflows in Q3 2020 as concerns about the struggle to contain COVID-19 persisted. Indonesia had total net outflows of USD0.3 billion during the quarter due to fund withdrawals in August and September that offset the foreign buying in July. Investor concerns about a potential weakening of Bank Indonesia's independence also sparked the capital outflows. In September, Indonesia's parliament received a recommendation to give government ministers voting rights at monetary policy meetings and to allow the central banks to fund fiscal deficits.

In the Philippines, net foreign funds outflow amounted to USD0.3 billion in Q3 2020, an improvement from the previous quarter's USD2.0 billion withdrawals. Foreign investors sold Philippine government bonds from March to August. In the months of Q3 2020, outflows in July amounted to USD0.2 billion, tapering off in August to USD92.0 million, before registering inflows of USD46.9 million in September. This improvement was likely brought about by some optimism with the gradual reopening of the economy and progress in COVID-19 containment as evidenced by declining daily cases.

Local Currency Bond Issuance

Total LCY bond sales in emerging East Asia climbed to USD2.2 trillion in Q3 2020, as governments borrowed to support large-scale stimulus programs.

LCY bond issuance in emerging East Asian markets continued to expand in Q3 2020, buoyed by governments seeking to fund large-scale stimulus programs and recovery measures amid the COVID-19 outbreak. Total bond sales reached USD2.2 trillion in Q3 2020 on a 6.4% q-o-q expansion (**Table 3**). Growth, however, moderated due to a high base effect following the 21.5% q-o-q issuance hike posted in the preceding quarter. Issuance in Q3 2020 was largely driven by higher sales of Treasury instruments and other government bonds. Central bank issuance also contributed to the growth but to a much lower extent. In contrast, the volume of issuance by corporates fell short of the previous quarter's volume. Seven out of nine emerging East Asian bond markets posted a higher issuance volume in Q3 2020 than in the previous quarter, with the Republic of Korea and Malaysia as the exceptions. Both markets recorded q-o-q declines in issuance in Q3 2020 vis-à-vis Q2 2020.

On an annual basis, issuance growth expanded at a faster pace of 39.8% y-o-y in Q3 2020 compared with 32.5% y-o-y in Q2 2020. Except for Viet Nam, all regional bond markets recorded y-o-y increases in bond issuance in Q3 2020. Viet Nam was the sole market that posted a y-o-y contraction in issuance.

Government bonds continued to account for a larger share of issuance than corporate bonds, representing 61.2% of the region's issuance total during the quarter, up from the previous quarter's 58.5%. In Q3 2020, LCY government bond issuance totaled USD1,374.1 billion on growth of 11.4% q-o-q and 51.8% y-o-y. Driving much of the growth in government bond issuance was Treasury instruments and other government bonds, which comprised 75.2% of the total government bond issuance during the quarter. The markets of the PRC, Indonesia, the Philippines, Thailand, and Viet Nam saw q-o-q increases in their issuance of Treasury and other government bonds during the quarter. On the other hand, lower issuance volumes of Treasury and other government bonds were observed in Hong Kong, China; the Republic of Korea; and Malaysia. Singapore maintained the same volume of issuance in Q3 2020 compared with the previous quarter.

Central bank issuance recovered in Q3 2020, with growth rising 8.2% q-o-q after contracting 1.4% q-o-q in Q2 2020. Most of the region's central banks increased their issuance in Q3 2020, particularly in Hong Kong, China; Indonesia; the Philippines; Singapore; and Thailand. On the other hand, the Bank of Korea and Bank Negara Malaysia reduced their issuance, while the State Bank of Vietnam had no issuance.

In contrast, corporate bond issuance across the region declined a marginal 0.6% q-o-q to USD870.7 billion. On a y-o-y basis, however, corporate bond issuance grew 24.3% in Q3 2020, which was lower than the previous quarter's 38.8% rise. The PRC and the Republic of Korea, which are home to the region's first- and second-largest corporate bond markets, respectively, each recorded a low volume of issuance during the quarter. Corporates from Singapore and Viet Nam also had less issuance during the quarter.

The PRC continued to dominate LCY bond issuance in the region, constituting 70.1% of emerging East Asia's aggregate issuance volume in Q3 2020. Total bond sales reached USD1,573.5 billion in Q3 2020, of which

Table 3: Local-Currency–Denominated Bond Issuance (gross)

	Q3 2019		Q2 2020		Q3 2020		Growth Rate (LCY-base %)		Growth Rate (USD-base %)	
	Amount (USD billion)	% share	Amount (USD billion)	% share	Amount (USD billion)	% share	Q3 2020 q-o-q	y-o-y	Q3 2020 q-o-q	y-o-y
China, People's Rep. of										
Total	981	100.0	1,414	100.0	1,574	100.0	6.9	52.5	11.3	60.5
Government	467	47.6	736	52.1	866	55.1	13.1	76.3	17.7	85.6
Central Bank	0	0.0	0	0.0	0	0.0	–	–	–	–
Treasury and Other Govt.	467	47.6	736	52.1	866	55.1	13.1	76.3	17.7	85.6
Corporate	514	52.4	678	47.9	707	44.9	0.2	30.8	4.3	37.7
Hong Kong, China										
Total	130	100.0	137	100.0	145	100.0	5.2	9.8	5.2	11.1
Government	107	82.1	107	78.0	117	80.8	9.0	8.0	9.0	9.3
Central Bank	106	81.8	106	77.2	117	80.7	10.0	8.4	10.0	9.7
Treasury and Other Govt.	0.5	0.4	1	0.8	0.1	0.1	(87.8)	(73.7)	(87.8)	(73.4)
Corporate	23	17.9	30	22.0	28	19.2	(8.2)	17.9	(8.2)	19.3
Indonesia										
Total	24	100.0	30	100.0	41	100.0	44.3	78.5	38.3	70.3
Government	21	87.2	29	98.0	39	93.9	38.2	92.2	32.5	83.3
Central Bank	8	33.5	8	26.4	9	21.6	17.9	15.0	13.0	9.7
Treasury and Other Govt.	13	53.7	21	71.6	30	72.3	45.7	140.4	39.7	129.4
Corporate	3	12.8	1	2.0	3	6.1	340.7	(14.7)	322.5	(18.6)
Korea, Rep. of										
Total	164	100.0	208	100.0	189	100.0	(11.5)	12.6	(9.1)	15.1
Government	63	38.6	96	46.4	85	44.8	(14.5)	30.6	(12.1)	33.5
Central Bank	30	18.3	33	16.0	31	16.2	(10.5)	(0.4)	(8.0)	1.9
Treasury and Other Govt.	33	20.3	63	30.3	54	28.6	(16.7)	58.5	(14.3)	62.1
Corporate	101	61.4	112	53.6	104	55.2	(8.9)	1.2	(6.4)	3.5
Malaysia										
Total	20	100.0	22	100.0	22	100.0	(4.5)	6.3	(1.5)	7.1
Government	9	45.6	14	63.7	12	57.4	(14.0)	33.7	(11.3)	34.7
Central Bank	2	10.2	0.2	1.1	0	0.0	(100.0)	(100.0)	(100.0)	(100.0)
Treasury and Other Govt.	7	35.4	14	62.6	12	57.4	(12.5)	72.1	(9.8)	73.3
Corporate	11	54.4	8	36.3	9	42.6	12.1	(16.7)	15.6	(16.1)
Philippines										
Total	7	100.0	14	100.0	25	100.0	77.0	254.0	81.9	278.5
Government	5	78.5	13	96.0	23	89.8	65.4	304.5	69.9	332.5
Central Bank	0	0.0	0	0.0	1	4.1	–	–	–	–
Treasury and Other Govt.	5	78.5	13	96.0	22	85.7	57.9	286.2	62.3	312.9
Corporate	1	21.5	1	4.0	3	10.2	358.3	69.0	370.9	80.7
Singapore										
Total	124	100.0	136	100.0	148	100.0	6.8	18.1	9.0	19.6
Government	120	96.8	131	96.8	144	97.5	7.5	18.9	9.8	20.4
Central Bank	94	75.9	106	78.2	118	80.0	9.3	24.6	11.6	26.1
Treasury and Other Govt.	26	21.0	25	18.6	26	17.5	0.0	(1.7)	2.1	(0.5)
Corporate	4	3.2	4	3.2	4	2.5	(16.1)	(6.4)	(14.4)	(5.2)
Thailand										
Total	78	100.0	79	100.0	93	100.0	20.9	23.4	18.3	19.5
Government	65	82.8	71	89.6	83	89.0	20.2	32.7	17.6	28.5
Central Bank	59	75.7	59	75.2	65	69.1	11.2	12.6	8.8	9.1
Treasury and Other Govt.	5	7.0	11	14.4	19	19.9	67.1	248.1	63.5	237.1
Corporate	13	17.2	8	10.4	10	11.0	27.4	(21.3)	24.6	(23.8)

continued on next page

Table 3 *continued*

	Q3 2019		Q2 2020		Q3 2020		Growth Rate (LCY-base %)		Growth Rate (USD-base %)	
	Amount (USD billion)	% share	Amount (USD billion)	% share	Amount (USD billion)	% share	Q3 2020		Q3 2020	
							q-o-q	y-o-y	q-o-q	y-o-y
Viet Nam										
Total	22	100.0	6	100.0	8	100.0	34.3	(63.7)	34.4	(63.7)
Government	22	99.4	2	39.6	5	63.7	116.2	(76.8)	116.3	(76.7)
Central Bank	19	89.2	0	0.0	0	0.0	–	(100.0)	–	(100.0)
Treasury and Other Govt.	2	10.2	2	39.6	5	63.7	116.2	126.0	116.3	126.2
Corporate	0.1	0.6	4	60.4	3	36.3	(19.3)	2,048.7	(19.2)	2,050.4
Emerging East Asia										
Total	1,550	100.0	2,046	100.0	2,245	100.0	6.4	39.8	9.7	44.8
Government	879	56.7	1,201	58.7	1,374	61.2	11.4	51.8	14.4	56.3
Central Bank	319	20.6	313	15.3	340	15.2	8.2	6.3	8.7	6.6
Treasury and Other Govt.	560	36.1	888	43.4	1,034	46.1	12.5	76.7	16.5	84.7
Corporate	671	43.3	845	41.3	871	38.8	(0.6)	24.3	3.0	29.8
Japan										
Total	411	100.0	406	100.0	533	100.0	28.3	26.5	31.3	29.6
Government	357	86.9	370	91.1	484	90.8	27.9	32.2	30.9	35.5
Central Bank	0	0.0	20	5.0	0	0.0	(100.0)	–	–	–
Treasury and Other Govt.	357	86.9	350	86.1	484	90.8	35.3	32.2	38.5	35.5
Corporate	54	13.1	36	8.9	49	9.2	32.4	(11.4)	35.5	(9.2)

( ) = negative, – = not applicable, LCY = local currency, q-o-q = quarter-on-quarter, Q2 = second quarter, Q3 = third quarter, USD = United States dollar, y-o-y = year-on-year.
Notes:
1. Corporate bonds include issues by financial institutions.
2. Bloomberg LP end-of-period LCY–USD rates are used.
3. For LCY base, emerging East Asia growth figures are based on 30 September 2020 currency exchange rates and do not include currency effects.
Sources: People's Republic of China (CEIC); Hong Kong, China (Hong Kong Monetary Authority); Indonesia (Bank Indonesia; Directorate General of Budget Financing and Risk Management, Ministry of Finance; and Indonesia Stock Exchange); Republic of Korea (*EDAILY BondWeb* and The Bank of Korea); Malaysia (Bank Negara Malaysia); Philippines (Bureau of the Treasury and Bloomberg LP); Singapore (Singapore Government Securities and Bloomberg LP); Thailand (Bank of Thailand and ThaiBMA); Viet Nam (Bloomberg LP and Vietnam Bond Market Association); and Japan (Japan Securities Dealers Association).

55.1% was government bonds and the remaining 44.9% was corporate bonds. Growth moderated to 6.9% q-o-q in Q3 2020 after surging 31.2% q-o-q in Q2 2020 as the government continued to stimulate the economy, leading to a high base effect. Government bond issuance drove much of the growth, particularly Treasury bonds and local government bonds, driven by government directives for increased spending to support fiscal policies and pursue projects that were derailed by the COVID-19 pandemic. The government also increased its quota of local government bonds by CNY1.6 trillion in 2020 compared to last year's and pushed local governments to tap the quota for issuing bonds in a bid to boost economic recovery. Local governments were also required to complete their 2020 issuances by October. Corporate bond issuance posted marginal growth of 0.2% in Q3 2020 from 15.9% q-o-q in Q2 2020 due to rising interest rates. On an annual basis, the PRC's issuance activities quickened to 52.5% y-o-y in Q3 2020 from 48.2% y-o-y in Q2 2020.

LCY bond issuance in the Republic of Korea totaled USD189.2 billion in Q3 2020, down 11.5% q-o-q following a 4.0% q-o-q hike in the preceding quarter. All bond segments recorded declines in issuance during the quarter. Government bond issuance slowed by 14.5% q-o-q, but with the volume still relatively high, as the government sought to finance its supplemental budgets. Issuance of central bank instruments also dropped during the quarter, falling 10.5% q-o-q as the Bank of Korea added liquidity. For the third consecutive quarter, the volume of new corporate bond issuance decelerated, falling 8.9% q-o-q as corporates reconsidered their borrowing plans due to uncertainties in the economy. On a y-o-y basis, bond issuance moderated to 12.6% in Q3 2020 from 16.2% in Q2 2020.

In Hong Kong, China, bond issuance climbed to USD144.7 billion in Q3 2020 on growth of 5.2% q-o-q that followed a 1.4% q-o-q hike in the prior quarter. Issuance of Exchange Fund Bills and Exchange Fund

Notes picked up during the quarter, rebounding to expand 10.0% q-o-q after contracting 1.5% q-o-q in Q2 2020 due to the Hong Kong Monetary Authority's decision in the earlier quarter to reduce issuance to increase liquidity. On the other hand, the issuance of Hong Kong Special Administrative Region Bonds declined in Q3 2020. Meanwhile, corporate bond sales contracted 8.2% q-o-q in Q3 2020 following growth of 9.8% q-o-q in Q2 2020. On a y-o-y basis, LCY bond issuance surged 9.8% in Q3 2020, up from 2.2% in Q2 2020.

Total bonds sales from ASEAN economies tallied USD337.4 billion in Q3 2020, with the share of the regional total climbing to 15.0%. Aggregate bond issuance swelled to 17.5% q-o-q and 23.5% y-o-y in Q3 2020 from 4.8% q-o-q and 2.1% y-o-y in Q2 2020. Five out of six ASEAN economies for which data are available recorded q-o-q increases in bond issuance during the quarter, including Indonesia, the Philippines, Singapore, Thailand, and Viet Nam. The exception was Malaysia, which pared its issuance volume in Q3 2020 compared with the previous quarter. Among ASEAN economies, the largest issuers in Q3 2020 were Singapore, Thailand, and Indonesia.

LCY bond issuance from Singapore summed to USD147.7 billion in Q3 2020, with growth inching up to 6.8% q-o-q from 6.2% q-o-q in Q2 2020. The hike stemmed from an increase in the issuance of government bonds, while corporate bond issuance contracted during the quarter. Government bond issuance edged higher on growth of 7.5% q-o-q, driven largely by the 9.3% q-o-q hike in the issuance of Monetary Authority of Singapore bills. The volume of issuance of Singapore Government Securities bills and bonds was unchanged from the previous quarter. Corporate bond issuance during the quarter weakened 16.1% q-o-q following a 50.8% q-o-q expansion in Q2 2020. On an annual basis, LCY bond issuance in Singapore slipped to 18.1% y-o-y from 19.9% y-o-y in Q2 2020.

Thailand saw total bond sales in Q3 2020 of USD93.3 billion, as growth accelerated 20.9% q-o-q from only 3.1% q-o-q in Q2 2020. Much of the q-o-q expansion stemmed from increased issuance volume by the government, particularly Treasury and other government bonds. Treasury bond issuance surged 67.1% q-o-q as the government aimed to boost economic growth through increased fiscal spending. New issuance of central bank instruments also rebounded during the

quarter, rising 11.2% q-o-q following a decline of 0.4% in the previous quarter. Corporate bond issuance also recovered, rising 27.4% q-o-q in Q3 2020 after contracting 23.7% q-o-q in the previous quarter. LCY bond issuance in Thailand rebounded on growth of 23.4% y-o-y following a decline of 14.1% y-o-y in Q2 2020.

In Indonesia, LCY bond issuance remained active as issuance reached USD41.4 billion in Q3 2020, with growth accelerating to 44.3% q-o-q from 37.5% q-o-q in Q2 2020. Growth was boosted by increased issuance of Treasury instruments as the government expedited fiscal spending to pump-prime the economy in response to the adverse impact of the COVID-19 pandemic. Issuance of central bank bills also climbed during the quarter, rising 17.9% q-o-q. Corporate bond sales were quite active during the quarter, as issuance rose more than four-fold in Q3 2020. On a y-o-y basis, issuance volume slightly dipped to 78.5% from 79.4% in Q2 2020.

LCY bond sales in Malaysia totaled USD21.6 billion in Q3 2020 on a 4.5% q-o-q contraction. The decline in issuance stemmed from lower bond sales of Treasury instruments and the absence of Bank Negara Malaysia issuance during the quarter. On the other hand, corporate bond issuance climbed 12.1% q-o-q in Q3 2020 after declining 15.7% q-o-q in the preceding quarter. On a y-o-y basis, bond issuance grew 6.3% in Q3 2020 following a 16.7% contraction in Q2 2020.

In the Philippines, LCY bond sales nearly doubled to reach USD25.4 billion in Q3 2020. Overall growth soared 77.0% q-o-q after a decline of 19.6% q-o-q in the prior quarter. Government bond issuance grew 65.4% q-o-q on the back of a 57.9% q-o-q hike in the issuance of Treasury instruments and the resumption of issuance of central bank bills by the Bangko Sentral ng Pilipinas (BSP). Q3 2020 marked the first issuance of central banks bills by the BSP since the 1980s. Beginning on 18 September, the BSP issued central bank bills once a week as part of efforts to expand its monetary policy tools. Corporate bond issuance during the quarter also rebounded strongly, as issuance climbed more than four-fold. On an annual basis, bond issuance growth surged to 254.0% y-o-y in Q3 2020 from 58.6% y-o-y in the prior quarter.

LCY bond issuance in Viet Nam hit USD7.9 billion in Q3 2020, owing to a 34.3% q-o-q rise after a decline of 25.2% q-o-q in Q2 2020. The increase was dominated by a 116.2% q-o-q gain in Treasury bond issuance, as the government sought funding for its stimulus programs. In addition, the State Bank of Vietnam has not issued central bank bills for the past 2 quarters to help maintain liquidity. In contrast, corporate bonds issuance fell 19.3% q-o-q in Q3 2020. On a yearly basis, Viet Nam's LCY bond issuance contracted 63.7% y-o-y in Q3 2020, which was slightly better than the 75.0% y-o-y contraction in Q2 2020.

Cross-Border Bond Issuance

Cross-border bond issuance in emerging East Asia reached USD1.8 billion in Q3 2020.

Intraregional bond issuance in emerging East Asia reached USD1.8 billion in Q3 2020, a 39.7% q-o-q decline from the USD3.0 billion raised in Q2 2020, and amounted to only half of the aggregate issuance in Q3 2019. The decline was primarily due to tepid cross-border issuance from the PRC, whose share of the region's aggregate issuance volume plunged to 21.4% in Q3 2020 from 56.6% in Q2 2020. Hong Kong, China had the highest share in Q3 2020 at 39.4% (**Figure 4**). Other economies that issued cross-border bonds during the quarter included the Republic of Korea, the Lao People's Democratic Republic, Malaysia, and Singapore. Monthly issuance volumes amounted to USD552.2 million, USD506.1 million, and USD757.4 million for the months of July, August, and September, respectively.

Figure 4: Origin Economies of Intra-Emerging East Asian Bond Issuance in the Third Quarter of 2020

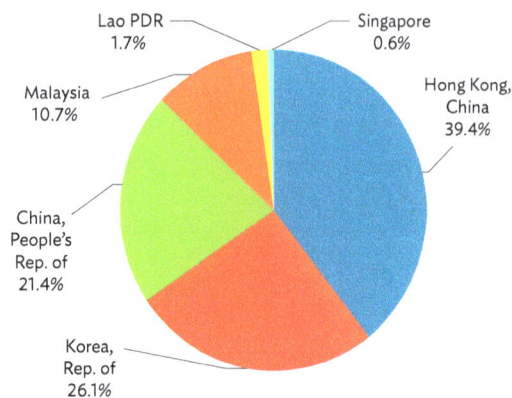

Lao PDR 1.7%
Singapore 0.6%
Hong Kong, China 39.4%
Malaysia 10.7%
China, People's Rep. of 21.4%
Korea, Rep. of 26.1%

Lao PDR = Lao People's Democratic Republic.
Source: *AsianBondsOnline* calculations based on Bloomberg LP data.

In Q3 2020, Hong Kong, China dominated the region's cross-border issuance market with aggregate issuance of USD715.7 million, which was almost at par with the volume issued in the previous quarter. Six institutions from Hong Kong, China issued cross-border bonds in Q3 2020, and all were denominated in Chinese yuan. Real estate company Wharf REIC Finance was the largest issuer in Hong Kong, China with USD191.4 million of 3-year and 5-year bonds. The Hong Kong Mortgage Corporation followed with issuance totaling USD160.5 million from bonds of various tenors. China Travel Services Group, which had the second-largest single issuance in the region in Q3 2020, raised USD147.3 million via a short-term bond.

In the Republic of Korea, cross-border bond issuances reached USD474.4 million in Q3 2020 and comprised over a quarter of the regional total. Three government-related institutions issued intraregional bonds in Q3 2020, led by the Export–Import Bank of Korea, which raised a total of USD187.3 million worth of 2-year and 3-year CNY-denominated bonds. Korea Development Bank also raised USD140.7 million via issuance of 1-year and 2-year bonds denominated in Chinese yuan, Hong Kong dollars, and Singapore dollars; and Korea Gas Corporation, which issued USD58.1 million worth of HKD-denominated 7-year bonds. The only private corporation that issued cross-border bonds for the quarter was Hyundai Capital at USD88.4 million.

Only two institutions raised funds via issuance of intraregional bonds in the PRC in Q3 2020, with the aggregate volume falling to USD388.8 million from USD1.5 billion and USD1.7 billion in the first and second quarters of the year, respectively. China Construction Bank issued SGD-denominated 3-year bonds amounting to USD366.2 million and Gemstones International issued short-term bonds worth USD22.6 million denominated in Hong Kong dollars.

Malayan Banking was the sole issuer of cross-border bonds from Malaysia, raising USD195.1 million worth of bonds denominated in Hong Kong dollars and Chinese yuan, and in various tenors ranging from 1 year to 7 years.

In the Lao People's Democratic Republic, hydroelectric power plant Nam Ngum 2 Power Company issued 3-year and 5-year THB-denominated bonds worth

USD31.6 million. In Singapore, Nomura International Fund issued 5-year CNY-denominated bonds worth USD10.0 million.

The top 10 issuers of cross-border bonds in the region had an aggregate issuance volume of USD1.7 billion in Q3 2020 and accounted for 91.6% of the regional total. Half of the list comprised firms from Hong Kong, China, which issued a total of USD684.7 million. The PRC's China Construction Bank was the largest issuer in the region at USD366.2 million, followed by Malayan Banking at USD195.1 million. The remaining firms on the top 10 list were from the Republic of Korea and had an aggregate issuance volume of USD416.4 million.

The Chinese yuan was the predominant currency of cross-border bonds in emerging East Asia in Q3 2020, surpassing the Hong Kong dollar, with a total of USD1.2 billion and a share of 63.5% of the regional total (**Figure 5**). Firms that issued in this currency were from Hong Kong, China; the Republic of Korea; Malaysia; and Singapore. The second-most widely used currency in Q3 2020 was the Singapore dollar with a total of USD395.5 million and share of 21.8%. Other cross-border issuance currencies included the Hong Kong dollar (USD236.3 million, 13.0%) and the Thai baht (USD31.6 million, 1.7%).

Figure 5: Currency Shares of Intra-Emerging East Asian Bond Issuance in the Third Quarter of 2020

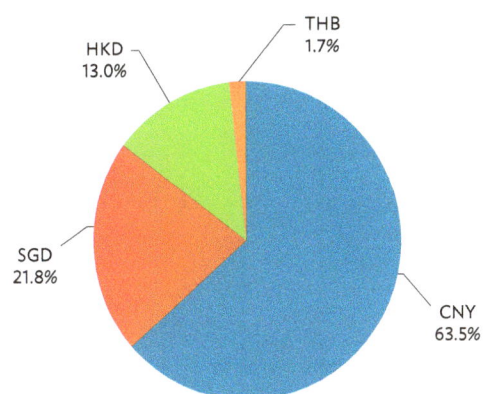

CNY = Chinese renminbi, HKD = Hong Kong dollar, SGD = Singapore dollar, THB = Thai baht.
Source: *AsianBondsOnline* calculations based on Bloomberg LP data.

G3 Currency Issuance

Total G3 currency bond issuance in emerging East Asia amounted to USD288.7 billion in January–September.

The value of G3 currency bonds issued in emerging East Asia from January to September totaled USD288.7 billion, an increase of 12.3% y-o-y from USD257.1 billion in the same period in 2019 (**Table 4**).[5] The expansion was driven by higher G3 issuance volumes in all of the region's economies compared with a year earlier, except in Viet Nam, which did not issue any G3 bonds during the review period.

Of all G3 currency bonds issued during the review period, a total of 93.0% was denominated in US dollars, 6.3% in euros, and 0.7% in Japanese yen. In January–September, a total of USD268.5 billion worth of bonds denominated in US dollars was issued in emerging East Asia, representing a jump of 12.4% y-o-y. The equivalent of USD18.2 billion of EUR-denominated bonds was issued during the review period, an increase of 70.0% y-o-y, as more economies issued such bonds. Bonds issued in Japanese yen totaled USD2.0 billion, a decline of 73.3% y-o-y from a high base that was largely driven by Malaysia's samurai bond issuance in March 2019. In addition, most of the region's economies opted not to issue in Japanese yen during the review period.

The PRC continued to dominate the region's issuance of G3 currency bonds, totaling USD171.9 billion during the January–September period, mainly supported by issuances in US dollars. This was followed by Hong Kong, China with USD27.1 billion and Indonesia with USD24.3 billion, both issuing mainly in US dollars as well.

In the first 9 months of 2020, G3 currency bond issuance increased on a y-o-y basis in the Philippines (115.2%); Thailand (55.0%); Indonesia (54.4%); Malaysia (40.1%); Singapore (16.1%); the Republic of Korea (7.7%); the PRC (4.5%); and Hong Kong, China (3.9%). Cambodia issued G3 currency bonds during the January–September period after not issuing any during the same period in 2019. On the other hand, Viet Nam chose not to issue any G3 currency bonds in January–September 2020 after issuing during the same period in 2019.

---

[5]   G3 currency bonds are denominated in either euros, Japanese yen, or US dollars.

Table 4: G3 Currency Bond Issuance

2019 Issuer	Amount (USD billion)	Issue Date	January–September 2020 Issuer	Amount (USD billion)	Issue Date
Cambodia	**0.0**		**Cambodia**	**0.4**	
China, People's Rep. of	**225.2**		**China, People's Rep. of**	**122.9**	
Tencent Holdings 3.975% 2029	3.0	11-Apr-19	Industrial and Commercial Bank of China 3.58% Perpetual	2.9	23-Sep-20
People's Republic of China (Sovereign) 0.125% 2026	2.2	12-Nov-19	Bank of China 3.60% Perpetual	2.8	4-Mar-20
People's Republic of China (Sovereign) 1.950% 2024	2.0	3-Dec-19	Tencent Holdings 2.39% 2030	2.3	3-Jun-20
Others	218.0		Others	164.0	
Hong Kong, China	**31.9**		**Hong Kong, China**	**27.1**	
Celestial Miles 5.75% Perpetual	1.0	31-Jan-19	AIA Group 3.200% 2040	1.8	16-Sep-20
Hong Kong, China (Sovereign) 2.50% 2024	1.0	28-May-19	MTR Corporation 1.625% 2030	1.2	19-Aug-20
AIA Group 3.60% 2029	1.0	9-Apr-19	AIA Group 3.375% 2030	1.0	7-Apr-20
Others	28.9		Others	23.2	
Indonesia	**22.4**		**Indonesia**	**24.3**	
Perusahaan Penerbit SBSN *Sukuk* 4.45% 2029	1.3	20-Feb-19	Indonesia (Sovereign) 4.20% 2050	1.7	15-Apr-20
Indonesia (Sovereign) 1.40% 2031	1.1	30-Oct-19	Indonesia (Sovereign) 3.85% 2030	1.7	15-Apr-20
Indonesia (Sovereign) 3.70% 2049	1.0	30-Oct-19	Indonesia (Sovereign) 2.85% 2030	1.2	14-Jan-20
Others	19.0		Others	19.8	
Korea, Rep. of	**29.4**		**Korea, Rep. of**	**24.2**	
Republic of Korea (Sovereign) 2.500% 2029	1.0	19-Jun-19	Korea Housing Finance Corporation 0.010% 2025	1.2	5-Feb-20
Export–Import Bank of Korea 0.375% 2024	0.8	26-Mar-19	Korea Development Bank 1.250% 2025	1.0	3-Jun-20
LG Display 1.500% 2024	0.7	22-Aug-19	Export–Import Bank of Korea 0.829% 2025	0.8	27-Apr-20
Others	26.8		Others	21.2	
Lao People's Democratic Republic	**0.2**		**Lao People's Democratic Republic**	**0.0**	
Malaysia	**13.7**		**Malaysia**	**15.2**	
Malaysia (Sovereign) 0.530% 2029	1.8	15-Mar-19	Petronas Capital 4.55% 2050	2.8	21-Apr-20
Resorts World Las Vegas 4.625% 2029	1.0	16-Apr-19	Petronas Capital 3.50% 2030	2.3	21-Apr-20
Others	10.9		Others	10.2	
Philippines	**6.7**		**Philippines**	**11.7**	
Philippines (Sovereign) 3.750% 2029	1.5	14-Jan-19	Philippines (Sovereign) 2.950% 2045	1.4	5-May-20
Philippines (Sovereign) 0.875% 2027	0.8	17-May-19	Philippines (Sovereign) 2.457% 2030	1.0	5-May-20
Others	4.4		Others	9.3	
Singapore	**9.7**		**Singapore**	**9.6**	
DBS Group 2.85% 2022	0.8	16-Apr-19	Oversea-Chinese Banking Corporation 1.832% 2030	1.0	10-Sep-20
BOC Aviation 3.50% 2024	0.8	10-Apr-19	BOC Aviation 3.250% 2025	1.0	29-Apr-20
Others	8.2		Others	7.6	
Thailand	**6.4**		**Thailand**	**4.4**	
Bangkok Bank (Hong Kong, China) 3.733% 2034	1.2	25-Sep-19	Bangkok Bank (Hong Kong, China) 5.0% Perpetual	0.8	23-Sep-20
Kasikornbank 3.343% 2031	0.8	2-Oct-19	PTT Treasury 3.7% 2070	0.7	16-Jul-20
Others	4.4		Others	2.9	
Viet Nam	**1.0**		**Viet Nam**	**0.0**	
Emerging East Asia Total	**346.6**		**Emerging East Asia Total**	**288.7**	
Memo Items:			Memo Items:		
India	**21.9**		**India**	**11.9**	
Indian Oil Corporation 4.75% 2024	0.9	16-Jan-19	Vedanta Holdings Mauritius II 13.00% 2023	1.4	21-Aug-20
Others	21.0		Others	10.5	
Sri Lanka	**4.9**		**Sri Lanka**	**0.4**	
Sri Lanka (Sovereign) 7.55% 2030	1.5	28-Jun-19	Sri Lanka (Sovereign) 6.57% 2021	0.1	30-Jul-20
Others	3.4		Others	**0.3**	

USD = United States dollar.
Notes:
1. Data exclude certificates of deposit.
2. G3 currency bonds are bonds denominated in either euros, Japanese yen, or US dollars.
3. Bloomberg LP end-of-period rates are used.
4. Emerging East Asia comprises Cambodia; the People's Republic of China; Hong Kong, China; Indonesia; the Republic of Korea; the Lao People's Democratic Republic; Malaysia; the Philippines; Singapore; Thailand; and Viet Nam.
5. Figures after the issuer name reflect the coupon rate and year of maturity of the bond.
Source: *AsianBondsOnline* calculations based on Bloomberg LP data.

The PRC accounted for 59.5% of all G3 currency issuance in emerging East Asia in January–September, issuing USD163.3 billion in US dollars and the equivalent of USD8.6 billion in euros. In August, internet-based services provider Prosus issued a 30-year callable bond denominated in US dollars. It also sold a dual-tranche EUR-denominated callable bond with tenors of 8 years and 12 years. Both issuances came under the company's Global Medium-Term Note Programme and will be used for general corporate purposes. In September, the Bank of Communications (Hong Kong) issued a 3-year and a 5-year bond totaling USD1.2 billion.

The Republic of Korea accounted for an 8.4% share of all G3 currency bonds issued during the review period: USD18.8 billion in US dollars and the equivalent of USD5.5 billion in euros. In August and September, the Export–Import Bank of Korea extended its issuance of USD-denominated bonds by issuing seven bonds with tenors ranging from 1 year to 5 years. In September, Korea Development Bank offered two 1-year bonds, a USD-denominated bond with a 0.64% coupon rate, and a zero-coupon bond denominated in euros.

Hong Kong, China accounted for a 9.4% share of G3 currency bond issuance in January–September. By currency, USD25.7 billion was issued in US dollars, while EUR-denominated and JPY-denominated bonds amounted to USD0.9 billion and USD0.5 billion, respectively. In September, multinational insurance and finance corporation AIA Group issued a 20-year USD-denominated callable bond worth USD1.8 billion ahead of new capital regulations for insurers set to be introduced by Hong Kong, China's Insurance Authority. Real estate business operator Elect Global Investments sold two perpetual callable bonds denominated in US dollars in August and September, totaling USD0.5 billion and with a coupon rate of 4.85% each.

G3 currency bond issuance among ASEAN member economies increased 47.8% y-o-y to USD65.1 billion in January–September from USD44.0 billion in the same period in 2019 as all ASEAN economies except for Viet Nam ramped up issuance during the period. As a share of emerging East Asia's total during the review period, ASEAN's G3 currency bond issuance accounted for 22.5%, up from 17.1% during the same period in the previous year. Indonesia and Malaysia led all ASEAN members in terms of G3 currency bond issuance, followed by the Philippines, Singapore, and Thailand, with

issuances amounting to USD11.7 billion, USD9.6 billion, and USD4.4 billion, respectively.

Indonesia's G3 currency bond issuance in January–September accounted for 8.4% of the total in emerging East Asia, comprising USD22.2 billion in US dollars, the equivalent of USD1.2 billion in euros, and the equivalent of USD0.9 billion in Japanese yen. In August and September, Bank Indonesia issued two 1-year zero-coupon bonds denominated in US dollars. In September, FPC Resources, a subsidiary of the investment management firm First Pacific Company, sold a 7-year USD-denominated callable bond to pay and refinance its existing debt obligations.

G3 currency bonds issued by Malaysia accounted for 5.2% of emerging East Asia's total, including USD-denominated bonds worth USD14.6 billion and JPY-denominated bonds worth USD0.6 billion. In August, telecommunications company Axiata was able to raise USD1.5 billion from a dual-tranche offering of USD-denominated callable bonds with tenors of 10 years (*sukuk*) and 30 years, the longest tenor ever for the company. During the same month, Malayan Banking Berhad sold a callable zero-coupon bond denominated in US dollars with a tenor of 40 years, the longest-dated tenor issued in the region in August.

The Philippines accounted for 4.0% of total G3 currency bond issuance in emerging East Asia during the January–September period, comprising bonds denominated in US dollars and euros amounting to USD10.3 billion and USD1.4 billion, respectively. In August, Rizal Commercial Banking Corporation issued a perpetual callable bond denominated in US dollars. The issuance was the Philippines' first additional Tier 1 capital under the Basel III regulations. Proceeds will be used for the bank's green and social activities. In September, conglomerate Filinvest Development offered a USD-denominated 5-year bond, proceeds from which will be used to refinance debt obligations and invest in green projects and information technology infrastructure.

Singapore's share of G3 currency bond issuance in emerging East Asia was 3.3% in January–September, comprising USD9.5 billion in US dollars and the equivalent of USD0.1 billion in euros. Oversea-Chinese Banking Corporation increased its USD-denominated bonds outstanding in August and September after issuing two bonds with tenors of 4 years and 10 years. In September, commercial aircraft sales and leasing company BOC Aviation raised USD0.8 billion from a 10-year callable bond denominated in US dollars. The issuance was drawn from its global medium-term note program.

During the January–September period, 1.5% of all G3 currency bonds issued in the region were from Thailand, comprising USD3.9 billion worth of bonds denominated in US dollars and USD0.5 billion in euros. In September, Bangkok Bank (Hong Kong, China) issued a USD-denominated perpetual callable bond. The issuance will be part of the bank's Basel III additional Tier 1 capital.

Cambodia issued USD0.4 billion worth of G3 currency bonds in July, contributing a 0.1% share of such bonds issued in the region during the review period. The USD-denominated bond issuance from casino and resort operator Nagacorp has a tenor of 4 years and a coupon rate of 7.95%. Proceeds from the issuance will be used to redeem part of the company's outstanding bonds.

Figure 6 presents the monthly G3 currency issuance in emerging East Asia for the period September 2019 to September 2020. G3 issuance has been quite active since June of this year. However, a dip in issuance was observed in August, before spiking in September. The decline in August was mainly due to the drop in G3 currency bond

Figure 6: G3 Currency Bond Issuance in Emerging East Asia

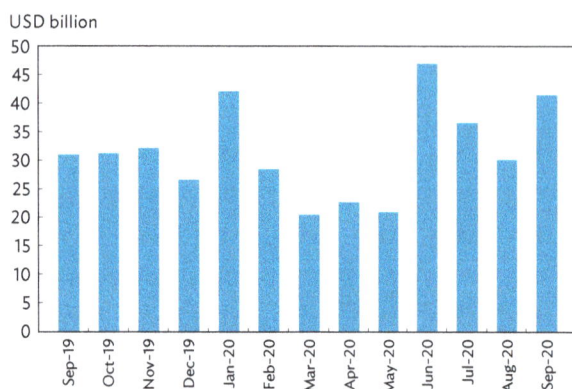

USD billion

USD = United States dollar.
Notes:
1. Emerging East Asia comprises Cambodia; the People's Republic of China; Hong Kong, China; Indonesia; the Republic of Korea; the Lao People's Democratic Republic; Malaysia; the Philippines; Singapore; Thailand; and Viet Nam.
2. G3 currency bonds are bonds denominated in either euros, Japanese yen, or US dollars.
3. Figures were computed based on 30 September 2020 currency exchange rates and do not include currency effects.
Source: *AsianBondsOnline* calculations based on Bloomberg LP data.

issuances in Indonesia, the Republic of Korea, and the Philippines. On the other hand, September issuances jumped mainly due to significant increases from the PRC; Hong Kong, China; the Republic of Korea; and Singapore. August and September saw several issuances of bonds, with tenors ranging from 10 years to 40 years, as institutional investors sought longer-term bonds to match the duration of their long-term liabilities.

Government Bond Yield Curves

Government bond yield curves shifted down between 31 August and 30 October in most markets in emerging East Asia.

COVID-19 continued to weigh on market outlook between 31 August and 30 October, creating a highly uncertain economic outlook. In particular, rising COVID-19 cases, such as in the US and the euro area are placing pressure on the economic recovery. Additionally, uncertainties regarding the direction of the US economic policy and stimulus also dampened investor sentiment.

In the US, the Federal Reserve left monetary policy unchanged during its 15–16 September meeting. The Federal Reserve noted that data indicate that the US economy improved in Q3 2020; however, uncertainty remains due to COVID-19. Federal Reserve Chairman Jerome Powell has said that it would take time before the economy returns to its pre-COVID-19 levels and that it would require additional support, including fiscal stimulus. The Federal Reserve's updated forecast in September was not substantially different from that in June, but the new forecast for full-year growth in 2020 improved to –3.7% from –6.5%. The Federal Reserve also left monetary policy unchanged during its 4-5 November meeting.

Both the European Central Bank (ECB) and the Bank of Japan (BOJ) left their monetary policies unchanged at their respective monetary policy meetings on 29 October. Both central banks noted improvements in Q3 2020, while also stating that concerns remained. In the euro area, the ECB indicated that it may make adjustments to monetary policy in December, while the BOJ downgraded its GDP forecast for fiscal 2020 from previous forecasts made in July.

In emerging East Asia, the uncertain economic outlook led central banks in the region to maintain its accommodative monetary policy. This largely impacted the shorter-end of the curve in most markets, as the region's 2-year yields trended downwards, with the exception of the PRC, Singapore, and Thailand. The PRC's 2-year yield has consistently risen as its economy recovers after having successfully dealt with the COVID-19 epidemic (**Figure 7a**). Both Singapore and Thailand's 2-year yields rose as investors shunned shorter tenors, preferring longer ones (**Figure 7b**).

In contrast to the 2-year yield movements, 10-year yields climbed among a majority of markets. The steepest rise came from the PRC and the Philippines. The PRC's

10-year yield moved upward 16 basis points (bps) between 31 August and 30 October, on continued economic growth (**Figure 8a**). In contrast, continued investor uncertainty regarding the direction of the Philippine economy led to a jump of 17 bps in its 10-year yield (**Figure 8b**). Hong Kong, China's; the Republic of Korea's; and Malaysia's 10-year yields also rose, but the increases were marginal.

The largest decline in 10-year yields was seen in Viet Nam, with a 33-bps drop for the review period as its

Figure 7a: 2-Year Local Currency Government Bond Yields

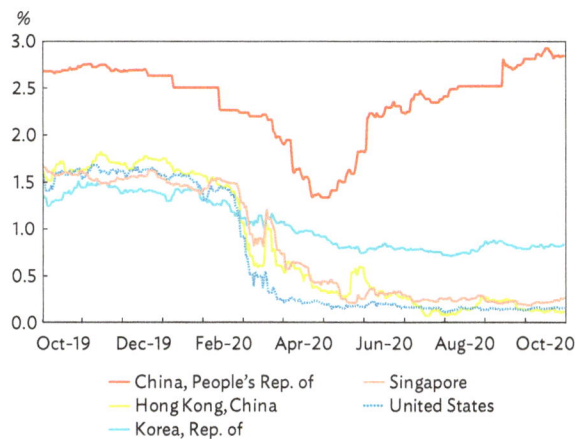

Note: Data as of 30 October 2020.
Source: Based on data from Bloomberg LP.

Figure 7b: 2-Year Local Currency Government Bond Yields

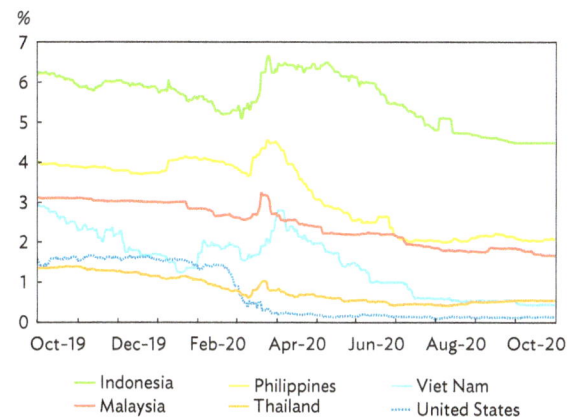

Note: Data as of 30 October 2020.
Source: Based on data from Bloomberg LP.

Figure 8a: 10-Year Local Currency Government Bond Yields

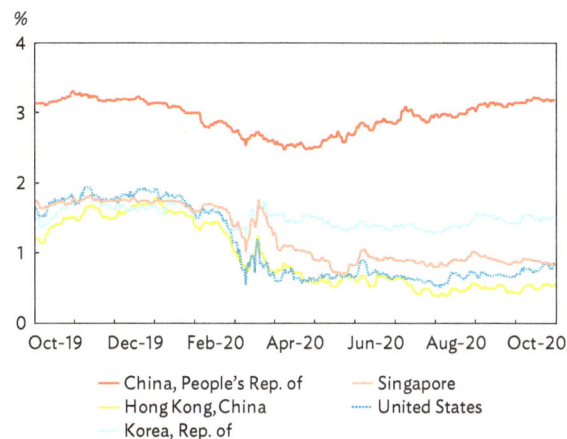

Note: Data as of 30 October 2020.
Source: Based on data from Bloomberg LP.

Figure 8b: 10-Year Local Currency Government Bond Yields

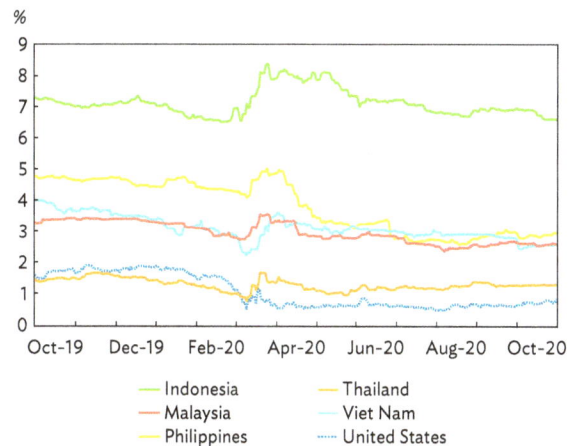

Note: Data as of 30 October 2020.
Source: Based on data from Bloomberg LP.

central bank was the only one to reduce rates in October. Indonesia's 10-year yields also plunged, as investor interest returned in October, following the passage of an Omnibus Law, which provided easing regulations for businesses and labor.

Singapore's 10-year yield fell, the opposite of its 2-year yield, as the economy is expected to slow down into the fourth quarter as the resurgence of cases in other economies will cap external demand. Similarly, Thailand saw an increase in the 2-year yield but a drop in its 10-year yield, as concerns over debt oversupply dissipated. The government announced that it would only borrow THB1.47 trillion for the fiscal year beginning 1 October 2020, which is 11% lower than the preceding year.

Yield curves overall shifted downward for most markets in emerging East Asia, but the rationale for each market's movement was different (**Figure 9**). The PRC, with the entire yield curve shifting upward, and Malaysia, whose yield curve movements were mixed, were the exceptions.

Viet Nam's entire yield curve shifted downward following the central bank's easing, while Indonesia's yield curve shifted downward for nearly all tenors amid renewed investor interest. Singapore's yield curve also shifted downward for most tenors over a lack of inflationary pressures and uncertainty over the global economic recovery. In the Republic of Korea, yields largely fell for most maturities amid fears of new wave of COVID-19 cases.

In the Philippines, yields at the shorter-end fell, but rose at the longer-end, due to higher investor risk aversion. In Thailand, yields rose at the shorter-end but fell at the longer end, buoyed by a recovery in bond inflows in October.

The 2-year versus 10-year yield spreads were mixed across the region (**Figure 10**). The PRC, Indonesia, Singapore, Thailand, and Viet Nam showed a decline in the spread. All other emerging East Asian economies showed a rising yield spread during the review period.

While economic growth remains a concern, some economies' GDP recovered in Q3 2020. In the PRC, GDP growth accelerated to 4.9% y-o-y in Q3 2020 from 3.2% y-o-y in Q2 2020, reflecting steady but gradual recovery. Viet Nam's economy likewise recovered in Q3 2020, with GDP growth rising to 2.6% y-o-y from

0.4% y-o-y in the previous quarter, the only market in the region which consistently posted positive growth despite the COVID-19 pandemic. The remaining markets continued to post negative y-o-y growth rates in Q3 2020, but at a slower pace compared to the previous quarter. This includes Hong Kong, China (–3.5% from –9.0%); Indonesia (–3.5% from –5.3%); the Republic of Korea (–1.3% from –2.7%); Malaysia (–2.7% from –17.1%); the Philippines (–11.5% from –16.9%); and Thailand (6.4% from –12.1%).

The overall weak economic environment led to a decline in inflation in August and September in most emerging East Asian markets for which data are available. In particular, Hong Kong, China; Malaysia; and Thailand remained in deflationary territory during the review period, while Indonesia's inflation was stable (**Figure 11a**). The main exception to the regional trend was the Republic of Korea, which has experienced a steady rise in inflation since having moved out of deflation in June (**Figure 11b**).

Despite declines in inflation, central banks in the region have largely held off on raising policy rates during the review period after having aggressively eased monetary policy in previous months. During the review period, the Philippines reduced rates by a cumulative 175 bps (**Figure 12a**). In July, Bank Negara Malaysia and Bank Indonesia further reduced rates. The lone exception was Viet Nam, whose central bank reduced its policy rate on 1 October by 50 bps, for a cumulative rate reduction of 200 bps year-to-date through 30 October (**Figure 12b**). Subsequently, both Bangko ng Sentral ng Pilipinas and Bank Indonesia implemented a surprise rate cut of 25 bps on 19 November.

The movement of corporate spreads was largely mixed across the region.

AAA-rated corporate versus government yield spreads fell in the PRC between 31 August and 15 October as the economy continued to recover from the impact of COVID-19. Corporate spreads also narrowed in Thailand during the review period. Yield spreads rose for longer tenors in Malaysia and shifted upward in the Republic of Korea (**Figure 13a**).

For lower-rated corporate bonds, spreads fell in both the PRC and Malaysia, while they rose in Thailand, and were unchanged in the Republic of Korea (**Figure 13b**).

Figure 9: Benchmark Yield Curves—Local Currency Government Bonds

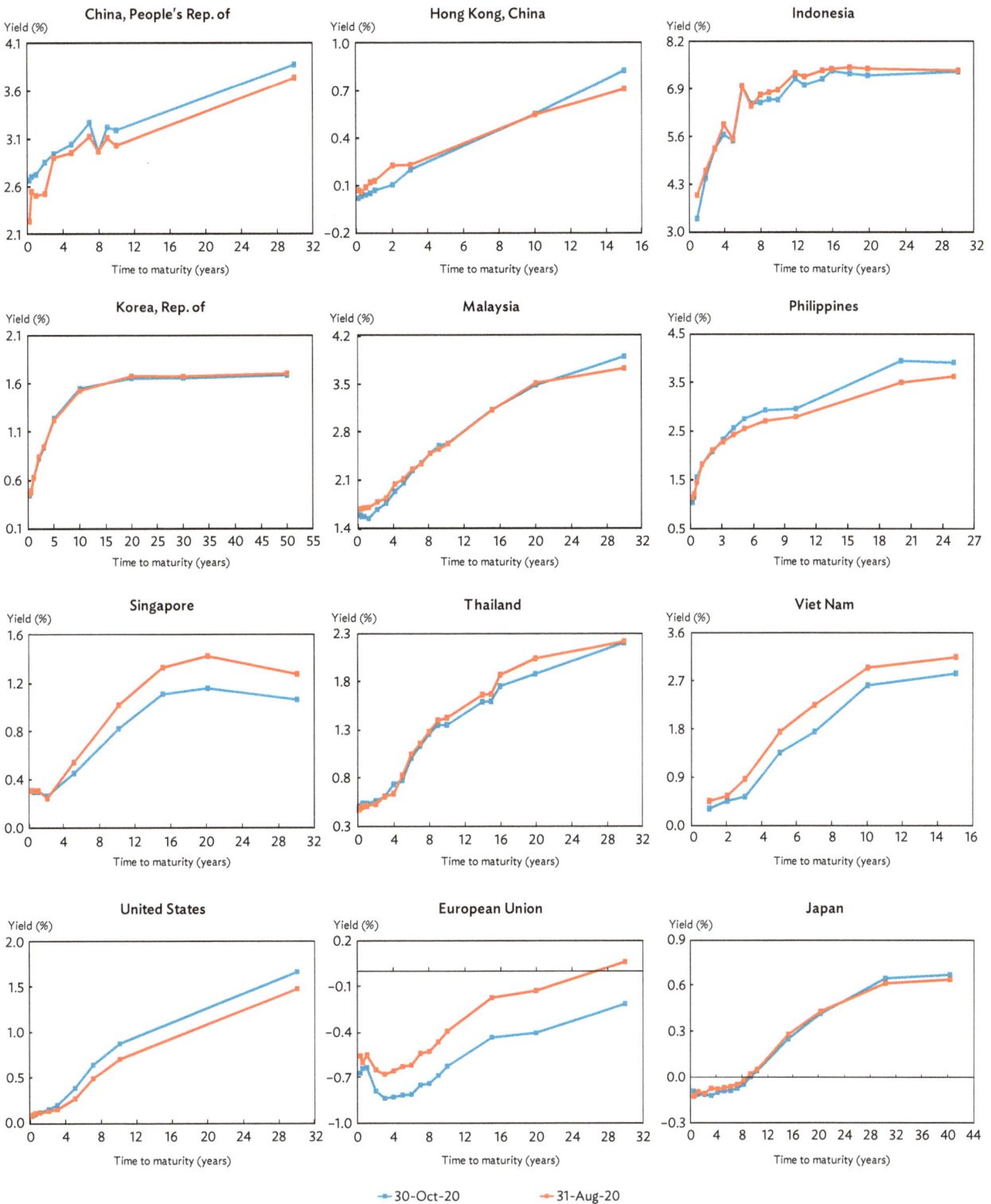

China, People's Rep. of

Hong Kong, China

Indonesia

Korea, Rep. of

Malaysia

Philippines

Singapore

Thailand

Viet Nam

United States

European Union

Japan

30-Oct-20   31-Aug-20

Sources: Based on data from Bloomberg LP and Thai Bond Market Association.

Figure 10: Yield Spreads between 2-Year and 10-Year Government Bonds

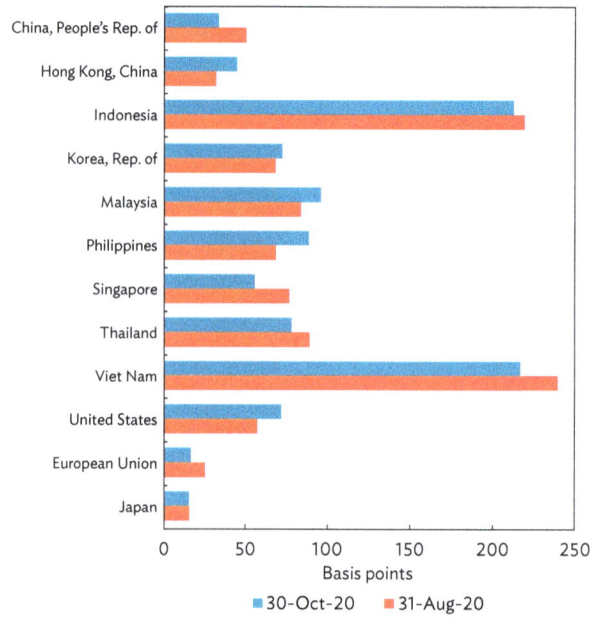

Source: *AsianBondsOnline* computations based on Bloomberg LP data.

Figure 11a: Headline Inflation Rates

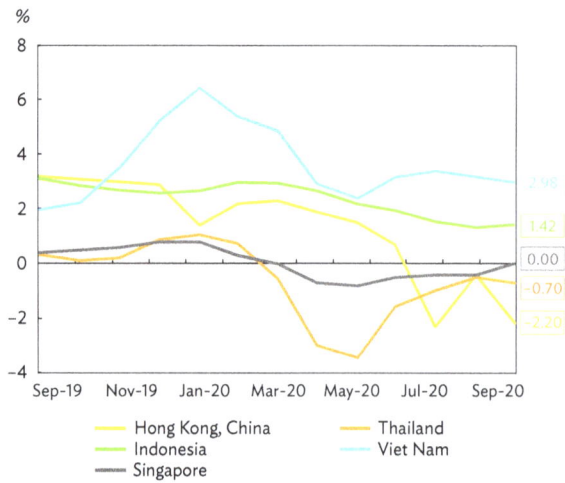

Note: Data as of 30 September 2020.
Source: Based on data from Bloomberg LP.

Figure 11b: Headline Inflation Rates

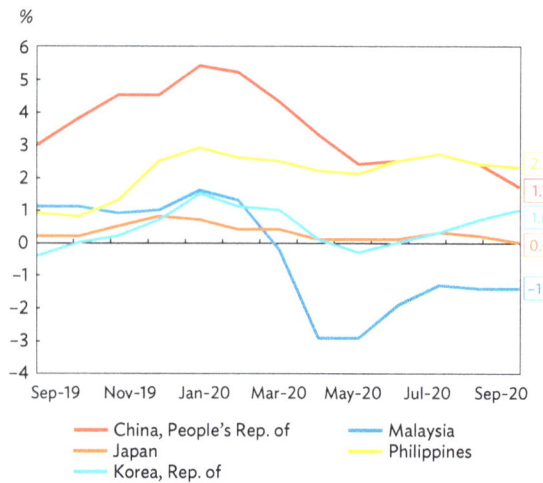

Note: Data as of 30 September 2020.
Source: Based on data from Bloomberg LP.

Figure 12a: Policy Rates

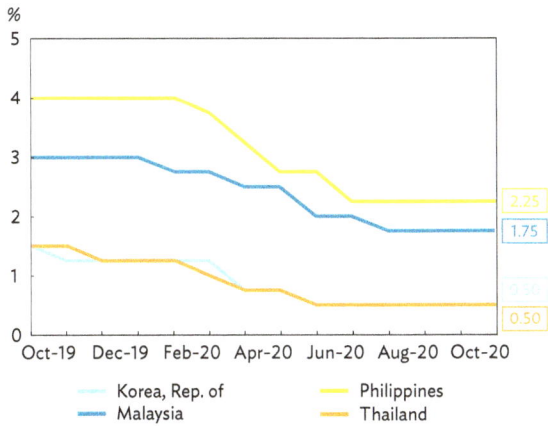

%

Korea, Rep. of
Malaysia
Philippines
Thailand

Note: Data as of 30 October 2020.
Source: Based on data from Bloomberg LP.

Figure 12b: Policy Rates

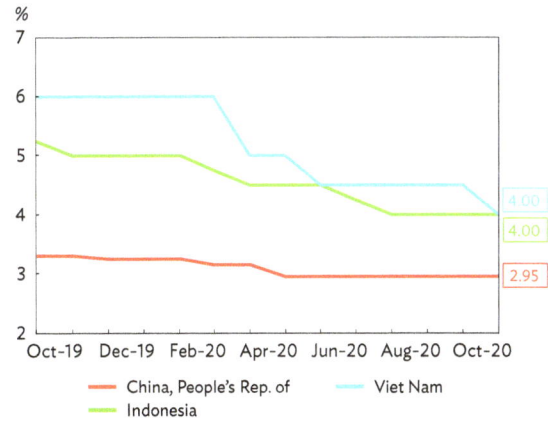

%

China, People's Rep. of
Indonesia
Viet Nam

Notes:
1. Data as of 30 October 2020.
2. For the People's Republic of China, data used in the chart is the 1-year medium-term lending facility rate. While the 1-year benchmark lending rate is the official policy rate of the People's Bank of China, market players use the 1-year medium-term lending facility rate as a guide for the monetary policy direction of the People's Bank of China.
Source: Based on data from Bloomberg LP.

Figure 13a: Credit Spreads—Local Currency Corporates Rated AAA vs. Government Bonds

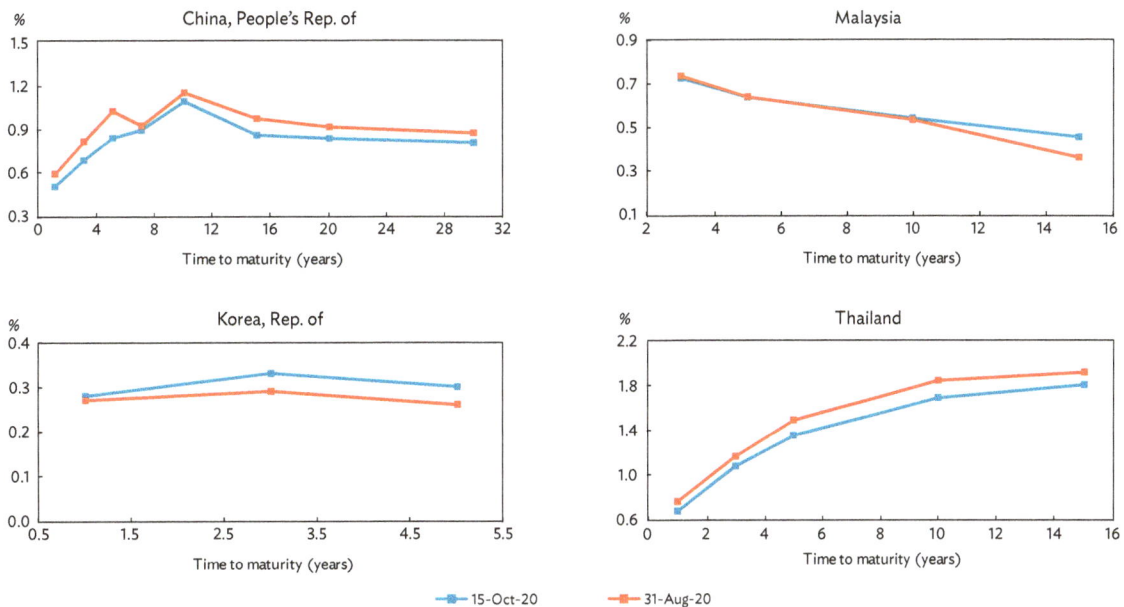

China, People's Rep. of

Malaysia

Korea, Rep. of

Thailand

15-Oct-20   31-Aug-20

Notes:
1. Credit spreads are obtained by subtracting government yields from corporate indicative yields.
2. For Malaysia, data on corporate bonds yields are as of 28 August 2020 and 14 October 2020.
3. For Thailand, data for corporate bond yields are as of 31 August 2020 and 9 October 2020.
Sources: People's Republic of China (Bloomberg LP); Republic of Korea (*EDAILY BondWeb*); Malaysia (Fully Automated System for Issuing/Tendering Bank Negara Malaysia); and Thailand (Bloomberg LP).

Figure 13b: Credit Spreads—Lower-Rated Local Currency Corporates vs. AAA

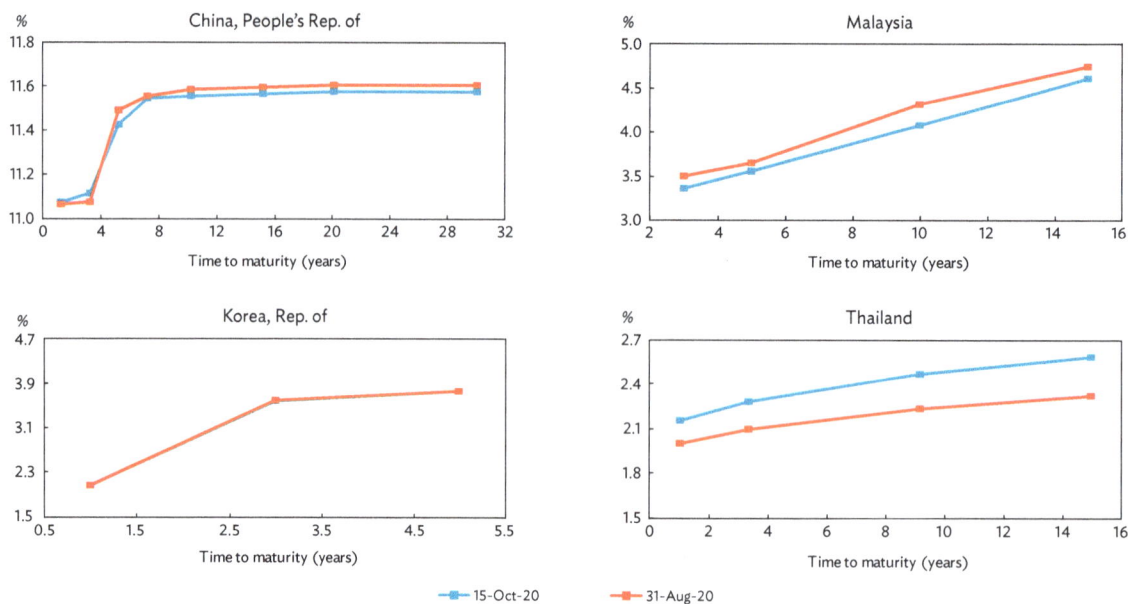

China, People's Rep. of

Malaysia

Korea, Rep. of

Thailand

15-Oct-20   31-Aug-20

Notes:
1. For the People's Republic of China and the Republic of Korea, credit spreads are obtained by subtracting corporate indicative yields rated AAA from corporate indicative yields rated BBB+.
2. For Malaysia, data on corporate bonds yields are as of 28 August 2020 and 14 October 2020.
3. For Thailand, data for corporate bond yields are as of 31 August 2020 and 9 October 2020.
Sources: People's Republic of China (Bloomberg LP); Republic of Korea (*EDAILY BondWeb*); Malaysia (Fully Automated System for Issuing/Tendering Bank Negara Malaysia); and Thailand (Bloomberg LP).

Policy and Regulatory Developments

People's Republic of China

The People's Republic of China Eases Foreign Capital Entry Rules

In September, the People's Republic of China (PRC) streamlined the existing regulations for the Renminbi Qualified Foreign Institutional Investor program and the Qualified Foreign Institutional Investor program. The new rules combined the two existing regulations into one and also made application requirements easier and simplified procedures. The new regulations took effect on 1 November.

The People's Republic of China Issues USD-Denominated Bonds

In October, the Government of the PRC issued USD6.0 billion worth of 3-year, 5-year, 10-year, and 30-year bonds. The bonds are the first USD-denominated bonds issued by the Government of the PRC since 1996 that are marketed to United States (US) investors under 144a Rules. The USD1.25 billion 3-year bond was issued with a coupon rate of 0.40%, while the USD2.25 billion 5-year bond was issued with a coupon rate of 0.55%. The USD2.0 billion 10-year bond was issued with a coupon rate of 1.2%, and the USD0.5 billion 30-year bond was issued with a coupon rate of 2.25%.

Hong Kong, China

Hong Kong Monetary Authority Holds Countercyclical Capital Buffer at 1.0%

On 12 October, the Hong Kong Monetary Authority (HKMA) announced that the countercyclical capital buffer (CCyB) would remain unchanged at 1.0%. The HKMA noted that the latest data based on the second quarter indicators signaled the need for a higher CCyB of 2.5%. However, the HKMA deemed that considering the high level of uncertainty facing the economy, holding the CCyB steady at 1.0% was more appropriate. A lower CCyB releases additional liquidity into the banking system by raising banks' lending capacity to support the economy. The CCyB is an integral part of the Basel III regulatory capital framework designed to increase the resilience of the banking sector in periods of excess credit growth.

Indonesia

Indonesia's Parliament Approves 2021 State Budget

In September, the Indonesian Parliament approved the 2021 state budget, which calls for a deficit equivalent to 5.7% of gross domestic product (GDP). The 2021 state budget estimates revenue will reach IDR1,743.7 trillion, while state spending is expected to total IDR2,750.0 trillion. The underlying macroeconomic assumptions for the 2021 state budget include (i) economic growth of 5.0%, (ii) average inflation of 3.0%, (iii) an exchange rate of IDR14,600 per USD1, (iv) an average 10-year bond yield of 7.29%, and (v) Indonesian crude oil price of USD45 per barrel.

Republic of Korea

The National Assembly Passed the Fourth Supplementary Budget

On 22 September, the National Assembly passed the fourth supplementary budget of 2020 worth KRW7.8 trillion. This brings the aggregate amount of all four supplementary budgets to KRW62.2 trillion. The budget is expected to fund additional coronavirus disease (COVID-19) relief programs to support small businesses and low-income households.

The Republic of Korea Announces New Fiscal Rules

On 5 October, the Government of the Republic of Korea announced new fiscal rules to address the rapid increase in national debt. Although the economy's fiscal soundness and debt ratios are still considered low compared to its similarly rated peers, the government aims to maintain its fiscal sustainability. One rule is to maintain the government-debt-to-GDP ratio below 60% and the consolidated fiscal balance deficit at 3% or less of GDP. Implementation is expected to take effect starting in 2025 after a transition period of 3 years.

Malaysia

FTSE Russell Keeps Malaysia in Its FTSE World Government Bond Index

On 24 September, FTSE Russell decided to keep Malaysia in its FTSE World Government Bond Index, but the economy remained on the data provider's FTSE Russell Fixed Income Watch List for possible exclusion. In its September 2020 fixed-income review, FTSE Russell acknowledged Bank Negara Malaysia's policy reforms to enhance secondary market bond liquidity and improve foreign exchange market structure. FTSE Russell will continue to monitor developments in the Malaysian bond market as Bank Negara Malaysia's policies take effect and assess whether these regulatory reforms translate into practical improvements for international participants.

Philippines

Bangko Sentral ng Pilipinas Issues Central Bank Securities

The Bangko Sentral ng Pilipinas (BSP) started issuing BSP securities on 18 September as an additional instrument to manage liquidity in the financial system. According to the BSP, this initiative will help the central bank shift to more market-based monetary operations and support the implementation of monetary policy under the interest rate corridor framework. The addition of BSP securities to the supply of risk-free financial instruments in the banking system could help in the development of the local currency bond market. The BSP securities will be one of the monetary policy tools to mop up excess liquidity. Initial offerings will be small in volume and have shorter tenors but will eventually be scaled up and have longer maturities. The issuance of the securities is allowed under the New Central Bank Act that was signed in February 2019.

Bangko Sentral ng Pilipinas Approves Provisional Advance to the Government of the Philippines

On 1 October, the BSP approved the Government of the Philippines' request for a provisional advance of PHP540.0 billion to be used for budget deficit financing amid the COVID-19 pandemic. This came after the Bureau of the Treasury fully settled the previous PHP300.0 billion repurchase agreement on 29 September. The fresh funds will be settled on or before 29 December and will have zero interest. The new tranche is pursuant to Section 89 of the New Central Bank Act as amended in the Bayanihan II Act, which allows the government to avail of provisional advances from the central bank of up to PHP846.0 billion. Market participants expect the new funds to lift some burden from the government to increase borrowing.

Singapore

Monetary Authority of Singapore Expands Access to Liquidity Facilities

On 3 September, the Monetary Authority of Singapore (MAS) announced various measures to enhance financial institutions' access to Singapore dollar and US dollar funding. On 28 September, a Singapore Dollar Term Facility was launched to provide financial institutions flexible options in terms of SGD-denominated borrowing at longer tenors. The facility, which compliments the overnight MAS Standing Facility, offers SGD-denominated funds with 1-month and 3-month tenors. The new facility makes available more options for collateral composed of cash and other marketable securities in various currencies. For domestic systemically important banks, residential property loans may be pledged as collateral with the Singapore Dollar Term Facility. MAS also enhanced the US Dollar Facility, established in March, which allows banks to borrow US dollars by pledging SGD-denominated collateral. Similar to the Singapore Dollar Term Facility guidelines, options for collateral for the US Dollar Facility were also expanded.

Thailand

Securities and Exchange Commission and Thai Bond Market Association Launch Environment, Social, and Governance Bond Hub

On 21 October, the Securities and Exchange Commission and the Thai Bond Market Association jointly launched an environment, social, and governance (ESG) information platform to support investors and issuers of ESG bonds by making information publicly available. The ESG bond information hub was created by the Thai Bond Market Association from a platform developed by Luxembourg Green Exchange.

Viet Nam

Ministry of Finance Issues Guidance on Bond Issuance Information Disclosure

On 14 August, the Ministry of Finance issued Circular No. 77/2020/TT-BTC to provide guidance on its existing decrees, Decree No. 81/2020/ND-CP and Decree No. 163/2018/ND-CP, on the provision of bond issuance information in the domestic market. In particular, the circular guides the (i) information disclosure regime of bond issuers; (ii) information disclosure on the corporate bond website; and (iii) reporting regime of the stock exchange, corporate bond issuance consulting organizations, and bond depository organizations.[6]

---

[6] The Ministry of Finance guides the issuance of corporate bonds. See https://english.luatvietnam.vn/circular-no-77-2020-tt-btc-dated-august-14-2020-of-the-ministry-of-finance-on-guiding-a-number-of-provisions-of-the-governments-decree-no-81-2020-189347-Doc1.html.

Financing a Sustainable Recovery

This special section discusses the importance of developing green and social finance in ensuring a sustainable recovery from the global recession triggered by the outbreak of coronavirus disease (COVID-19). A global economy that is more resilient to shocks will help people around the world to live a better life.

Before the outbreak of COVID-19, emerging Asian economies were progressing in their pursuit of the United Nations Sustainable Development Goals through various policies. Climate change, which poses a long-term challenge to sustainable development, has hit the poor especially hard and could potentially push more than 100 million people back into poverty by 2030. There is now plenty of evidence showing that negative environmental and social externalities have significant negative impacts on economic development. **Box 5** reviews extant knowledge on how various environmental and social challenges can hamper economic growth.

The pandemic has sharply curtailed global economic growth and worsened social conditions worldwide. Furthermore, COVID-19 poses a disproportionately larger threat to poor and vulnerable groups such as low-income households and small and medium-sized enterprises. In many economies, the process of sustainable development has been disrupted by falling fiscal revenues and increased expenditures to contain COVID-19 and mitigate its negative economic impacts. Nevertheless, global policy makers are aware that pursuing a sustainable development path is important to prevent future shocks. With limited policy scope, mobilizing private financial resources for green and inclusive investments becomes vital to achieving a sustainable recovery.

The importance of environmental and social externalities is now widely acknowledged in financial markets. Amid the market turmoil caused by COVID-19 during the first quarter of 2020, environmental- and social-themed financing instruments showed resilience and even outperformed conventional funds. As a result, more attention is being paid to financing that integrates social impacts such as social bonds, sustainable bonds, sustainable loans, and sustainability-linked bonds. **Box 6** reviews the development of green and social finance during the COVID-19 pandemic.

While conventional wisdom may have once suggested that investors only care about financial returns and therefore do not consider environmental and social externalities, this is no longer the case. **Box 7** reviews existing knowledge and outlines a few reasons why externalities matter, including lower systematic and idiosyncratic risks, client demands and fund flow concerns, hedging for climate-related risks, and social pressure.

In addition to investors, existing evidence shows that sustainable finance also benefits other stakeholders by delivering economic benefits in terms of rising shareholder value, lower funding costs, a broader investor base, innovation, and increased growth and employment. **Box 8** summarizes the findings in the literature and details the positive economic impacts of green and social finance.

Box 5: Environmental and Social Externalities and Economic Growth and Development

Rapid population growth and economic development is upsetting the world's ecological balance.[a] Environmental degradation is evident in air, water, land, and noise pollution, as well as in the loss of natural habitat. Environmental deterioration has given rise to reproductive, mental health, and other public health problems. The 1997 Kyoto Protocol, which was succeeded by the Paris Agreement in 2016, required countries to make concrete commitments in the fight against global climate change. The agreements reflect a growing recognition that the international community must mitigate the disastrous effects of climate change and environmental destruction, including natural hazards and occurrences of infectious diseases, to achieve the United Nations (UN) Sustainable Development Goals (SDGs).

Rapid environmental pollution has been linked to climate change. It also directly affects health, as evident in rising morbidity and mortality rates. Many studies find evidence that air pollution leads to a deterioration of productivity and growth. Air pollution is a silent killer since the poisonous pollutants are invisible to the human eye. While most studies document outdoor air quality, the World Bank (2019) has also found that many people die from poor indoor air quality, especially in developing economies, where households are exposed to dirty fuels. A study of the People's Republic of China (PRC), the world's most populous country and a manufacturing powerhouse, show that a decline in air pollutants can translate into higher labor productivity. Fu, Viard, and Zhang (2017) estimate that reducing PM2.5 (sulfur dioxide) by 1% through methods other than lowering manufacturing output would generate annual productivity gains of CNY57,600 (110.5) for the average firm and CNY9.2 billion (17.6), or 0.06% (0.12%) of the PRC's gross domestic product (GDP), across all firms.[b]

The effect of pollutants is not unidirectional. Ho, Oueghlissi, and el Ferktaji (2019) find that there is bidirectional causality between GDP and carbon dioxide emissions. This implies that either a virtuous or a vicious cycle can ensue between a country's environmental state and its economic growth. The negative externalities from polluted cities harm neighboring cities, where nearby cities that stand in the way of wind from a polluted city show increased pollution. In addition, air pollution can induce an exodus of highly skilled workers from urban areas who want to avoid such pollution, as the harmful effects of air pollution impair the productivity of the workforce

and its quality of life (Fu, Viard, and Zhang 2017). Air pollution also harms mental health. As the average concentration of particulate matter increases, the probability that the exposed population will experience a deterioration of mental health also rises. Chen, Oliva, and Zhang (2018) estimated that, in the PRC, the annual increase in health expenditures resulting from air pollution totaled USD22.88 billion in 2014–2015.

Water pollution, which is known to affect ecosystems, agriculture, and health, is an important driver of economic growth. According to Damania et al. (2019), when the biological oxygen demand, an indicator of water pollution, exceeds 8 milligrams per liter then the annual GDP growth of downstream regions is reduced by 0.83 percentage points relative to a mean growth rate of 2.33% used in the study (**Figure B5**). Access to water is important since shortages limit economic growth and job creation. The UN (2016) has estimated that about 50% of the world's workers are employed in eight key water-based and natural-resource-dependent industries. An improved water supply in Africa, for example, could generate an estimated economic return of about USD28.4 billion a year, or nearly 5% of the continent's GDP. There is also evidence that water quality exceeds the effect of water quantity on growth. El Khanji and Hudson (2016), using a panel of 177 economies covering the period

Figure B5: Water Pollution and Gross Domestic Product Growth

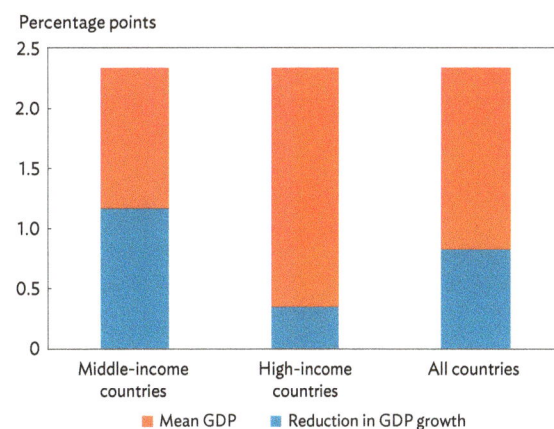

Percentage points

GDP = gross domestic product
Note: Annual mean GDP growth is 2.33%.
Source: Damania et al. 2019. *Quality Unknown: The Invisible Water Crisis.* Washington, DC: World Bank.

---

[a]   This box was written by Cynthia Castillejos-Petalcorin (Senior Economics Officer) and Donghyun Park (Principal Economist) in the Economic Research and Regional Cooperation Department of the Asian Development Bank.
[b]   PM 2.5 is particulate matter (PM) that have a diameter of less than 2.5 micrometers that can be inhaled and cause serious health problems.

continued on next page

Box 5: Environmental and Social Externalities and Economic Growth and Development
continued

1960–2009, found out that the quality of water affected economic growth in both the short and long run to a greater degree than water quantity. Thus, the study suggests that improving water quality will also strengthen economic growth.

Social development can contribute to sustainable economic growth. Investment in areas such as education, sanitation, health care, gender equality, and affordable housing fosters social development, which in turn fosters economic development. An especially important contribution of social investment is that it promotes the type of inclusive growth that enables vulnerable groups to take part in and benefit from development.

Small and medium-sized enterprises (SMEs) comprise a vulnerable group that plays a vital role in economic development. In particular, SMEs are an engine of job creation and a catalyst for mobilizing local resources for rural development. The World Bank (2020) has estimated that formal SMEs contribute up to 40% of GDP in many emerging economies. SMEs also contribute to the achievement of the UN Sustainable Development Goals via income distribution and poverty alleviation. In Asia and the Pacific, SMEs have also greatly contributed to the growth of exports (Jabbour et al. 2020).

Another vulnerable group is women. Reducing gender inequality benefits social development and inclusive growth. Based on indicators of education performance in science, technology, engineering and mathematics, labor market activity, wages, and work-life balance, the European Institute for Gender Equality (2017) found that measures to improve gender equality would add about 10.5 million jobs and lift per capita GDP by 4%–10% in the European Union by 2050. In Asia and the Pacific, reducing barriers to female participation in the labor force would mitigate the negative economic impact of population aging on the region's economic growth (Asian Development Bank 2011). However, Kabeer and Natali (2013) found that while promoting gender equality fosters growth, there is no guarantee that economic growth will foster gender equality on its own in the absence of supportive measures such as promoting female education. Girls and women often suffer from unequal access to education, health care, finance, and technology, especially in developing economies.

Many economies have yet to tap the full potential of female participation in the workforce. A vast literature on gender inequality shows that female labor participation contributes tangibly to social development and inclusive growth. The

United Nations Children's Fund (UNICEF) (2019) reported that 132 million school-aged girls are currently not in school, and about 14.95 million girls are married off as child brides. The economic cost of child marriage may be as high as USD1.7 billion in Niger relative to delaying the girls' marriage age to 20 (World Economic Forum 2018, World Bank 2019). Using industry-level data for a group of developing economies in the 1990s, Bertay, Dordevic, and Sever (2020) found that allocating female labor to more productive uses significantly boosts economic growth. As such, increased female labor participation is imperative and should be given high priority in the public policy agenda.

Poor sanitation and lack of access to affordable housing are social problems that reduce human well-being and social and economic development (World Health Organization [WHO] 2019). A large number of economy-level studies confirm that the failure to address these issues heightens the risk of health problems and lowers productivity. UNICEF and WHO (2017) report that while 2.1 billion people gained access to basic sanitation services between 2000 and 2017, 2.0 billion people still lack such access. A cost–benefit analysis by WHO in 2012 found that USD1.0 invested in sanitation generates an average economic return of USD5.5 in terms of lower health costs, higher productivity, and fewer premature deaths. Within Asia, the returns are USD8.8 in East Asia and USD5.0 in Southeast Asia.

Based on UN data, only 13 of the world's cities have adequate affordable housing (UN HABITAT 2016). Affordable housing policies not only promote social stability but also provide economic opportunities. For instance, many SMEs are home-based enterprises that provide work, income, and services for many people (Tipple 2005). In addition, affordable housing enables the clustering of younger people who are indispensable for the knowledge economy (Florida 2019).

The coronavirus disease (COVID-19) is a multidimensional global public health crisis (Manisalidis et al. 2020). The pandemic's lingering effects on physical and mental health will be more numerous and varied than what medical experts initially expected (Mayo Clinic 2020, Couzin-Frankel 2020). While a healthy and productive workforce is an important ingredient of sustainable and inclusive economic growth (UN 2019), COVID-19's persistent effects will impact the productivity of the workforce in many economies.

Encouragingly, many economies have begun to adopt sustainable and socially responsible practices. Economy-level evidence points to a significant and positive impact

continued on next page

Box 5: Environmental and Social Externalities and Economic Growth and Development
continued

of improved environment, social, and governance (ESG) policies on economic growth (Wang, Yu, and Zhong 2020). The effect is larger in countries with stronger ESG incentives, more robust corporate and social responsibility, and effective law enforcement systems (Wang, Yu, and Zhong 2020). In a similar vein, governments with a better ESG performance can improve market risk perception and thus benefit from lower government bond spreads and financing costs (Crifo, Diaye, and Oueghlissi 2017). Granular firm-level studies show that stronger ESG policies in the corporate sector have a significant and positive effect on national-level economic performance. In a study of 30 economies at different income levels, Zhou et al. (2020) show that a 1-percentage-point increase in average economic, social, and governance performance leads to gains of 0.06%, 0.09%, and 0.16%, respectively, in the log of GDP per capita. The results hold for both developed economies with more systematic ESG policies and, more interestingly, for developing economies too. This suggests that a proactive adoption of stronger ESG policies can contribute to growth (Tarmuji, Maelah, and Tarmuji 2016).

A fresh perspective that recognizes and strengthens the nexus between environmental and social factors on one hand, and economic growth on the other, is the blueprint for sustainable development in the future. With appropriate and conducive policies that protect the environment and address various social needs, governments can become catalysts of sustainable development.

References

Asian Development Bank (ADB). 2011. *Asian Development Outlook 2011 Update: Preparing for Demographic Transition*. Manila. https://www.adb.org/publications/asian-development-outlook-2011-update-preparing-demographic-transition.

A. C. Bertay, L. Dordevic, and C. Sever. 2020. Gender Inequality and Economic Growth: Evidence from Industry-Level Data. *IMF Working Paper*. No. WP/20/119. Washington, DC: International Monetary Fund.

S. Chen, P. Oliva, and P. Zhang. 2018. Air Pollution and Mental Health: Evidence from China. *National Bureau of Economic Research Working Papers*. No. w24686. https://www.nber.org/papers/w24686.

J. Couzin-Frankel. 2020. From 'brain fog' to heart damage, COVID-19's lingering problems alarm scientists. Science. https://www.sciencemag.org/news/2020/07/brain-fog-heart-damage-covid-19-s-lingering-problems-alarm-scientists.

P. Crifo, M. A. Diaye, and R. Oueghlissi. The Effect of Countries' ESG Ratings on Their Sovereign Borrowing Costs. *The Quarterly Review of Economics and Finance*. 66 (2017). pp. 13–20. http://www.sciencedirect.com/science/article/pii/S1062976917301497.

R. Damania, S. Desbureaux, A. S. Rodella, J. Russ, and E. Zaveri. 2019. *Quality Unknown: The Invisible Water Crisis*. Washington, DC: World Bank. https://openknowledge.worldbank.org/handle/10986/32245.

S. El Khanji and J. Hudson. 2016. Water Utilization and Water Quality in Endogenous Economic Growth. *Environment and Development Economics*. 21 (2016): pp. 626–48.

European Institute for Gender Equality. 2017. *Economic Benefits of Gender Equality in the European Union: Report on the Empirical Application of the Model*. https://eige.europa.eu/publications/economic-benefits-gender-equality-european-union-report-empirical-application-model.

R. Florida. 2019. *How Affordable Housing Can Improve the American Economy*. https://www.bloomberg.com/news/articles/2019-02-05/how-affordable-housing-can-boost-the-economy.

S. Fu, B. Viard, and P. Zhang. 2017. Air Quality and Manufacturing Firm Productivity: Comprehensive Evidence from China. *MPRA Paper*. No. 78914. https://mpra.ub.uni-muenchen.de/78914/.

S. H. Ho, R. Oueghlissi, and R. el Ferktaji. 2019. The Dynamic Causality between ESG and Economic Growth: Evidence from Panel Causality Analysis. *MPRA Paper*. No. 95390. https://mpra.ub.uni-muenchen.de/95390/.

A. B. L. S. Jabbour, N. O. Ndubisi, B. M. R. P. Seles. 2020. Sustainable Development in Asian Manufacturing SMEs: Progress and Directions. *International Journal of Production Economics*. 225 (2020). 107567. https://doi.org/10.1016/j.ijpe.2019.107567.

N. Kabeer and L. Natali. 2013. Gender Equality and Economic Growth: Is there a Win–Win? *IDS Working Papers*. No. 2013: 1–58. https://onlinelibrary.wiley.com/doi/full/10.1111/manc.12274.

continued on next page

Box 5: Environmental and Social Externalities and Economic Growth and Development
continued

I. Manisalidis, E. Stavropoulou, A. Stavropoulos, and E. Bezirtzoglou. 2020. Environmental and Health Impacts of Air Pollution: A Review. *Front Public Health*. 20 February. doi:10.3389/fpubh.2020.00014.

Mayo Clinic. 2020. COVID-19: *Long-Term Effects*. https://www.mayoclinic.org/diseases-conditions/coronavirus/in-depth/coronavirus-long-term-effects/art-20490351.

I. Tarmuji, R. Maelah, and N. H. Tarmuji. 2016. The Impact of Environmental, Social, and Governance Practices on Economic Performance: Evidence from ESG Score. *International Journal of Trade, Economics, and Finance*. 7 (3).

G. Tipple. 2005. The Place of Home-Based Enterprises in the Informal Sector: Evidence from Cochabamba, New Delhi, Surabaya, and Pretoria. *Urban Studies*. 42 (4): 611–32. doi:10.1080/00420980500060178.

J. Wang, J. Yu, and R. Zhong. 2020. *Country Sustainable Development and Economic Growth: The International Evidence*. 11 February. https://ssrn.com/abstract=3350232 or http://dx.doi.org/10.2139/ssrn.3350232.

United Nations. 2016. *United Nations World Water Development Report: Water and Jobs*. https://en.unesco.org/news/water-drives-job-creation-and-economic-growth-says-new-report.

————. 2019. *Transforming Our World: The 2030 Agenda for Sustainable Development*. https://sustainabledevelopment.un.org/post2015/transformingourworld.

United Nations Framework Convention on Climate Change. 2016. *Paris Climate Change Agreement*. https://unfccc.int/process-and-meetings/the-paris-agreement/the-paris-agreement.

UN Habitat. 2016. *Only 13 of World's Cities Have Affordable Housing According to New Research*. https://unhabitat.org/only-13-of-worlds-cities-have-affordable-housing-according-to-new-research.

UNICEF and WHO. 2017. *Progress on Household Drinking Water, Sanitation, and Hygiene 2000–2017*. https://washdata.org/sites/default/files/documents/reports/2019-07/jmp-2019-wash-households.pdf.

World Bank. 2015. *Economic Impacts of Child Marriage Report*. https://documents.worldbank.org/curated/en/530891498511398503/Economic-impacts-of-child-marriage-global-synthesis-report/.

————. 2020. *Small and Medium Enterprises Finance*. https://https://www.worldbank.org/en/topic/smefinance.

World Economic Forum. 2018. *This Is the Economic Cost of Child Marriage*. https://www.weforum.org/agenda/2018/06/the-cost-of-child-marriage.

World Health Organization. 2012. *Global Costs and Benefits of Drinking-Water Supply and Sanitation Interventions to Reach the MDG Target and Universal Coverage*. https://www.who.int/water_sanitation_health/publications/2012/globalcosts.pdf.

X. Zhou, B. L. Caldecott, E. Harnett, and K. Schumacher. 2020.The Effect of Firm-Level ESG Practices on Macroeconomic Performance. *University of Oxford Smith School of Enterprise and the Environment Working Paper*. No. 20-03. https://www.smithschool.ox.ac.uk/publications/wpapers/workingpaper20-03.pdf.

Box 6: Development in Green and Social Finance during COVID-19 Period in Developing Asia

According to the United Nations Economic and Social Commission for Asia and the Pacific, developing Asia needs to invest USD1.5 trillion annually to achieve the United Nations (UN) Sustainable Development Goals by 2030.[a] The Asian Development Bank's climate-adjusted annual investment requirement over the same period is USD200 billion.[b] Public sector resources alone are insufficient to finance such huge investments. This means that the region must leverage and mobilize resources from the private sector to finance investments promoting green and inclusive economic growth that reduces poverty, benefits vulnerable groups, and decreases inequality.

Extant environment, social, and governance (ESG) debt instruments can be broadly classified into two major categories: bonds and loans. Widely used bond instruments include green bonds, social bonds, sustainability bonds, and sustainability-linked bonds. These are fixed-income products designed to fund investments that generate positive environmental and social outcomes. On the other hand, ESG-themed loans such as green loans and sustainability-linked loans (SLLs) are bank products that finance or refinance, in whole or in part, new and/or existing eligible

projects with clear benefits to the environment and social sustainability.

Before the outbreak of the coronavirus disease (COVID-19), green and social financing was clearly on the rise, making it one of the most promising areas in development finance.[c] Green bonds were the forerunner of ESG bonds. The total global value of green bonds grew from USD1.5 billion to USD257.5 billion between 2007 and 2019. Green bonds comprised the largest category of ESG bond issuances in 2019, accounting for more than half (56%) of issuance in the sustainable debt market. **Figure B6.1** shows the growth of global green bonds, which have gained traction in Asia and the Pacific, with the region now accounting for 12% of global green bonds. According to Climate Bonds Initiative (CBI) data, the issuance of green bonds in Asia and the Pacific reached USD33.1 billion in 2019. In Southeast Asia, which accounts for about 25% of the regional total, issuance nearly doubled to USD8.1 billion in 2019 from USD4.1 billion in 2018.

Amid the COVID-19 pandemic, a slowdown in the green bond market's expansion has been observed and attributed to investors' shifting appetite toward social and sustainability

Figure B6.1: Green Bond Issuance

Figure B6.1a

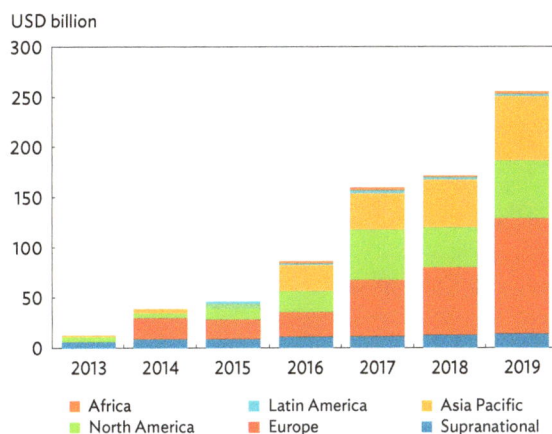

Figure B6.1b

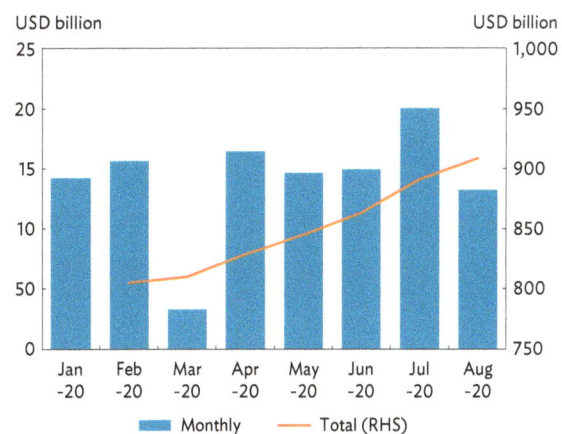

RHS = right-hand side, USD = United States dollar.
Sources: Authors' compilations based on data from Climate Bonds Initiative monthly market blogs and HSBC.

---

[a] This box was written by Cynthia Castillejos-Petalcorin (Senior Economics Officer) and Donghyun Park (Principal Economist) in the Economic Research and Regional Cooperation Department of the Asian Development Bank (ADB).
[b] ADB. 2017. *Meeting Asia's Infrastructure Needs*. https://www.adb.org/publications/asia-infrastructure-needs. Manila.
[c] S. Hyun, D. Park, and S. Tian. 2020. The Price of Going Green: The Role of Greenness in Green Bond Markets. *Account Finance*. 60 (1). pp. 73–95; O. D. Zerbib. 2019. The Effect of Pro-Environmental Preferences on Bond Prices: Evidence from Green Bonds. *Journal of Banking & Finance*. 98 (2019). pp. 39–60.

continued on next page

Box 6: Development in Green and Social Finance during COVID-19 Period in Developing Asia *continued*

bonds that address public health and economic inequalities. During the first half of 2020, global green bond issuance stood at USD91.8 billion, down about 22% from the same period in 2019. In Asia and the Pacific, the CBI noted that issuance in the second quarter (Q2) fell to its lowest level since the first quarter (Q1) of 2017, with January–June 2020 green bond issuance amounting to only USD10.7 billion. Despite the market downturn in 2020, green bonds have still held up better than investment-grade corporate credit.[d]

Even as green bond issuance slows, the COVID-19 pandemic has heightened the need to support vulnerable groups and improve public health and sanitization, underscoring the urgent need for social and sustainability financing. There has been significant growth in social and sustainability bond issuance as sovereigns and corporates tap the debt market. Social bond issuance rose from a mere USD277 million in 2014 to USD20.0 billion in 2019, according to the CBI. In the first half of 2020, social bond issuance reached USD10.9 billion in Q1 2020 and then tripled to USD33.0 billion in Q2 2020. The relative importance of social bonds in ESG investing has clearly increased substantially in 2020 (**Figure B6.2**).

Figure B6.2: ESG Bond Issuance

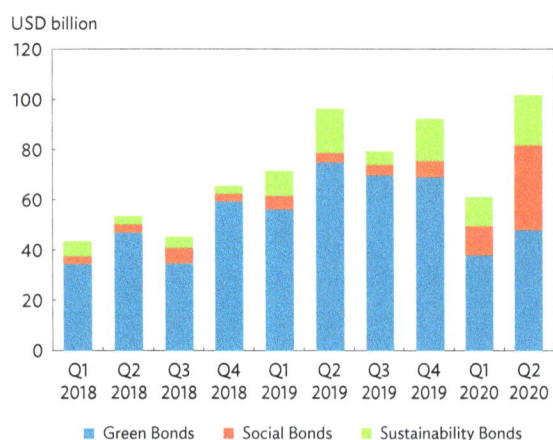

ESG = environment, social, and governance; Q1 = first quarter; Q2 = second quarter; Q3 = third quarter; Q4 = fourth quarter; USD = United States dollar.
Sources: Climate Bonds Initiative, Dealogic, and Moody's Investors Service.

Refinitiv estimates that the volume of sustainable bond issuance in January–June 2020 totaled USD194.5 billion, a 47% year-on-year increase from the same period in 2019. Issuance volume totaled USD63.6 billion in Q1 2020 before more than doubling to USD130.9 billion in Q2 2020. Consequently, Asia and the Pacific (including Japan) now accounts for 16% of the global sustainability bond market. Within the region, large social bond issuances, from both sovereigns and corporates, came from the Republic of Korea (USD9.5 billion), Japan (USD9.3 billion), the People's Republic of China (USD0.9 billion), India (USD0.5 billion), and the Philippines (USD0.4 billion).[e] A common use of the proceeds has been to extend loans to financially strapped small businesses and to finance development of coronavirus vaccines.

The issuance of sustainability bonds, whose proceeds are used for green and social projects, stood at USD46.0 billion in full-year 2019. With increased attention from investors, sustainability bond issuance volume exploded to USD56.7 billion during the first half of 2020, more than twice the amount issued in the first half of 2019. The number of issuances soared by 94% from the previous year, according to Refinitiv. Some of the largest issuances of sustainability bonds in Asia and the Pacific to date in 2020 include (i) Japan's Mitsubishi UFJ Financial Group issuance in September worth JPY150 billion (USD1.42 billion); (ii) the Government of Thailand's dual-tranche USD966 million bond issuance in September, the first of its kind among members of the Association of Southeast Asian Nations, which was three times oversubscribed; and (iii) a triple-tranche offer of USD-denominated bonds by the Government of Indonesia in June worth USD4.3 billion, including a USD1 billion bond with a 50-year tenor, a first in Indonesian history.[f] A *sukuk* (Islamic bond) variant of ESG-themed bonds was also issued by Indonesia in June 2020, raising another USD2.5 billion from a triple-tranche global *sukuk* that was 6.7 times oversubscribed.[g] The common theme of the aforementioned issuances is the financing of activities to help cope with the impact of the pandemic.

Interestingly, investors remain keen on pandemic-related bonds despite the risk associated with weaker global

---

[d] C. Bray. 2020. Green Bonds Gain Popularity, A Defensive Bet as Coronavirus Pandemic Weighs on Markets, Investment Managers Say. *SCMP*. 4 May. https://www.scmp.com/business/banking-finance/article/3082693/green-bonds-gain-popularity-defensive-bet-coronavirus.

[e] U. Volz. 2020. An Urgent Need for Social Bonds in Asia. *Background Paper for the Asian Development Outlook 2021*. Manila.

[f] A. W. Akhlas. 2020. Government Raises $2.5b through Global Sukuk Offering to Address Pandemic Deficit. *Jakarta Post*. 18 June. https://www.thejakartapost.com/news/2020/06/18/govt-raises-2-5b-through-global-sukuk-offering-to-address-pandemic-deficit.html.

[g] Footnote f.

continued on next page

Box 6: Development in Green and Social Finance during COVID-19 Period in Developing Asia   *continued*

economic prospects. The interest perhaps reflects a growing awareness of sustainability in investment strategies and business practices. Moody's Investors Service revised its forecast for social and sustainability bond volumes to USD150 billion in 2020, up from its previous forecast of USD100 billion.[h]

Similar trends have been observed for green and social-themed loans. The demand for SLL products picked up in 2019, peaking in the fourth quarter, as this modality facilitates the entry of companies into sustainable financing. SLL lending volume jumped 89% from USD188.3 billion in 2018 to USD122 billion in 2019.[i] However, in the first half of 2020, sustainable lending fell to USD79.1 billion, slightly declining from the same period in 2019. During Q2 2020, a total of USD31.9 billion of SLL products was issued (**Figure B6.3**).

Notwithstanding the strong demand for ESG blended bonds and loans, there are some concerns, especially as they relate to the lack of ESG ratings standardization. This should not impact the issuance of much-needed ESG financing, but rather could be a catalyst in fast-tracking efforts to harmonize and strengthen ESG ratings information. ESG financing is helping economies, in developing Asia and elsewhere, recover from the health and economic effects of the COVID-19 pandemic in an environmentally and socially sustainable way by influencing business conduct.

Finally, central banks can play a major role in supporting the development of green finance models and tools. They

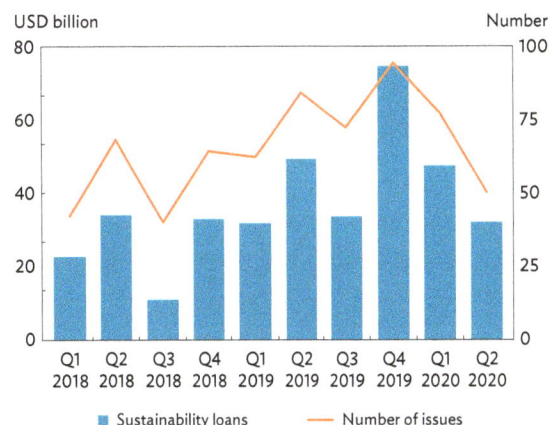

Figure B6.3: Sustainable Loans

Q1 = first quarter; Q2 = second quarter; Q3 = third quarter; Q4 = fourth quarter; USD = United States dollar.
Sources: Climate Bonds Initiative, Dealogic, and Moody's Investors Service.

can also enforce policies on climate-related financial disclosure reporting. The UN has proposed a list of central bank interventions for financing development needs during the COVID-19 recovery period and beyond. These include extensions of swap lines and specific measures in monetary and financial policy frameworks that could integrate risks—including those related to sustainability, climate and environment, gender, and inequality—in financial supervision and regulation.[j]

---

[h] M. Segal. 2020. Moody's Raises Forecast for Global Sustainable Bond Issuance After Q2 Rebound. *ESG Today*. 17 August. https://esgtoday.com/moodys-raises-forecast-for-global-sustainable-bond-issuance-after-q2-rebound/.
[i] *Refinitiv*. H1 2020 Sustainable Finance Review. https://www.refinitiv.com/perspectives/market-insights/refinitiv-analyzes-the-sustainable-finance-market/.
[j] UN. 2020. *Financing for Development in the Era of COVID-19 and Beyond (Part 1)*. https://www.un.org/sites/un2.un.org/files/financing_for_development_covid19_part_i_hosg.pdf.

Box 7: Why Environmental and Social Externalities Matter for Financial Markets

Green and social finance refers to investments that integrate environmental and social (E&S) impacts. It has become one of the fastest growing areas in development finance in recent years.[a] Green and social finance helps address E&S issues such as food security, renewable and clean energy, affordable and accessible housing, healthcare, quality jobs, environmental protection, and education, among others (Camilleri 2020). By allocating capital to socially responsible and environmentally sustainable projects, and pricing the risks of negative externalities, green and social finance can guide investments toward generating positive externalities for the natural environment and vulnerable groups.

The literature has discussed the different motivations of investors to avoid negative green and social externalities. First, E&S practice serves as insurance against systematic risk in the economy. Lins, Servaes, and Tamayo (2017) suggested that (i) corporates can build social capital via practicing social responsibility, and (ii) a high level of social capital strengthens the perception of trustworthiness and thus boosts trust among stakeholders. Lins, Servaes, and Tamayo (2017) found that social capital pays off during a crisis when overall confidence is low and the value of trust increases. Specifically, they document that, during a crisis, firms with a higher level of social responsibility show superior performance than their peers in terms of profitability, productivity, and fund-raising ability, as they are supported by stakeholders' commitment to help such as through credit lines and sales. Hence, investments with positive E&S externalities offer insurance benefits against systematic risk such as a financial crisis or a pandemic. Similarly, Albuquerque, Koskinen, and Zhang (2019) developed a model showing that firms with social responsibility policies have lower profit elasticity in response to aggregate shocks, resulting in less systematic risk and higher firm valuations. They document supportive empirical evidence for this prediction.

Second, E&S compliance helps hedge against negative corporate events and the idiosyncratic risks of firms. E&S practices serve as reputation capital that help cushion against shocks or future E&S negative incidents. Godfrey, Merrill, and Hansen (2009) found that businesses' voluntary actions to improve social conditions create moral capital that provides insurance-like benefits and gains positive attribution from stakeholders. Facing negative corporate

events, this buffering of goodwill from stakeholders will reduce negative judgement and sanctions, and reduce the loss of shareholder value. Empirical evidence shows that compared to firms following an E&S initiative, firms that do not have an E&S practice will face huge costs—which reduces capital expenditure and eventually affects their core business in the context of negative E&S incidents (Ho, Nguyen, and Vu 2020)—and experience greater reductions in firm value because of reputational damage (Aouadi and Marsat 2018). When corporates are involved in E&S scandals, investors face risk. Chen, Dong, and Lin (2020) have indicated that institutional investors can lower portfolio risk more by controlling negative externalities than by boosting positive externalities.

Third, E&S investment can be motivated by preferences and signaling for sustainability and social responsibility by various stakeholders such as managers, shareholders, clients, and society at large. Riedl and Smeets (2017) showed that both intrinsic social preference (without self-benefit) and social signaling (with self-benefit such as social image and reputation) of investors play important roles in investing in E&S assets, and investors forgo financial returns via sustainable and responsible mutual funds by bearing higher management fees and lower returns. Similarly, Białkowski and Starks (2016) found that flows into sustainable and responsible mutual funds show greater persistence than flows into conventional funds, as they are also driven by clients' nonfinancial considerations. Similarly, Ghoul and Karoui (2017) documented that fund flows are less sensitive to the performance of mutual funds that hold more assets with high social responsibility levels, which is driven by clients' nonfinancial utility. Social norms and pressures also motivate E&S investment. Dyck et al. (2019) showed that institutional investment has a causal impact on holding companies' E&S performance. This impact is more pronounced for investors committed to E&S activism and for foreign investors from countries with strong social norms.

Fourth, investing in E&S-themed assets can help manage portfolio risks during a transition to low-carbon investments. The Task Force on Climate-Related Financial Disclosures (2017) outlined key climate-related risks (transition risk and physical risk) and opportunities during a low-carbon transition that have financial implications for companies.[b]

---

[a] This box was written by Shu Tian (Economist) and Mai Lin Villaruel (Economics Officer) in the Economic Research and Regional Cooperation Department of the Asian Development Bank.

[b] Transition risk includes policy and legal risks due to changes in regulations and litigation, technology risk due to creative destruction in green technology, market risk due to climate-related changes in market supply and demand, and reputation risk due to stakeholders' changing perceptions toward green development. Physical risk includes acute risk from disasters and chronic risk driven by climate change patterns. Opportunities include resource efficiency and energy sources to save costs, products and services with low-emission features, markets with new opportunities, and resilience to better respond to climate-related risks.

continued on next page

Box 7: Why Environmental and Social Externalities Matter for Financial Markets   *continued*

Dafermos, Nikolaidi, and Galanis (2018) found that climate change will harm both the financial and nonfinancial sectors by weakening the economic fundamentals of firms, thereby leading to financial instability. Dikau and Volz (2020) indicated that climate-related risks challenge monetary and financial stability, which has led central banks to consider incorporating climate-related risks into their macroprudential policy framework to safeguard macro-financial stability. For example, climate change may adversely affect price stability by influencing food and energy prices, which indirectly affects core inflation (Volz 2017).

In recent years, climate- and social-related risks have attracted attention that may challenge financial stability and thus invite new macroprudential policies. The Bank for International Settlements (2019) has indicated that climate change risk may pose a new type of systematic risk to financial stability.

The outbreak of the coronavirus disease (COVID-19) has underscored the role of financial stability amid shocks when businesses, especially small and medium-sized enterprises, have difficulty repaying their liabilities (Asian Development Bank 2020). As risks associated with climate change and social inclusiveness have gained regulatory and central bank attention in terms of the need to improve macroprudential practices, investments with E&S impacts can help boost portfolio resilience and strengthen the financial sector regulatory framework.

Such risks already show a real impact on financing costs and investment portfolios. In financial markets, investors have different incentives with regard to E&S externalities. Investors influence business investments via different mechanisms, such as ownership and monitoring efforts (Chen, Dong, and Lin 2020) and by conveying a preference for improved E&S performance (Dyck et al. 2019). Ethical investors such as green investors are also essential in risk-sharing in financial markets and thus can affect the cost of capital among polluting firms shifting to low-carbon operations (Heinkel, Kraus, and Zechner 2001). Rich evidence has been documented showing that firms with environmental concerns have a less diversified investor base and a higher cost of capital (Seltzer, Starks, and Zhu 2020; Painter 2020; Battiston and Monasterolo 2020; de Greiff, Delis, and Ongena 2018; Ng and Rezaee 2015; and Beirne, Renzhi, and Volz 2020), while firms pursuing E&S practices, such as issuing green bonds, benefit from better investor profiles and a lower cost of capital (Ghoul et al. 2011, Chava 2014).

References

Asian Development Bank. 2020. *Asia Small and Medium-Sized Enterprise Monitor 2020*. Manila.

R. Albuquerque, Y. Koskinen, and C. Zhang. 2019. Corporate Social Responsibility and Firm Risk: Theory and Empirical Evidence. *Management Science*. 65 (10). pp. 4451–69.

A. Aouadi and S. Marsat. 2018. Do ESG Controversies Matter for firm Value? Evidence from International Data. *Journal of Business Ethics*. 151 (4). pp. 1027–47.

S. Battiston and I. Monasterolo. 2020. *The Climate Spread of Corporate and Sovereign Bonds*. https://ssrn.com/abstract=3376218.

J. Beirne, N. Renzhi, and U. Volz. 2020. Feeling the Heat: Climate Risks and the Cost of Sovereign Borrowing. *Asian Development Bank Institute Working Paper*. No. 1160. Tokyo.

J. Białkowski and L.T. Starks. 2016. *SRI Funds: Investor Demand, Exogenous Shocks, and ESG Profiles*. BlackRock Research Conference. San Francisco. 6 January.

Bank for International Settlements. 2019. Research on Climate-Related Risks and Financial Stability: An "Epistemological Break"? Basel.

M. A. Camilleri. 2020. The Market for Socially Responsible Investing: A Review of the Developments. *Social Responsibility Journal*. doi:10.1108/SRJ-06-2019-0194.

S. Chava. 2014. Environmental Externalities and Cost of Capital. *Management Science*. 60 (9). pp. iv–vi, 2111–380.

Chen, T., H. Dong, C. Lin, 2020. Institutional Shareholders and Corporate Social Responsibility. *Journal of Financial Economics*. 135 (2). pp. 483–504.

K. de Greiff. M.D. Delis, and S.R.G. Ongena. 2018. Being Stranded on the Carbon Bubble? Climate Policy Risk and the Pricing of Bank Loans. *CEPR Discussion Paper*. No. DP12928. https://ssrn.com/abstract=3178099.

Y. Dafermos, M. Nikolaidi, and G. Galanis. 2018. Climate Change, Financial Stability, and Monetary Policy. *Ecological Economics*. 152 (2018). pp. 219–34.

continued on next page

Box 7: Why Environmental and Social Externalities Matter for Financial Markets   *continued*

S. Dikau and U. Volz. 2020. Central Bank Mandates, Sustainability Objectives and the Promotion of Green Finance. *SOAS Department of Economics Working Paper.* No. 232. London: SOAS University of London.

A. Dyck, K. Lins, L. Roth, and H. Wagner. 2019. Do Institutional Investors Drive Corporate Social Responsibility? International Evidence. *Journal of Financial Economics.* 131 (2019). pp. 693–714.

S. Ghoul, O. Guedhami, C. Kwok, and D. Mishra. 2011. Does Corporate Social Responsibility Affect the Cost of Capital? *Journal of Banking & Finance.* 35 (9). pp. 2388–406.

S. Ghoul and A. Karoui. 2017. Does Corporate Social Responsibility Affect Mutual Fund Performance and Flows? *Journal of Banking & Finance.* 77 (C). pp. 53–63.

P.C. Godfrey, C.B. Merrill, and J.M. Hansen. 2009. The Relationship between Corporate Social Responsibility and Shareholder Value: An Empirical Test of the Risk Management Hypothesis. *Strategic Management Journal.* 30 (2009). 425–45.

R. Heinkel, A. Kraus, and J. Zechner. 2001 The Effect of Green Investment on Corporate Behavior. *Journal of Financial and Quantitative Analysis.* 36 (2001). pp. 431–49.

C. Ho, H. Nguyen, and V Vu. 2020. *The Real Effects of Environment and Social Scandals on the Corporate Sector.* Available at SSRN: 3601616 (2020).

K.V. Lins, H. Servaes, and A. Tamayo. 2017. Social Capital, Trust, and Firm Performance: The Value of Corporate Social Responsibility during the Financial Crisis. *The Journal of Finance.* 72 (4): 1785–824.

A. Ng and Z. Rezaee. 2015. Business Sustainability Performance and Cost of Equity Capital Business Sustainability Performance and Cost of Equity Capital. *Journal of Corporate Finance.* 34 (2015). pp. 128–49.

M. Painter. 2020. An Inconvenient Cost: The Effects of Climate Change on Municipal Bonds. *Journal of Financial Economics.* 135 (2020). pp. 468–82.

A. Riedl and P. Smeets. 2017. "Why Do Investors Hold Socially Responsible Mutual Funds?" *The Journal of Finance.* 72 (6). pp. 2505–50.

L. Seltzer, L.T. Starks, and Q. Zhu. 2020. *Climate Regulatory Risks and Corporate Bonds.* https://ssrn.com/abstract=3563271.

Task Force on Climate-Related Financial Disclosure. 2017. *Final Report–Recommendations of the Task Force on Climate-Related Financial Disclosures.* New York. https://www.fsb-tcfd.org/wp-content/uploads/2017/06/FINAL-TCFD-Report-062817.pdf.

U. Volz. 2017. *On the Role of Central Banks in Enhancing Green Finance: United Nations Environment Program Inquiry into the Design of a Sustainable Financial System.* Nairobi.

Box 8: Economic Consequences of Green and Social Finance

Green and social finance helps mobilize funding resources for investments with environmental and social impacts.[a] Aside from contributing to positive social externalities, it is important for policy makers, companies, investors, and various stakeholders to also understand the economic consequences of green and social finance. Such knowledge will facilitate policy making and increase market participation in green and social finance for sustainable development.

The literature has extensively discussed the economic impact of green and social finance from different aspects such as company value, cost of funding, employment, green innovation, and investor base. From the business and shareholder perspective, tapping green and social finance has positive impacts on firm value, and it therefore benefits shareholders. The literature has also documented that firms with superior social responsibility and environmental, social, and governance (ESG) performances have a lower cost of capital, a better credit rating, and improved financial performance (Goss and Roberts 2011, Chava 2014). Green and social finance provides direct funding for companies to make clean investments in climate change mitigation and adaptation, and signals a commitment to emissions reduction and sustainable production. With increasing awareness of social responsibility among the investor community, such signals generate positive feedback from financial markets, which benefits companies through higher firm values, lower funding costs, and a broadened investor base.

Evidence has shown that tapping green and social financing is related to higher firm values. Tang and Zhang (2020) showed that when companies announce a green bond issuance, their stocks witnessed an average 1.72% cumulative abnormal return over a 20-day event window and had about 7% more liquidity compared with matched firms. The authors attribute this favorable market reaction to positive signaling, better information transparency, greater investor attention, and an expanded investor base. Flammer (2020) also documented how positive stock market reactions to green bond issuance announcements are stronger for first-time green bond issuers and certified green bond issuers. Zhou and Cui (2019) found that companies' green bond issuances are associated with improved profitability such as return on invested capital, net profit margin on sales, and return on assets.

As a leading green and social finance instrument, the cost of green bonds has attracted extensive discussion. Green bonds are documented to generate similar or lower costs compared to matched conventional bonds (Ehlers and Packer 2017, Baker et al. 2018, Hachenberg and Schiereck 2018, and Zerbib 2019). A strong environmental commitment—as evidenced by green labels, green bond certification, and independent verification—also generates significant cost advantages for green bond issuers. Such issuers benefit from a yield reduction of 8 basis points compared to conventional bonds (Gianfrate and Peri 2019) and 6 basis points relative to peer green bonds (Hyun, Park, and Tian 2020). One key driver for the yield benefit on green bonds is the high demand for green bonds given their limited supply.[b] The Climate Bonds Initiative has frequently reported oversubscriptions for new green bond offerings in its series of market monitoring reports, indicating prevailing investor perceptions of excess demand for green bonds relative to supply.

The cost convenience of green bonds also holds when compared to bank loans. Alonso-Conde and Rojo-Suárez (2020) evaluated the impacts of green bonds versus conventional bank loan financing on the profitability of an environmentally friendly project. They found that investments financed by green bonds earn a higher internal rate of return for shareholders, which was driven by the lower financing costs of green bonds relative to bank loans. They argue that green finance provides economic and financial incentives for shareholders of green projects and helps align shareholders' objectives with the United Nations Sustainable Development Goals.

In addition to higher firm values and lower costs, tapping green and social financing has been shown to broaden the issuer base and attract new types of investors such as ethical investors and socially responsible investment funds. Giudice (2017) summarized a number of studies conducted by major investment banks and found that around 89% of all investors expressed an interest in or are familiar with sustainable investments, and 65% of them are already conducting sustainable investing. Rising awareness of sustainable investments enables the broadening of the investor base as companies signal their environmental and social commitment by tapping social and green finance. Empirical evidence indicates that green bond issuances help sovereigns and corporates attract new investors and that these green bond investors have a long-term investment horizon. By issuing green bonds, companies see increased bond ownership among long-term and ethical investors (Flammer 2020).

---

[a] This box was written by Shu Tian (Economist) and Mai Lin Villaruel (Economics Officer) in the Economic Research and Regional Cooperation Department of the Asian Development Bank. Research assistance from Adam Zhou of Harvard University is greatly appreciated.

[b] For example, see Climate Bonds Initiative. 2019. *Green Bond Pricing in the Primary Market and Green Bonds Market 2019*. http://climatebonds.net.

continued on next page

Box 8: Economic Consequences of Green and Social Finance   *continued*

From the investor perspective, instruments that feature environmental and social impacts not only deliver positive externalities but also offer greater resilience during shocks and help hedge against systematic risk, idiosyncratic risk, and climate-change-related risk. Nemoto and Lian (2020) showed that Japanese firms with higher corporate social responsibility rankings demonstrated greater resilience amid market turmoil in the first quarter of 2020 resulting from the coronavirus disease (COVID-19) outbreak. Amundi (2020) found that during the market sell-off in March 2020, ESG-themed funds showed greater resilience than conventional funds, with 62% of large ESG funds outperforming the MSCI World Index.

In addition, investing in green- and social-themed instruments helps investors to meet client demand and preferences for sustainability and responsibility. During the past decade, increasing awareness of climate change has directed more funding into many sustainability-themed sectors, such as clean energy, green building, sustainable transport, energy efficiency, pollution prevention, climate adaptation, and sustainable agriculture (Lee, Thwing-Eastman, and Marshall 2020). Such awareness among stakeholders has also directed investors, especially institutional investors, to invest in environmental initiatives. Recent developments in the green and social finance market—such as international standards, principles, and independent certifiers—has strengthened investor confidence in terms of reputation risk.

Green and social finance also provides funding to support a low-carbon transition. Policy makers face complex decision-making scenarios in which some sectors will be negatively affected during the redistribution of investment toward a low-carbon economy. Evidence shows that green and social finance contributes to economic development by directing investment toward high value-added sectors. Glomsrød and Taoyuan (2016, 2018) found that green finance (i.e., labeled green bonds) can help shift investment from coal industries to other high value-added industries, which will increase future savings and investment, and lead to a 1.6% increase in gross domestic product among sample economies. The reallocation of investment via green finance also leads to a 2%–4% lower rate of return on capital, as well as income redistribution since income is shifted from investors to wage earners. The income redistribution also contributes to demand and gross domestic product growth.

Employment is a key factor to consider as the energy sector experiences low-carbon reform. Renewable energies are widely recognized for their potential for green job creation, given their less capital-intensive and more labor-intensive business nature. Ram, Aghahosseini, and Breyer (2020) argue that renewable technologies can create jobs during the low-carbon transition. Under the assumption that the world's electricity generation will be entirely from renewable sources by 2050, they project that the number of jobs directly related to energy will be 35 million globally, or 1.5 times as high as the 2015 level of around 21 million jobs, with solar photovoltaic replacing coal as the leading job-creating technology in the electricity sector and accounting for around 64% of total jobs in the sector by 2050. Green finance through the direct funding of low-carbon investments will contribute to employment and local economic development. Using both computable general equilibrium and input–output models, Perrier and Quirion (2018) find that shifting investment toward low-carbon sectors yields jobs if the investment is directed to sectors with relatively lower wages and a higher share of labor in value added. They suggest that a double dividend (employment and environmental) can be achieved by encouraging the development of low-carbon, labor-intensive sectors.

Another important issue that matters for economic development is innovation. Green and social finance can provide funding to facilitate innovation in green technologies. For example, Zhou and Cui (2019) showed that green bond issuance is positively associated with the innovation capacity of companies, as evidenced by year-on-year growth in total research and development expenses, and in research and development expenses as a share of total operational income. Green innovation has also been found to be positively related to firms' profitability (Aguilera-Caracuel and Ortiz-De-Mandojana 2013).

Green and social finance can facilitate the transition to an environmentally friendly and inclusive future. Besides the positive externalities it delivers, green and social finance can also provide the world with economic benefits. However, given the huge amount of funding needed to meet the pledged climate change targets, the size of green and social finance remains relatively small. Action is needed to develop the market and mobilize more resources to address social and environmental challenges.

continued on next page

Box 8: Economic Consequences of Green and Social Finance   *continued*

References

J. Aguilera-Caracuel and N. Ortiz-De-Mandojana. 2013. Green Innovation and Financial Performance: An Institutional Approach. *Organization & Environment.* 26 (4): pp. 365–85.

Amundi. 2020. ESG *Resilience During the COVID Crisis: Is Green the New Gold?* https://research-center.amundi.com/page/Article/2020/05/The-day-after-3-ESG-Resilience-During-the-Covid-Crisis-Is-Green-the-New-Gold.

A.B. Alonso-Conde and J. Rojo-Suárez. 2020. On the Effect of Green Bonds on the Profitability and Credit Quality of Project Financing. *Sustainability 2020.* 12 (2020). pp. 6695. doi:10.3390/su12166695.

M. Baker, D. Bergstresser, G. Serafeim, and J. Wurgler. 2018. Financing the Response to Climate Change: The Pricing and Ownership of US Green Bonds. *NBER Working Paper.* No. 25194. Cambridge, MA: NBER.

S. Chava. 2014. Environmental Externalities and Cost of Capital. *Management Science.* 60 (9). pp. 2223–47.

T. Ehlers and F. Packer. 2017. Green Bond Finance and Certification. *BIS Quarterly Review.* pp. 89–104.

A. Goss and G. Roberts. 2011. The Impact of Corporate Social Responsibility on the Cost of Bank Loans. *Journal of Banking & Finance.* 35 (7). pp. 1794–810.

C. Flammer. 2020. Corporate Green Bonds. *Journal of Financial Economics.* Forthcoming. https://ssrn.com/abstract=3125518.

G. Gianfrate and M. Peri. 2019. The Green Advantage: Exploring the Convenience of Issuing Green Bonds. *Journal of Cleaner Production.* 219 (2019). pp. 127–35.

E. L. Giudice. 2017. The Green Bond Market, Explained. World Economic Forum. 25 July. https://www.weforum.org/agenda/2017/07/what-are-green-bonds-explainer/.

B. Hachenberg and D. Schiereck. 2018. Are Green Bonds Priced Differently from Conventional Bonds? *Journal of Asset Management.* 19 (6). pp. 371–83.

S. Hyun, D. Park, and S. Tian. 2020. The Price of Going Green: The Role of Greenness in Green Bond Markets. *Accounting & Finance.* 60 (1). pp. 73–95.

L. Lee, M. Thwing-Eastman, R. Marshall. 2020. *2020 ESG Trends to Watch.* MSCI, MSCI ESG Research LLC, January. www.msci.com/documents/10199/02f6473f-6fd8-aaf8-be72-443196478ec3.

M. Ram, A. Aghahosseini, and C. Breyer. 2020. Job Creation during the Global Energy Transition towards 100% Renewable Power System by 2050. *Technological Forecasting and Social Change.* 151 (2020). 119682.

N. Nemoto and L. Liu. 2020. ESG Investment growth amid the COVID-19 Crisis. https://www.asiapathways-adbi.org/2020/06/esg-investment-growth-amid-covid-19-crisis/.

Q. Perrier and P. Quirion. 2018. How Shifting Investment towards Low-Carbon Sectors Impacts Employment: Three Determinants under Scrutiny. *Energy Economics.* 75 (2018). 464–83.

S. Glomsrød and W. Taoyuan. 2016. Business as Unusual: The Implications of Fossil Divestment and Green Bonds for Financial Flows, Economic Growth, and Energy Markets. *CICERO Working Paper.* No. 2016:01.

———. 2018. Business as Unusual: The Implications of Fossil Divestment and Green Bonds for Financial Flows, Economic Growth, and Energy Markets. *Energy for Sustainable Development.* 44 (2018). pp. 1–10.

D. Tang and Y. Zhang. 2020. Do Shareholders Benefit from Green Bonds? *Journal of Corporate Finance.* 61 (2020). pp. 101–27.

O.D. Zerbib. 2019. The Effect of Pro-Environmental Preferences on Bond Prices: Evidence from Green Bonds. *Journal of Banking & Finance.* 98 (2019). pp. 39–60.

X. Zhou and Y. Cui. 2019. Green Bonds, Corporate Performance, and Corporate Social Responsibility. *Sustainability.* 11 (23). 6881. doi:10.3390/su1123688.

Bank Efficiency and Bond Markets: Evidence from Asia and the Pacific

Financial intermediation promotes economic growth, creating liquidity and extending credit to facilitate resource allocation and risk sharing.[7] The efficiency of the banking sector is a major concern of regulators and policy makers, and it remains a topical issue in the literature. While most existing empirical studies focus on various factors that affect bank profit and/or cost efficiency, this study adds to the literature by examining how bond market development is related to bank profit and cost efficiency.

Banks are an indirect financing channel that primarily provide credit to the private sector, while bond markets serve as a direct financing channel that provide credit to both the public and private sectors. Bond market development can affect bank efficiency in many aspects. First, bond markets compete with the banking sector not only for loans but also for deposits. Government bonds serve as an alternative risk-free investment vehicle for depositors; therefore, banks need to increase deposit rates to attract more funding. Meanwhile, corporate bond markets provide an alternative source of financing for the private sector, which becomes a potential competitor of banks. Firms with the highest credit quality have the option to tap bond markets for financing via corporate bond issuances. Hence, a large bond market will force banks to improve the efficiency of their asset allocation to maintain profitability and challenge banks' cost efficiency given possible higher funding costs. Second, bond markets offer more investment instruments for banks' asset portfolios. Banks can invest in government bonds and high-rated corporate bonds, thus better managing the liquidity and credit quality of their asset portfolios, albeit at the cost of lower returns. Third, banks can issue corporate bonds to obtain stable financing with the desired maturity, which can mitigate the duration gap between assets and liabilities on banks' balance sheets, albeit with higher funding costs. Fourth, bond markets provide market-based benchmarking for banks to price their loans and deposits. Hence, bond market development affects banks' operation in terms of assets and liability management, as well as liquidity risk management.

While many developing economies' financial systems remain largely bank-centered, recent decades have seen the rapid development of capital markets. Thus, it is important to understand how bond market development is related to the profit and cost efficiencies of commercial banks. This study constructs a sample of commercial banks from 27 economies in Asia and the Pacific from 2004 to 2017 and considers how their efficiency is related to three bond market development indicators: (i) aggregated bond market size as a share of gross domestic product (GDP), (ii) government bond market size as share of GDP, and (iii) corporate bond market size as a share of GDP. In addition to bond market development, a number of other related variables are also considered in this study, including economic, banking-industry, and bank-specific attributes such as GDP growth, inflation, income level, banking sector openness and regulation, bank size, and leverage ratio. This study utilizes parametric stochastic frontier analysis to estimate bank efficiency. This technique provides unbiased systematic estimates for an unbalanced panel data sample during which bank efficiency can be influenced by country-specific and bank-specific factors, and thus is widely used in cross-economy studies. The dependent variable is bank profit or cost inefficiency; thus, the negative sign of a coefficient will indicate that the variable has a positive impact on bank profit or cost efficiency.

The empirical results are presented in two parts. The first is the effect of overall bond market development. The development of all three bond market types

---

[7] This is shortened version of D. Park, S. Tian, and Q. Wu. 2020. Bank Efficiency and the Bond Markets: Evidence from the Asia and Pacific Region. *Asian Development Bank Economics Working Paper Series*. No. 612. https://www.adb.org/publications/bank-efficiency-bond-markets-asia-pacific.

(i.e., aggregate, corporate, and government) has a positive effect on bank profit efficiency but a negative effect on bank cost efficiency. The results are robust when control variables are introduced. The effect is persistently significant for the total bond market and the government bond market, but not for the corporate bond market. The results indicate that banks are generally more profit-efficient, but less cost-efficient, in an economy with a relatively more developed bond market (**Figure 14**). This finding confirms the competitor role of bond markets. When large clients can tap corporate bond markets for financing, banks are forced to lend to smaller clients by improving asset management skills and profitability. Meanwhile, a larger government bond market means deposit pricing is more market-based, which will increase banks' funding costs. In addition, when banks issue bonds to finance themselves, they also face higher costs. Thus, a developed bond market is associated with lower cost efficiency. Consistent with the relevant literature, the results show that banks are generally more efficient in economies with a higher degree of capital account openness, more constraints on cross-border investment, faster economic growth, a lower inflation rate, and higher income levels. As for bank attributes, larger banks are more profit-efficient but less cost-efficient, and a higher capital ratio reduces (increases) bank profit (cost) efficiency. Banking-industry specific characteristics have a mixed effect on bank efficiency. Less stringent banking entry requirements, higher asset concentration, greater supervisory independence and private monitoring power,

and a higher rate of foreign ownership of banks all help to improve bank profit efficiency, while the impacts of these factors on bank cost efficiency are trivial.

The second part of the results looks beyond the level of bond market development and examines the impact of bond market structure on bank profit and cost efficiencies. The result shows that while total bond market development has a positive and significant impact on bank profit efficiency, the share of corporate bonds to total bond market size has a positive but insignificant effect on bank profit efficiency (**Figure 15**). Furthermore, a larger share of local currency (LCY) corporate bonds as share of total LCY bonds is found to significantly improve bank profit efficiency, while the positive and significant impact of total bond market size remains. The structure of the corporate bond market has a mixed effect on bank cost efficiency. The role of total bond market size on banks' cost efficiency remains insignificant, but a larger share of corporate bonds to total bonds shows a significant role in improving banks' cost efficiency. However, when LCY corporate bonds as a share of total LCY bonds is considered in the analysis, total bond market size showed a significant negative impact on bank cost efficiency.

Overall, we find that bond market development has important implications for the banking sector. Bond

Figure 14: Effect of the Level of Bond Market Development on Bank Inefficiency (% of GDP)

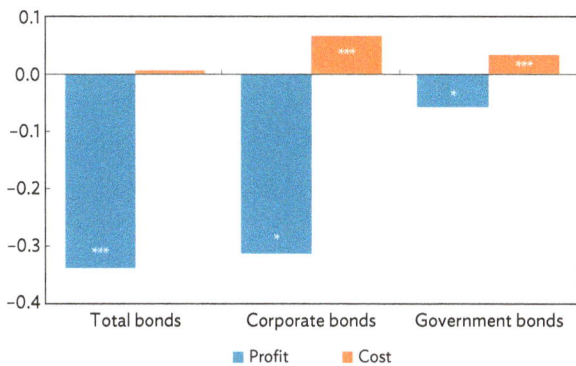

GDP = gross domestic product.
Notes: The dependent variable is bank profit (cost) inefficiency. A negative impact indicates improved bank profit (cost) efficiency, while a positive impact indicates reduced bank profit (cost) efficiency. The ***, **, and * indicate significance at the 1%, 5%, and 10% levels, respectively.
Source: Authors' calculations.

Figure 15: Effect of the Aggregate Bond Market Structure on Bank Inefficiency

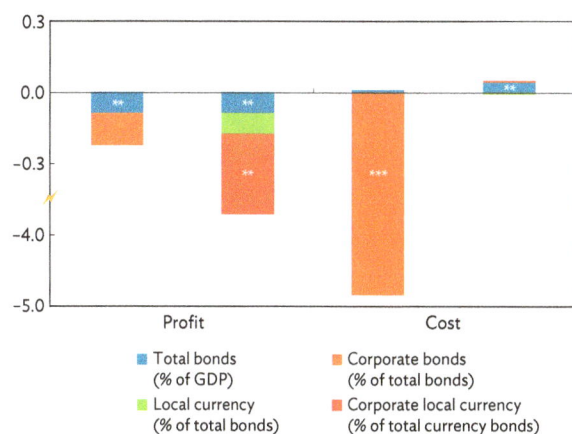

GDP = gross domestic product.
Notes: The dependent variable is bank profit (cost) inefficiency. A negative impact indicates improved bank profit (cost) efficiency, while a positive impact indicates reduced bank profit (cost) efficiency. The ***, **, and * indicate significance at the 1%, 5%, and 10% levels, respectively.
Source: Authors' calculations.

markets serve as a competitor for bank depositors and borrowers, an investment asset pool with government bonds and corporate bonds as portfolio assets, and an alternative financing vehicle in the form of bank bond issuances. They also offer asset and liability pricing benchmarks. On the assets end, the competition and asset pool effects benefit banks with higher profit efficiency as banks improve asset allocation and build capacity to extend more loans to smaller clients that do not have access to capital markets that could increase returns on assets. Meanwhile, a larger bond market lowers banks' overall cost efficiency because government bonds compete for depositors and force banks to raise costs on deposits, and bank bond issuance also comes with higher costs than deposits. The structure of the bond market also matters to bank efficiency as government bonds and corporate bonds have different implications for banks.

The findings of this paper have important policy implications for economies with a very low level of bond market development, or those without a functioning bond market, and for economies with a high level of bond market development but an unbalanced bond market structure. The bond market works like a double-edged sword for bank management. On the asset side, banks can invest in the corporate bond market to diversify risk in their asset portfolios, but they also face competition from the corporate bond market in that some clients will use direct financing from the bond market. On the liability side, banks may obtain stable funding from the corporate bond market, but they need to pay higher financing costs as government bonds compete for deposits and lead to higher funding costs for bank bond financing. Policy makers need to ensure a well-functioning and balanced bond market to better finance economic growth and development.

Market Summaries

People's Republic of China

Yield Movements

The People's Republic of China's (PRC) yield curve for local currency (LCY) bonds shifted upward between 31 August and 30 October (**Figure 1**). The largest shift in yields was seen in the 3-month tenor, which rose 43 basis points (bps). Other tenors that showed a strong rise were the 1-year and 2-year tenors. The 2-year tenor rose 33 bps, while the 1-year tenor rose 22 bps. The other remaining tenors rose between 4 bps and 16 bps. As a result, the 2-year versus 10-year yield spread narrowed from 50 bps to 34 bps between 31 August and 30 October.

The PRC's yields rose as its economy continued to grow, following the successful containment of its coronavirus disease (COVID-19) outbreak. The PRC's gross domestic product (GDP) growth rate accelerated from 3.2% year-on-year (y-o-y) in the second quarter (Q2) of 2020 to 4.9% y-o-y in the third quarter (Q3) of 2020. Growth in all three major sectors of the PRC's economy accelerated in Q3 2020. The fastest y-o-y acceleration was in the tertiary sector (from 1.9% to 4.3%), followed by the secondary sector (from 4.7% to 6.0%). The primary sector's growth accelerated from 3.3% y-o-y to 3.9% y-o-y.

The PRC's industrial production growth momentum also continued. In September, industrial production growth rose to 6.9% y-o-y from 5.6% y-o-y in August. The PRC's industrial production was negative in Q1 2020 and had a growth rate of 3.9% in April. The PRC's inflation rate fell to 1.7% y-o-y in September from 2.4% y-o-y in August.

Size and Composition

LCY bonds outstanding in the PRC rose 5.4% quarter-on-quarter (q-o-q) in Q3 2020, after expanding 5.6% q-o-q in Q2 2020, to reach CNY98.2 trillion (USD14.5 trillion) at the end of September. On a y-o-y basis, LCY bonds outstanding grew 19.9% y-o-y (**Table 1**).

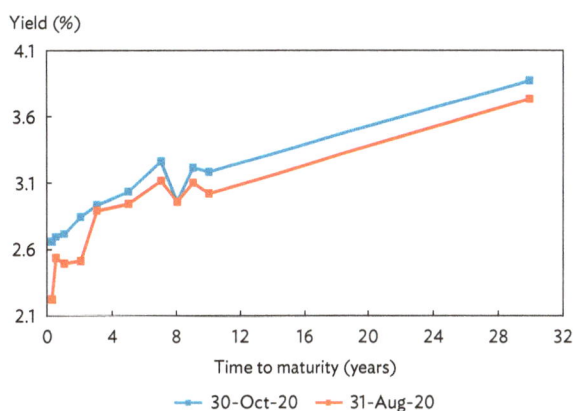

Figure 1: The People's Republic of China's Benchmark Yield Curve—Local Currency Government Bonds

Source: Based on data from Bloomberg LP.

Government bonds. The PRC's government bond market growth accelerated in Q3 2020 to 6.6% q-o-q from 5.4% q-o-q in Q2 2020 as the central government continued to fund its fiscal stimulus programs. The growth rate of Treasury bonds outstanding sped up to 8.7% q-o-q from 5.5% q-o-q during the same period.

While local governments continued to issue special bonds and received a quota increase in 2020 of CNY1.6 trillion compared with 2019, growth slowed slightly to 6.1% q-o-q in Q3 2020 from 6.2% q-o-q in Q2 2020 due to a high base effect. Growth in policy bank bonds accelerated to 5.0% q-o-q from 4.2% q-o-q in the same period.

Corporate bonds. The PRC's corporate bond market's growth slowed to 3.2% q-o-q in Q3 2020 from 5.9% q-o-q in Q2 2020. The slowdown in growth was largely due to the increased cost of funding as interest rates rose.

Rising interest rates led to a decline in commercial paper outstanding of 4.6% q-o-q in Q3 2020 (**Table 2**). Higher interest rates make the refinancing of short-term commercial paper more expensive. Other types of

Table 1: Size and Composition of the Local Currency Bond Market in the People's Republic of China

| | Outstanding Amount (billion) | | | | | | Growth Rates (%) | | | |
| | Q3 2019 | | Q2 2020 | | Q3 2020 | | Q3 2019 | | Q3 2020 | |
	CNY	USD	CNY	USD	CNY	USD	q-o-q	y-o-y	q-o-q	y-o-y
Total	81,916	11,459	93,187	13,189	98,178	14,457	3.6	14.9	5.4	19.9
Government	52,913	7,402	58,867	8,332	62,747	9,240	3.5	12.9	6.6	18.6
Treasury Bonds and Other Government Bonds	15,963	2,233	17,775	2,516	19,327	2,846	3.2	11.2	8.7	21.1
Central Bank Bonds	14	2	15	2	15	2	250.0	–	0.0	7.1
Policy Bank Bonds	15,445	2,161	16,662	2,358	17,489	2,575	1.5	8.9	5.0	13.2
Local Government Bonds	21,491	3,006	24,415	3,456	25,915	3,816	5.1	17.3	6.1	20.6
Corporate	29,003	4,057	34,320	4,857	35,432	5,217	3.9	18.6	3.2	22.2
Policy Bank Bonds										
China Development Bank	8,665	1,212	9,138	1,293	9,415	1,386	1.0	8.6	3.0	8.7
Export–Import Bank of China	2,601	364	3,086	437	3,395	500	2.7	13.2	10.0	30.5
Agricultural Devt. Bank of China	4,179	585	4,438	628	4,679	689	1.9	7.0	5.4	12.0

– = not applicable, CNY = Chinese yuan, q-o-q = quarter-on-quarter, Q2 = second quarter, Q3 = third quarter, USD = United States dollar, y-o-y = year-on-year.
Notes:
1. Calculated using data from national sources.
2. Treasury bonds include savings bonds and local government bonds.
3. Bloomberg LP end-of-period local currency–USD rates are used.
4. Growth rates are calculated from local currency base and do not include currency effects.
Sources: CEIC.

Table 2: Corporate Bonds Outstanding in Key Categories

| | Amount (CNY billion) | | | Growth Rate (%) | | | |
| | | | | Q3 2019 | | Q3 2020 | |
	Q3 2019	Q2 2020	Q3 2020	q-o-q	y-o-y	q-o-q	y-o-y
Financial Bonds	5,505	6,803	7,166	1.1	33.5	5.3	30.2
Enterprise Bonds	3,840	3,771	3,826	1.0	(3.2)	1.5	(0.3)
Listed Corporate Bonds	7,250	8,996	9,619	1.0	21.6	6.9	32.7
Commercial Paper	2,152	2,825	2,694	1.0	13.5	(4.6)	25.2
Medium-Term Notes	6,141	7,300	7,351	1.0	16.5	0.7	19.7
Asset-Backed Securities	2,081	2,406	2,519	1.1	54.9	4.7	21.1

( ) = negative, CNY = Chinese yuan, q-o-q = quarter-on-quarter, Q2 = second quarter, Q3 = third quarter, y-o-y = year-on-year.
Source: CEIC.

corporate bonds outstanding showed a q-o-q increase, with listed corporate bonds growing the fastest.

Issuance of commercial paper declined in Q3 2020, leading to a decline in commercial paper outstanding. Issuance of medium-term notes also declined during the quarter (**Figure 2**).

The PRC's LCY corporate bond market continued to be dominated by a few big issuers (**Table 3**). At the end of Q3 2020, the top 30 corporate bond issuers accounted for a combined CNY8.9 trillion of corporate bonds outstanding, or about 25.2% of the total market. Of the top 30, the 10 largest issuers accounted for an aggregate

CNY5.9 trillion. China Railway, the top issuer, had more than three times the outstanding amount of bonds as the second-largest issuer, Agricultural Bank of China. The top 30 issuers included 16 banks, which continued to generate funding to strengthen their capital bases, improve liquidity, and lengthen their maturity profiles amid ongoing uncertainty resulting from the COVID-19 pandemic.

Table 4 lists the largest corporate bond issuances in Q3 2020. The top issuers consisted largely of financial institutions as they sought to improve their capital bases and liquidity in light of the ongoing economic impact of COVID-19.

Figure 2: Corporate Bond Issuance in Key Sectors

CNY billion

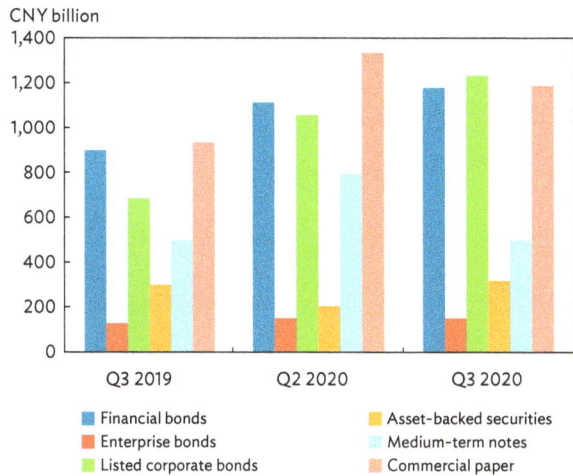

CNY = Chinese yuan, Q2 = second quarter, Q3 = third quarter.
Source: CEIC.

Investor Profile

Among the major government bond categories, banks were the single-largest holder at the end of September (**Figure 3**), with banks holding about 66% of Treasury bonds, 57% of policy bank bonds, and 57% of local government bonds. The share of banks in local government bonds was a significant drop from its previous share of 88% in the same period a year ago.

Liquidity

The volume of interest rate swaps rose 17.3% q-o-q in Q3 2020. The 7-day repurchase agreement remained the most used interest rate swap, comprising an 83.1% share of the total interest rate swap volume during the quarter (**Table 5**).

Policy, Institutional, and Regulatory Developments

The People's Republic of China Eases Foreign Capital Entry Rules

In September, the PRC streamlined the existing regulations for the Renminbi Qualified Foreign Institutional Investor program and the Qualified Foreign Institutional Investor program. The new rules combined the two existing regulations into one and also made application requirements easier and simplified procedures. The new regulations took effect on 1 November.

The People's Republic of China Issues USD-Denominated Bonds

In October, the Government of the PRC issued USD6.0 billion worth of 3-year, 5-year, 10-year, and 30-year bonds. The bonds are the first USD-denominated bonds issued by the Government of the PRC since 1996 that are marketed to US investors under 144a Rules. The USD1.25 billion 3-year bond was issued with a coupon rate of 0.40%, while the USD2.25 billion 5-year bond was issued with a coupon rate of 0.55%. The USD2.0 billion 10-year bond was issued with a coupon rate of 1.2%, and the USD0.5 billion 30-year bond was issued with a coupon rate of 2.25%.

Table 3: Top 30 Issuers of Local Currency Corporate Bonds in the People's Republic of China

	Issuers	Outstanding Amount		State-Owned	Listed Company	Type of Industry
		LCY Bonds (CNY billion)	LCY Bonds (USD billion)			
1.	China Railway	2,173.5	320.1	Yes	No	Transportation
2.	Agricultural Bank of China	645.1	95.0	Yes	Yes	Banking
3.	Bank of China	530.6	78.1	Yes	Yes	Banking
4.	Industrial and Commercial Bank of China	517.3	76.2	Yes	Yes	Banking
5.	Central Huijin Investment	449.0	66.1	Yes	No	Asset Management
6.	Bank of Communications	391.6	57.7	No	Yes	Banking
7.	Shanghai Pudong Development Bank	340.7	50.2	No	Yes	Banking
8.	China Construction Bank	307.1	45.2	Yes	Yes	Banking
9.	China National Petroleum	274.9	40.5	Yes	No	Energy
10.	Industrial Bank	273.2	40.2	No	Yes	Banking
11.	China Minsheng Banking	264.0	38.9	No	Yes	Banking
12.	State Grid Corporation of China	261.5	38.5	Yes	No	Public Utilities
13.	China CITIC Bank	223.0	32.8	No	Yes	Banking
14.	State Power Investment	193.6	28.5	Yes	No	Energy
15.	Ping An Bank	178.7	26.3	No	Yes	Banking
16.	Tianjin Infrastructure Construction and Investment Group	159.0	23.4	Yes	No	Industrial
17.	Postal Savings Bank of China	155.0	22.8	Yes	Yes	Banking
18.	PetroChina	153.0	22.5	Yes	Yes	Energy
19.	China Southern Power Grid	153.0	22.5	Yes	No	Energy
20.	Huaxia Bank	143.0	21.1	Yes	No	Banking
21.	China Everbright Bank	141.8	20.9	Yes	Yes	Banking
22.	China Merchants Bank	139.2	20.5	Yes	Yes	Banking
23.	Shaanxi Coal and Chemical Industry Group	132.5	19.5	Yes	No	Energy
24.	Datong Coal Mine Group	123.4	18.2	Yes	No	Coal
25.	China Three Gorges Corporation	106.0	15.6	Yes	No	Power
26.	CITIC Securities	105.2	15.5	Yes	Yes	Brokerage
27.	China Datang	105.1	15.5	Yes	Yes	Energy
28.	Bank of Beijing	102.9	15.2	No	Yes	Banking
29.	Shougang Group	100.0	14.7	Yes	No	Steel
30.	Bank of Ningbo	99.1	14.6	No	Yes	Banking
	Total Top 30 LCY Corporate Issuers	**8,941.8**	**1,316.7**			
	Total LCY Corporate Bonds	**35,431.7**	**5,217.5**			
	Top 30 as % of Total LCY Corporate Bonds	**25.2%**	**25.2%**			

CNY = Chinese yuan, LCY = local currency, USD = United States dollar.
Notes:
1. Data as of 30 September 2020.
2. State-owned firms are defined as those in which the government has more than a 50% ownership stake.
Source: *AsianBondsOnline* calculations based on Bloomberg LP data.

Table 4: Notable Local Currency Corporate Bond Issuances in the Third Quarter of 2020

Corporate Issuers	Coupon Rate (%)	Issued Amount (CNY billion)
China State Railway Group		
10-year bond	3.57	20
10-year bond	3.74	15
5-year bond	3.47	15
10-year bond	3.68	15
20-year bond	4.04	5
5-year bond	4.15	5
0-year bond	3.93	5
Bank of China		
10-year bond	4.20	15
15-year bond	4.70	15
3-year bond	2.92	15
5-year bond	2.71	6
5-year bond	3.29	6
5-year bond	2.61	6

Corporate Issuers	Coupon Rate (%)	Issued Amount (CNY billion)
Industrial Bank		
3-year bond	2.17	23
3-year bond	2.58	22
5-year bond	2.67	7
5-year bond	2.95	5
Shanghai Pudong Development Bank		
3-year bond	2.08	50
Bank of Communications		
3-year bond	3.18	50

CNY = Chinese yuan.
Source: Based on data from Bloomberg LP.

Figure 3: Local Currency Treasury Bonds and Policy Bank Bonds Investor Profile

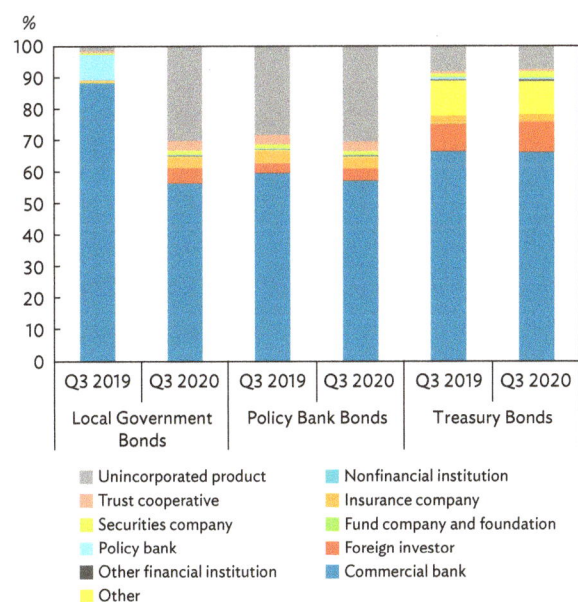

Legend:
- Unincorporated product
- Trust cooperative
- Securities company
- Policy bank
- Other financial institution
- Other
- Nonfinancial institution
- Insurance company
- Fund company and foundation
- Foreign investor
- Commercial bank

Q3 = third quarter.
Source: CEIC.

Table 5: Notional Values of the People's Republic of China's Interest Rate Swap Market in the Third Quarter of 2020

Interest Rate Swap Benchmarks	Notional Amount (CNY billion)	Share of Total Notional Amount (%)	Growth Rate (%)
	Q3 2020		q-o-q
7-Day Repo Rate (Deposit Institutions)	38,694.0	83.1	20.1
Overnight SHIBOR	35.0	0.1	(51.0)
3-Month SHIBOR	6,617.6	14.2	10.1
1-Year Lending Rate	518.5	1.1	(30.7)
5-Year Lending Rate	10.0	0.0	(45.8)
10-Year Treasury Yield	242.0	0.5	30.5
China Development Bank 10-Year Bond Yield	226.5	0.5	(11.2)
10-Year Bond Yield/10-Year Government Bond Yield	225.0	0.5	(11.2)
Total	46,568.6	100.0	17.3

( ) = negative, CNY = Chinese yuan, q-o-q = quarter-on-quarter, Q3 = third quarter, Repo = repurchase, SHIBOR = Shanghai Interbank Offered Rate.
Note: Growth rate computed based on notional amounts.
Sources: *AsianBondsOnline* and *ChinaMoney*.

Hong Kong, China

Yield Movements

Movements in Hong Kong, China's local currency (LCY) bond market yields were mixed between 31 August and 30 October (**Figure 1**). Yields fell at the shorter-end of the yield curve as bonds with maturities of 3 years or less shed an average of 6 basis points (bps). The 2-year tenor showed the largest drop at 12 bps. Yields rose at the longer-end of the curve, with the yield for the 10-year tenor inching up 1 bp, while the 15-year tenor gained 12 bps. The spread between the 2-year and 10-year tenors widened from 32 bps to 45 bps during the review period.

Heightened uncertainty, brought about by the lingering impact of the coronavirus disease (COVID-19) and exacerbated by political risks, led to the drop in yields at the shorter-end of the curve. The rise in yields at the longer-end of the curve reflected concerns about the debt burden implied by the rising cost of the government's relief efforts to boost the economy.

Declining yields also reflected the lingering weakness in Hong Kong, China's economy. Hong Kong, China's gross domestic product fell 3.5% year-on-year (y-o-y) in the third quarter (Q3) of 2020, a narrower decline than the 9.0% y-o-y contraction in the second quarter (Q2). The improvement stemmed mainly from increased exports, particularly to the People's Republic of China (PRC). Merchandise exports rose 3.9% y-o-y in Q3 2020, rebounding from the 2.2% y-o-y decline in the prior quarter. Although the economy is showing initial signs of improvement amid the PRC's recovery and the local containment of COVID-19, economic performance is still below its level prior to the recession. Unemployment reached a 16-year high of 6.4% in Q3 2020.

Demand for the Hong Kong dollar, fueled by high profile initial public offerings, continued to surge during the review period. High demand continued to push the Hong Kong dollar to the strong-side of its trading band against the US dollar, prompting repeated interventions from the Hong Kong Monetary Authority (HKMA). The HKMA's actions brought the aggregate balance— an indicator of liquidity in the financial system—from HKD193.1 billion (USD24.9 billion) to a record high of HKD457.5 billion (USD59.0 billion) during the review period.

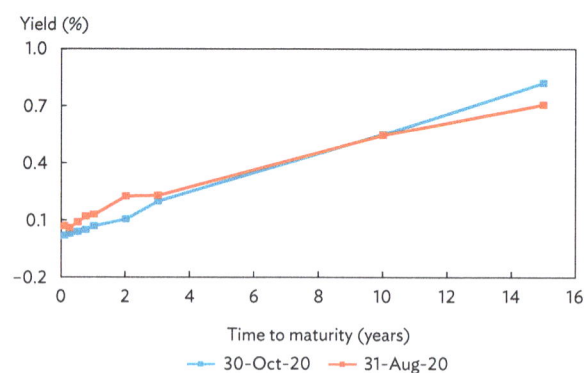

Figure 1: Hong Kong, China's Benchmark Yield Curve— Exchange Fund Bills and Notes

Source: Based on data from Bloomberg LP.

Hong Kong, China's consumer prices fell amid a deflationary stretch in Q3 2020. Consumer prices declined 2.2% y-o-y in September, following a 0.4% y-o-y dip in August and a 2.3% y-o-y contraction in July. The government's relief measures, which include waivers of public housing rents and weak demand due to the economic recession, drove deflationary pressures.

Uncertainty over the prolonged global pandemic, frictions between the PRC and the United States, and political risks continued to affect Hong Kong, China's economy and bond market.

Size and Composition

Hong Kong, China's LCY bonds outstanding amounted to HKD2,287.0 (USD295.1 billion) at the end of September, up from HKD2,267.6 billion at the end of June (**Table 1**). The LCY bond market's quarter-on-quarter (q-o-q) growth rose to 0.9% q-o-q in Q3 2020 from 0.5% q-o-q in Q2 2020, driven by a rebound in the government bond segment. On an annual basis, aggregate bonds outstanding increased 1.0% y-o-y in Q3 2020, reversing the 0.8% y-o-y contraction in the previous quarter. The share of government bonds to total LCY bonds outstanding slipped to 50.6% in Q3 2020 from 51.0% in Q2 2020.

Government bonds. At the end of September, LCY government bonds outstanding reached HKD1,157.6 billion, up slightly from HKD1,156.2 billion at the end of March. Although weak at 0.1% q-o-q, the

Table 1: Size and Composition of the Local Currency Bond Market in Hong Kong, China

| | Outstanding Amount (billion) | | | | | | Growth Rate (%) | | | |
| | Q3 2019 | | Q2 2020 | | Q3 2020 | | Q3 2019 | | Q3 2020 | |
	HKD	USD	HKD	USD	HKD	USD	q-o-q	y-o-y	q-o-q	y-o-y
Total	2,264	289	2,268	293	2,287	295	(0.9)	4.2	0.9	1.0
Government	1,170	149	1,156	149	1,158	149	0.5	1.4	0.1	(1.1)
Exchange Fund Bills	1,048	134	1,042	134	1,042	134	0.6	2.4	0.03	(0.6)
Exchange Fund Notes	28	4	26	3	26	3	(3.4)	(16.5)	0.0	(9.2)
HKSAR Bonds	94	12	89	11	90	12	1.0	(2.9)	1.1	(4.4)
Corporate	1,094	140	1,111	143	1,129	146	(2.4)	7.4	1.6	3.2

( ) = negative, HKD = Hong Kong dollar, HKSAR = Hong Kong Special Administrative Region, q-o-q = quarter-on-quarter, Q2 = second quarter, Q3 = third quarter, USD = United States dollar, y-o-y = year-on-year.
Notes:
1. Calculated using data from national sources.
2. Bloomberg LP end-of-period local currency–USD rates are used.
3. Growth rates are calculated from local currency base and do not include currency effects.
Source: Hong Kong Monetary Authority.

growth of aggregate government bonds outstanding in Q3 2020 reversed the 1.1% q-o-q contraction in the prior quarter. Strong growth in outstanding Hong Kong Special Administrative Region Bonds was the main driver of the expanding government bonds stock. Outstanding Exchange Fund Bills (EFBs) and Exchange Fund Notes (EFNs) posted positive but weak growth in Q3 2020. On a y-o-y basis, outstanding LCY government bonds continued to contract, dropping 1.1% in Q3 2020 after a 0.7% decline in Q2 2020. All components of LCY government bonds outstanding showed a decline in y-o-y growth in Q3 2020.

Exchange Fund Bills. The outstanding stock of EFBs inched up to HKD1,042.3 billion at the end of September from HKD1,041.9 billion at the end of June. Although weak, the 0.03% q-o-q growth in Q3 2020 reversed the 1.7% q-o-q decline posted in the previous quarter. Issuance of EFBs amounted to HKD903.8 billion in Q3 2020, rising 10.0% q-o-q.

Exchange Fund Notes. Since 2015, the HKMA has limited its issuance of EFNs to 2-year tenors. In August, the HKMA issued a 2-year EFN worth HKD1.2 billion. Due to maturities during the quarter, the amount of outstanding EFNs remained steady in Q3 2020 at HKD25.8 billion. On a y-o-y basis, the outstanding stock of EFNs continued to contract, falling 9.2% in Q3 2020 after a 12.2% decline in the previous quarter.

Hong Kong Special Administrative Region Bonds.
HKSAR Bonds outstanding rose 1.1% q-o-q to reach HKD89.5 billion at the end of September. The government issued a 15-year bond worth HKD1.0 billion

in September under the Institutional Bond Issuance Programme. On a y-o-y basis, the 4.4% contraction in outstanding HKSAR Bonds in Q3 2020 extended the 4.5% decline posted in the prior quarter.

Corporate bonds. Corporate bonds outstanding expanded 1.6% q-o-q to reach HKD1,129.4 billion at the end of September. On a y-o-y basis, corporate bonds outstanding rose 3.2% in Q3 2020, rebounding from a 0.9% contraction in the previous quarter.

Hong Kong, China's top 30 nonbank issuers had a combined HKD256.0 billion of LCY bonds outstanding at the end of September, accounting for 22.5% of the total corporate bond market (**Table 2**). Hong Kong Mortgage Corporation, Sun Hung Kai & Co., Hong Kong and China Gas Company, MRT, and Link Holdings maintained their positions as the top five issuers with outstanding LCY bonds outstanding of HKD40.7 billion, HKD18.6 billion, HKD16.1 billion, HKD13.0 billion, and HKD12.5 billion, respectively. The top 30 issuers were predominantly finance and real estate companies. Finance companies together accounted for a total of HKD105.5 billion of outstanding corporate bonds, while real estate firms had an aggregate corporate bonds stock of HKD58.0 billion. A majority of the top 30 nonbank issuers were listed on the Hong Kong Stock Exchange; only three were state-owned companies.

Corporate bond issuance totaled HKD215.2 billion at the end September, contracting 8.2% q-o-q amid weak business confidence due to economic and political uncertainties. **Table 3** lists the notable corporate bond issuances in Q3 2020. Among the largest issuances

Table 2: Top 30 Nonbank Corporate Issuers of Local Currency Corporate Bonds in Hong Kong, China

	Issuers	Outstanding Amount		State-Owned	Listed Company	Type of Industry
		LCY Bonds (HKD billion)	LCY Bonds (USD billion)			
1.	Hong Kong Mortgage Corporation	40.7	5.2	Yes	No	Finance
2.	Sun Hung Kai & Co.	18.6	2.4	No	Yes	Finance
3.	The Hong Kong and China Gas Company	16.1	2.1	No	Yes	Utilities
4.	MTR	13.0	1.7	Yes	Yes	Transportation
5.	Link Holdings	12.5	1.6	No	Yes	Finance
6.	Hongkong Land	12.5	1.6	No	No	Real Estate
7.	New World Development	12.1	1.6	No	Yes	Diversified
8.	Henderson Land Development	12.0	1.6	No	Yes	Real Estate
9.	Swire Pacific	10.3	1.3	No	Yes	Diversified
10.	Hang Lung Properties	9.4	1.2	No	Yes	Real Estate
11.	Hongkong Electric	8.5	1.1	No	No	Utilities
12.	CLP Power Hong Kong Financing	7.7	1.0	No	No	Finance
13.	Swire Properties	7.6	1.0	No	Yes	Diversified
14.	Guotai Junan International Holdings	7.3	0.9	No	Yes	Finance
15.	Wharf Real Estate Investment	6.9	0.9	No	Yes	Real Estate
16.	Smart Edge	6.8	0.9	No	No	Finance
17.	Airport Authority Hong Kong	6.6	0.9	Yes	No	Transportation
18.	AIA Group	6.3	0.8	No	Yes	Insurance
19.	CK Asset Holdings	6.2	0.8	No	Yes	Real Estate
20.	Hysan Development	5.7	0.7	No	Yes	Real Estate
21.	The Wharf Holdings	5.5	0.7	No	Yes	Finance
22.	Future Days	5.0	0.6	No	No	Transportation
23.	Lerthai Group	3.0	0.4	No	Yes	Real Estate
24.	Cathay Pacific	2.5	0.3	No	Yes	Transportation
25.	China Dynamics Holdings	2.4	0.3	No	Yes	Automotive
26.	Champion REIT	2.3	0.3	No	Yes	Real Estate
27.	South Shore Holdings	2.2	0.3	No	Yes	Industrial
28.	Emperor Capital Group	2.2	0.3	No	Yes	Finance
29.	Emperor International Holdings	2.2	0.3	No	Yes	Finance
30.	IFC Development	2.0	0.3	No	No	Finance
	Total Top 30 Nonbank LCY Corporate Issuers	**256.0**	**33.0**			
	Total LCY Corporate Bonds	**1,129.4**	**145.7**			
	Top 30 as % of Total LCY Corporate Bonds	**22.5%**	**22.5%**			

HKD = Hong Kong dollar, LCY = local currency, REIT = real estate investment trust, USD = United States dollar.
Notes:
1. Data as of 30 September 2020.
2. State-owned firms are defined as those in which the government has more than a 50% ownership stake.
Source: *AsianBondsOnline* calculations based on Bloomberg LP data.

Table 3: Notable Local Currency Corporate Bond Issuances in the Third Quarter of 2020

Corporate Issuers	Coupon Rate (%)	Issued Amount (HKD million)
Hong Kong Mortgage Corporation		
1.5-year bond	0.74	0.50
2-year bond	0.76	0.10
3-year bond	0.93	0.50
5-year bond	0.90	0.17
Guotai Junan International Holdings		
1-year bond	0.00	0.60
1-year bond	2.00	0.38
1-year bond	1.80	0.28
Hongkong Land		
15-year bond	2.65	0.80
15-year bond	2.90	0.40
Hang Lung Properties		
5-year bond	2.35	0.50
5-year bond	2.25	0.42
5-year bond	2.25	0.24
The Hong Kong and China Gas Company		
10-year bond	1.98	0.70
10-year bond	1.98	0.22

HKD = Hong Kong dollar.
Source: Bloomberg LP.

during the quarter were bonds issued by Hong Kong Mortgage Corporation, Guotai Junan International Holdings, Hongkong Land, Hang Lung Properties, and Hong Kong and China Gas Company.

Government-owned Hong Kong Mortgage Corporation issued a total of HKD10.3 billion of bonds in Q3 2020, including a 1.5-year bond with a 0.74% coupon worth HKD0.5 billion, a 2-year bond with a 0.76% coupon worth HKD0.1 billion, a 3-year bond with a 0.93% coupon worth

HKD0.5 billion, and a 5-year bond with a 0.90% coupon worth HKD0.2 billion.

Goutai Junan International Holdings, a financial firm, issued a total of HKD2.2 billion, including a zero coupon 1-year bond worth HKD0.6 billion, a 1-year bond with a 2.0% coupon worth HKD0.4 billion, and a 1-year bond with a 1.8% coupon worth HKD0.3 billion.

Hongkong Land issued two 15-year bonds with 2.65% and 2.90% coupons and worth a total of HKD1.20 billion. Hang Lung Properties issued three 5-year bonds worth a total of HKD1.16 billion with coupons ranging from 2.25% to 2.35%. The Hong Kong and China Gas Company raised HKD0.92 billion from two issuances of 10-year bonds, both with a 1.98% coupon.

Policy, Institutional, and Regulatory Developments

Hong Kong Monetary Authority Holds Countercyclical Capital Buffer at 1.0%

On 12 October, the HKMA announced that the countercyclical capital buffer (CCyB) would remain unchanged at 1.0%. The HKMA noted that the latest data based on Q2 2020 indicators signaled the need for a higher CCyB of 2.5%. However, the HKMA deemed that considering the high level of uncertainty facing the economy, holding the CCyB steady at 1.0% was more appropriate. A lower CCyB releases additional liquidity into the banking system by raising banks' lending capacity to support the economy. The CCyB is an integral part of the Basel III regulatory capital framework designed to increase the resilience of the banking sector in periods of excess credit growth.

Indonesia

Yield Movements

Local currency (LCY) government bond yields in Indonesia declined for most maturities between 31 August and 30 October (**Figure 1**). Yields for bonds with maturities of 4 years or less fell an average of 37 basis points (bps), while yields shed an average of 16 bps for maturities of 5 years or more. The exceptions to the declining trend in yields were the 7-year maturity, which gained by 7 bps, and the 3-year and 6-year bonds, which were unchanged during the review period. The 2-year versus 10-year spread narrowed from 219 bps on 31 August to 213 bps on 30 October.

The overall trend of declining yields was driven by expectations that Bank Indonesia would continue to maintain an easy monetary policy stance amid low inflation and a weak economic outlook. Bank Indonesia has kept its 7-day reverse repurchase rate steady at 4.00% since July. The policy rate had been lowered by a cumulative 100 bps year-to-date through the end of October. While there was still room to cut rates further, the central bank opted to utilize other monetary policy tools and macroprudential measures to ensure the stability of the Indonesian rupiah. In its meeting held on 12–13 October, Bank Indonesia's Board of Governors decided to hold its policy rate steady, while also keeping unchanged the deposit facility rate at 3.25% and the lending facility rate at 4.75%. At their current levels, the rates were deemed appropriate to ensure the rupiah's stability.

The coronavirus disease (COVID-19) outbreak in Indonesia has taken a toll on economic growth. A resurgence in the number of cases led the government to re-enforce social restrictions in September, further dampening investor sentiment in the bond market. This has led foreign investor holdings in the LCY government bond market to drop from 30.2% at the end of June to 27.0% at the end of September. In October however, investor interest picked up, leading to capital inflows for the first time since July, buoyed by the passage of the Omnibus Bill on Job Creation that is expected to improve investment climate in Indonesia.

Real gross domestic product (GDP) growth in the second quarter (Q2) of 2020 contracted 5.3% year-on-year

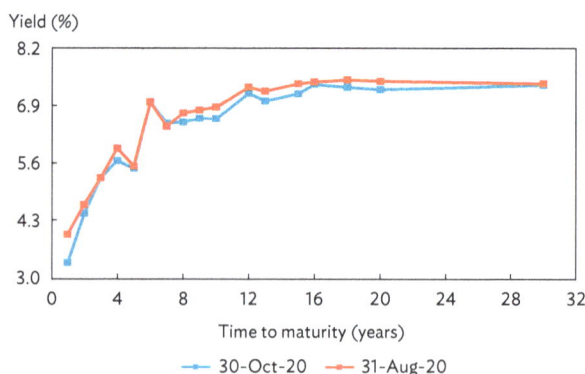

Figure 1: Indonesia's Benchmark Yield Curve— Local Currency Government Bonds

Source: Based on data from Bloomberg LP.

(y-o-y) after a 3.0% y-o-y expansion in the first quarter. While economic recovery has slowly taken ground, gross domestic product growth in the third quarter (Q3) of 2020 weakened but at a slower pace. GDP declined 3.5% y-o-y in Q3 2020 compared with -5.3% y-o-y in Q2 2020. For full-year 2020, the Ministry of Finance revised downward its economic growth projection in September to between −0.6% and −1.7% from its previous estimate of between −0.2% and −1.1% in August.

Among emerging East Asian currencies, the Indonesian rupiah depreciated the most year-to-date through 30 October, falling 5.2% vis-à-vis the United States dollar.

Size and Composition

The LCY bond market in Indonesia continued to expand to reach a size of IDR3,940.6 trillion (USD264.8 billion) at the end of September (**Table 1**). Overall growth accelerated to 9.9% quarter-on-quarter (q-o-q) in Q3 2020 after rising 7.8% q-o-q in Q2 2020. The faster growth stemmed largely from the expansion in government bonds, particularly Treasury bills and bonds, due to the government's increased borrowing needs to support its stimulus measures and recovery efforts amid the COVID-19 pandemic. Corporate bonds also contributed to growth, albeit to a lesser extent. On the other hand, the stock of central bank bills and bonds contracted during the review period. On a y-o-y basis,

Table 1: Size and Composition of the Local Currency Bond Market in Indonesia

| | Outstanding Amount (billion) | | | | | | Growth Rate (%) | | | |
| | Q3 2019 | | Q2 2020 | | Q3 2020 | | Q3 2019 | | Q3 2020 | |
	IDR	USD	IDR	USD	IDR	USD	q-o-q	y-o-y	q-o-q	y-o-y
Total	3,218,485	227	3,585,233	251	3,940,551	265	4.8	16.4	9.9	22.4
Government	2,780,941	196	3,155,519	221	3,499,812	235	4.8	18.6	10.9	25.8
Central Govt. Bonds	2,664,332	188	3,105,895	218	3,461,396	233	5.3	15.5	11.4	29.9
of which: Sukuk	456,844	32	579,263	41	617,771	42	8.8	20.8	6.6	35.2
Central Bank Bonds	116,609	8	49,624	3	38,416	3	(4.1)	201.2	(22.6)	(67.1)
of which: Sukuk	25,674	2	38,874	3	38,416	3	17.0	141.3	(1.2)	49.6
Corporate	437,544	31	429,715	30	440,739	30	4.9	4.4	2.6	0.7
of which: Sukuk	30,654	2	29,382	2	30,915	2	27.0	80.5	5.2	0.9

( ) = negative, IDR = Indonesian rupiah, q-o-q = quarter-on-quarter, Q2 = second quarter, Q3 = third quarter, USD = United States dollar, y-o-y = year-on-year.
Notes:
1. Calculated using data from national sources.
2. Bloomberg LP end-of-period local currency–USD rates are used.
3. Growth rates are calculated from local currency base and do not include currency effects.
4. Sukuk refers to Islamic bonds.
5. The total stock of nontradable bonds as of 30 September 2020 stood at IDR166.8 trillion.
Sources: Bank Indonesia; Directorate General of Budget Financing and Risk Management, Ministry of Finance; Indonesia Stock Exchange; and Bloomberg LP.

growth in the LCY bond market of Indonesia quickened to 22.4% in Q3 2020 from 16.8% in the previous quarter, making it the fastest-growing bond market in the region.

Government bonds continued to dominate the bond market, constituting nearly 90% of the entire stock of the Indonesian bond market at the end of September. About 11% of total bonds was accounted for by corporate bonds. The bulk of the aggregate bond stock comprised conventional bonds with a share of 82.6%. Sukuk (Islamic bonds) had a share of 17.4% at the end of the review period.

Government bonds. At the end of September, the stock of government bonds had expanded to a size of USD3,499.8 trillion. Growth accelerated to 10.9% q-o-q and 25.8% y-o-y amid increased issuance by the government. Driving growth was the increase in the stock of central government bonds, similar with the first 2 quarters of 2020.

Central government bonds. The outstanding stock of central government bonds totaled IDR3,461.4 trillion on double-digit growth of 11.4% q-o-q and 29.9% y-o-y in Q3 2020. This was up from the 9.6% q-o-q and 22.7% y-o-y expansions in Q2 2020. The uptick in size was due to active issuance by the government to fund stimulus and relief measures in its bid to shield the economy from further fallout due to the COVID-19 outbreak.

Total issuance of Treasury bills and Treasury bonds reached IDR445.5 trillion during the quarter. Issuance volume rose 45.7% q-o-q and 140.4% y-o-y. In addition to issuing in large sizes during the weekly Treasury auctions, the government also sold bonds through private placements of select government bonds. Issuance during the period also included government bond sales directly to Bank Indonesia, as part of their debt monetization agreement for this year. Also, the government sold conventional retail bonds and retail sukuk during the quarter, raising IDR18.3 trillion and IDR25.7 trillion, respectively. More active borrowing was necessitated by the need to fund large-scale stimulus and relief measures by the government.

Central bank bonds. At the end of September, the outstanding size of central bank bills and bonds reached IDR38.4 trillion. This represented a decline of 22.6% q-o-q in Q3 2020 following a 2.5% q-o-q hike in Q2 2020. On a y-o-y basis, the central bank bond stock declined 67.1% y-o-y in Q3 2020 after contracting 59.2% y-o-y in the preceding quarter. In Q3 2020, issuance of central bank bills and bonds summed to IDR133.2 trillion, up 17.9% q-o-q and 15.0% y-o-y.

Corporate bonds. The outstanding stock of corporate bonds totaled IDR440.7 trillion at the end of September, up 2.6% q-o-q in Q3 2020 following a decline of 3.0% q-o-q in the prior quarter. In the same period, corporate bonds grew a marginal 0.7% y-o-y after rising

Table 2: Top 30 Issuers of Local Currency Corporate Bonds in Indonesia

	Issuers	Outstanding Amount		State-Owned	Listed Company	Type of Industry
		LCY Bonds (IDR billion)	LCY Bonds (USD billion)			
1.	Perusahaan Listrik Negara	35,986	2.42	Yes	No	Energy
2.	Indonesia Eximbank	29,600	1.99	Yes	No	Banking
3.	Sarana Multi Infrastruktur	22,292	1.50	Yes	No	Finance
4.	Bank Rakyat Indonesia	20,882	1.40	Yes	Yes	Banking
5.	Sarana Multigriya Finansial	17,524	1.18	Yes	No	Finance
6.	Bank Tabungan Negara	15,975	1.07	Yes	Yes	Banking
7.	Bank Mandiri	14,000	0.94	Yes	Yes	Banking
8.	Bank Pan Indonesia	13,427	0.90	No	Yes	Banking
9.	Waskita Karya	13,096	0.88	Yes	Yes	Building Construction
10.	Indosat	13,013	0.87	No	Yes	Telecommunications
11.	Pegadaian	10,805	0.73	Yes	No	Finance
12.	Bank CIMB Niaga	9,339	0.63	No	Yes	Banking
13.	Pupuk Indonesia	8,897	0.60	Yes	No	Chemical Manufacturing
14.	Adira Dinamika Multi Finance	8,886	0.60	No	Yes	Finance
15.	Astra Sedaya Finance	8,458	0.57	No	No	Finance
16.	Permodalan Nasional Madani	7,689	0.52	Yes	No	Finance
17.	Semen Indonesia	7,078	0.48	Yes	Yes	Cement Manufacturing
18.	Telekomunikasi Indonesia	7,000	0.47	Yes	Yes	Telecommunications
19.	Hutama Karya	6,500	0.44	Yes	No	Nonbuilding Construction
20.	Medco-Energi Internasional	6,183	0.42	No	Yes	Petroleum and Natural Gas
21.	Federal International Finance	5,452	0.37	No	No	Finance
22.	Angkasa Pura II	5,000	0.34	Yes	No	Airport Management Serivces
23.	Bank Pembangunan Daerah Jawa Barat Dan Banten	5,000	0.34	Yes	Yes	Banking
24.	Mandiri Tunas Finance	4,978	0.33	No	No	Finance
25.	Bank Maybank Indonesia	4,849	0.33	No	yes	Banking
26.	Chandra Asri Petrochemical	4,139	0.28	No	Yes	Petrochemicals
27.	Adhi Karya	4,027	0.27	Yes	Yes	Building Construction
28.	Kereta Api Indonesia	4,000	0.27	Yes	No	Transportation
29.	Maybank Indonesia Finance	3,550	0.24	No	No	Finance
30.	XL Axiata	3,413	0.23	No	Yes	Telecommunications
	Total Top 30 LCY Corporate Issuers	**321,038**	**21.58**			
	Total LCY Corporate Bonds	**429,715**	**28.88**			
	Top 30 as % of Total LCY Corporate Bonds	**74.7%**	**74.7%**			

IDR = Indonesian rupiah, LCY = local currency, USD = United States dollar.
Notes:
1. Data as of 30 September 2020.
2. State-owned firms are defined as those in which the government has more than a 50% ownership stake.
Source: *AsianBondsOnline* calculations based on Indonesia Stock Exchange data.

3.0% y-o-y. While issuance rebounded strongly in Q3 2020, maturities capped the overall bond total.

The 30 largest issuers of corporate bonds in Indonesia had aggregate bonds of IDR321.0 trillion at the end of September, up from IDR318.7 trillion at the end of June (**Table 2**). Collectively, the top 30 issuers accounted for a 74.7% share of the aggregate corporate bond stock at the end of the review period. Firms from the banking and financing industry continued to dominate the list of top 30 issuers. Other institutions were from highly capitalized industries such as energy, telecommunications, construction, and transportation. Out of the 30 firms on the list, 18 were state-owned firms and 16 institutions had their shares listed on the Indonesia Stock Exchange.

Remaining in the top spot was state-owned energy firm Perusahaan Listrik Negara, whose outstanding bonds climbed to IDR36.0 trillion due to a multitranche issuance in September. Keeping its ranking from the previous quarter in the second spot was Indonesia Eximbank, with its bond stock rising to IDR29.6 trillion following a new bond issuance in July. Sarana Multi Infrastruktur rose to the third spot at the end of

September from the fifth spot at the end of June, following its issuance of a triple-tranche bond in July. Dropping to the fourth spot was Bank Rakyat Indonesia (IDR20.9 trillion), while Sarana Multigriya Finansial (IDR17.5 trillion) rose to the fifth spot via its issuance of a triple-tranche bond in July.

In Q3 2020, new issuance of corporate bonds totaled IDR37.7 trillion, a more than four-fold hike from issuance in Q2 2020. Corporates accelerated their issuance of new bonds amid the low-interest-rate environment, which made it conducive to borrow. A total of 38 firms borrowed funds via the debt market and added 116 new bond series to the corporate bond total during Q3 2020. There were 23 new series of *sukuk* that were issued, 14 series of which were structured as *sukuk ijarah* (Islamic bonds backed by lease agreements). The remaining nine series were structured as *sukuk mudharabah* (Islamic bonds backed by a profit-sharing scheme from a business venture or partnership). New bonds issued during the quarter had maturities ranging from 367 days to 15 years.

Among the new corporate debt issues in Q3 2020, the largest was state-owned pawnshop Pegadaian with total issuance amounting to IDR5,255 billion (**Table 3**). Its

Table 3: Notable Local Currency Corporate Bond Issuances in the Third Quarter of 2020

Corporate Issuers	Coupon Rate (%)	Issued Amount (IDR billion)	Corporate Issuers	Coupon Rate (%)	Issued Amount (IDR billion)
Pegadaian			Sarana Multigriya Finansial		
370-day bond	6.75	1,055.00	370-day bond	6.75	1,686.00
370-day bond	5.50	1,295.00	370-day bond *sukuk mudharabah*	6.75	346.00
370-day bond *sukuk mudharabah*	6.75	316.50	5-year bond	8.10	424.00
370-day bond *sukuk mudharabah*	5.50	704.00	Pupuk Indonesia		
3-year bond	7.60	303.00	3-year bond	7.00	1,146.83
3-year bond	6.45	1,125.00	5-year bond	7.70	857.84
3-year *sukuk mudharabah*	7.60	103.00	7-year bond	8.30	431.85
3-year *sukuk mudharabah*	6.45	131.00	Angkasa Pura II		
5-year bond	7.95	142.00	3-year bond	7.80	32.00
5-year *sukuk mudharabah*	7.95	80.50	5-year bond	8.50	159.00
Global Mediacom			7-year bond	9.10	1,602
370-day bond	10.75	331.43	10-year bond	9.25	457.00
370-day bond *sukuk ijarah*	10.75	297.97	Jasa Marga		
3-year bond	11.25	367.50	3-year bond	7.90	1,100.35
3-year *sukuk ijarah*	11.25	1.60	5-year bond	8.25	286.00
5-year bond	12.00	1,075.00	7-year bond	8.60	90.05
5-year *sukuk ijarah*	12.00	430.00	10-year bond	9.00	523.60

IDR = Indonesian rupiah.
Notes:
1. *Sukuk ijarah* are Islamic bonds backed by lease agreements.
2. *Sukuk mudharabah* are Islamic bonds backed by a profit-sharing scheme from a business venture or partnership.
Source: Indonesia Stock Exchange.

issuance comprised both conventional bonds and *sukuk mudharabah*, which were issued as multitranche bonds in July and September. Next was Global Mediacom's multitranche issuance of conventional bonds and *sukuk ijarah* totaling IDR2,503.5 billion. It was followed by Sarana Multigriya Finansial with a triple-tranche issuance amounting to IDR2,456.0 billion.

Investor Profiles

Net bond outflows in Indonesia totaled USD0.3 billion during Q3 2020. July was the only month during the quarter that experienced net bond inflows, which amounted to USD0.6 billion. However, bond outflows were recorded in August and September, with the largest outflows observed in September at USD0.6 billion.

As a result, the share of foreign holdings to bonds outstanding declined to 27.0% in Q3 2020 from 38.6% in Q3 2019 (**Figure 2**). The amount held by foreigners fell to IDR933.1 trillion from IDR1,029.4 trillion during the same review period. The share of foreign investors fell much more dramatically as government bonds outstanding growth accelerated as Indonesia issued more to fund its COVID-19 stimulus programs. The exodus of foreign investors was largely due to concerns regarding Indonesia's rising debt levels, debt monetization policy, and economic slowdown.

At the end of Q3 2020, foreign investor bond holdings were largely focused in tenors with maturities of between more than 5 years to 10 years, with a share of 35.3% (**Figure 3**). Bonds with maturities greater than 10 years were the next largest target of foreign investment, with a share of 31.2%. The share of bonds held by foreign investors with tenors of less than 1 year was 6.2%.

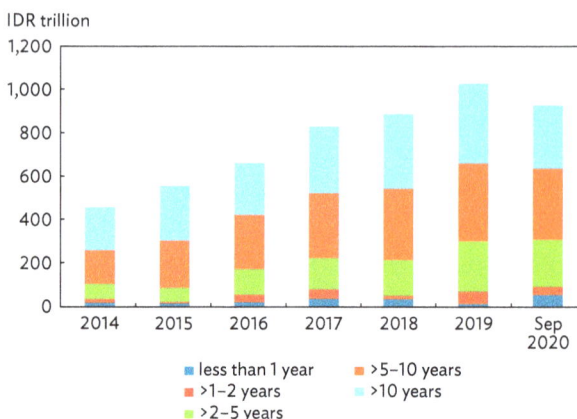

Figure 3: Foreign Holdings of Local Currency Central Government Bonds by Maturity

IDR = Indonesian rupiah.
Source: Directorate General of Budget Financing and Risk Management, Ministry of Finance.

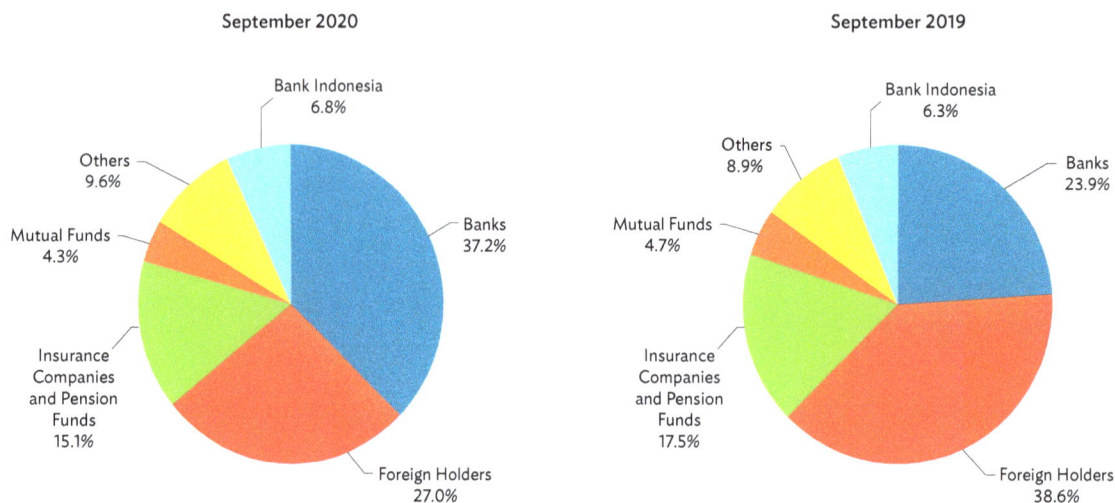

Figure 2: Local Currency Central Government Bonds Investor Profile

Source: Directorate General of Budget Financing and Risk Management, Ministry of Finance.

With the share of foreign holders declining in Q3 2020, Indonesian banks took up the slack as their share of total holdings shot up to 37.2% at the end of September from 23.9% a year earlier. Banks also bought significantly more government bonds in 2020 than in the previous year, with the amount held by banks rising to IDR1,289 trillion at the end of September from IDR637 trillion a year earlier.

The share of other institutional investors declined slightly on a y-o-y basis. The share of insurance companies fell to 15.1% from 17.5% during the review period, while the share of mutual funds dipped slightly to 4.3% from 4.7%. The share of Bank Indonesia rose to 6.8% at the end of Q3 2020 from 6.3% at the end of Q3 2019. The share of other investors also rose to 9.6% from 8.9%.

Policy, Institutional, and Regulatory Developments

Bank Indonesia and the People's Bank of China Establish Framework on the Use of Local Currencies

In September, Bank Indonesia and the People's Bank of China signed a memorandum of understanding to promote the use of the Indonesian rupiah and the Chinese yuan for the settlement of trade and direct investment. The agreement calls for the availability of direct quotation and interbank trading of the two currencies. In addition, information sharing and periodic discussions will be initiated by the respective central banks.

Indonesia's Parliament Approves 2021 State Budget

In September, the Indonesian Parliament approved the 2021 state budget, which calls for a deficit equivalent to 5.7% of GDP. The 2021 state budget estimates revenue will reach IDR1,743.7 trillion, while state spending is expected to total IDR2,750.0 trillion. The underlying macroeconomic assumptions for the 2021 state budget include (i) economic growth of 5.0%, (ii) average inflation of 3.0%, (iii) an exchange rate of IDR14,600 per USD1, (iv) an average 10-year bond yield of 7.29%, and (v) Indonesian crude oil price of USD45 per barrel.

Republic of Korea

Yield Movements

Between 31 August and 30 October, the Republic of Korea's local currency (LCY) government bond yield curve barely moved. Government bond yields remained range-bound during the review period, with yield changes almost negligible (**Figure 1**). Yields for 1-year, 5-year, and 10-year bonds rose 2 basis points (bps) on average. Meanwhile, the yield for tenors of less than 1 year fell 1 bp on average, and the yield for the remaining tenors fell 2 bps on average. The spread between the 2-year and 10-year yield inched up to 73 bps from 69 bps during the review period.

Yields at the shorter-end were almost unchanged amid expectations of the Bank of Korea maintaining the base rate in its October monetary policy meeting. Meanwhile, yield movements in the rest of the curve were minimal given continued supply–demand imbalances in the government bond market and uncertainties in the economic policy measures of major developing economies. Oversupply concerns continued to impact market sentiment amid expectations of increased bond issuance following the approval of the fourth supplementary budget and the release of the proposed 2021 fiscal budget.

In September, yields for tenors of more than 1 year saw a decline, albeit by only 10 bps on average, as the announcement of the Bank of Korea in the early part of the month—of plans to purchase up to KRW5 trillion of Korea Treasury Bonds by the end of 2020—was not enough to ease supply concerns. The pessimistic outlook on the Republic of Korea's economic growth also contributed to the downward trend. However, this trend was almost reversed in October leading up to the monetary policy meeting and as market players awaited the result of elections in the United States (US).

On 22 September, the National Assembly approved the fourth supplementary budget to be used to provide support to various sectors hit by the coronavirus disease (COVID-19) pandemic. The approved budget amounted to KRW7.8 trillion, bringing the aggregate supplementary budgets to KRW62.2 trillion. Earlier in the month, the government also submitted its 2021 fiscal budget plan of KRW555.8 trillion, an 8.5% increase from the original

Figure 1: The Republic of Korea's Benchmark Yield Curve—Local Currency Government Bonds

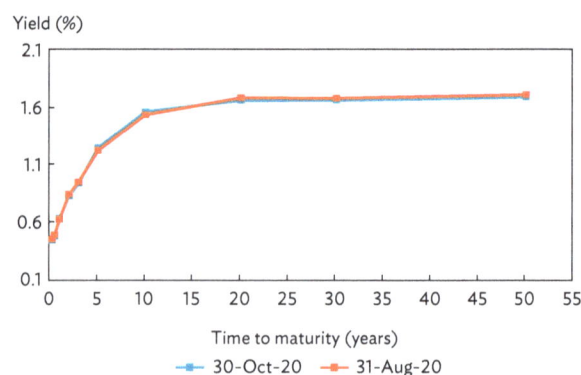

Source: Based on data from Bloomberg LP.

2020 budget. In October, the Ministry of Economy and Finance announced fiscal rules to address the rapid increase in national debt resulting from increased bond issuances.

On 14 October, the Bank of Korea decided to leave the base rate unchanged at 0.50% amid uncertainties that could affect the global and domestic economic outlook. The global economic recovery has slowed due to a resurgence in virus cases and uncertainties in economic policy measures to be implemented in major developing markets. The same trend has been observed in the domestic economy. Despite the recovery in exports, private consumption was dampened by the reimposition of lockdown measures as the number of new virus cases rose. The Bank of Korea expects risks to the economic outlook to remain elevated, maintaining its August forecast of a 1.3% contraction in economic growth in full-year 2020.

The Republic of Korea's economy rebounded in the third quarter (Q3) of 2020, posting growth of 1.9% quarter-on-quarter (q-o-q) in real gross domestic product (GDP) growth, based on advance estimates from the Bank of Korea, following a contraction of 3.2% q-o-q in the second quarter (Q2) of 2020. This was largely driven by the 15.6% q-o-q jump in exports in Q3 2020 after a sharp 16.1% q-o-q decline in the previous quarter. However, both government and private consumption declined in

Q3 2020. Private spending fell 0.1% q-o-q in Q3 2020, a reversal from the 1.4% q-o-q increase in Q2 2020, as stricter lockdowns were re-implemented. Government spending also posted a decline of 0.1% q-o-q from 1.5% q-o-q growth in the previous quarter. Meanwhile, gross fixed capital formation fell at a faster pace of 1.9% q-o-q versus 0.4% q-o-q during the same period in review. Consumer price inflation turned positive in July, reaching 0.3% y-o-y before gradually rising to 0.7% in August and 1.0% in September.

The Republic of Korea's LCY bond market registered its first net foreign outflows for the year in September at KRW31 billion as foreign investors took profits, particularly for short-term securities with tenors of less than 1 year. The outflows from this category surpassed the foreign buying volume of mid- to long-term tenors.

The Korean won strengthened during the review period, appreciating 4.7% versus the US dollar to KRW1,134.8 per USD1.0 as of 30 October. This can be attributed to the weakening of the US dollar. Furthermore, the currency appreciation has been tied to the strengthening of the Chinese yuan, as both currencies are linked through the People's Republic of China being one of the Republic of Korea's major trading partners.

Size and Composition

The size of the Republic of Korea's LCY bond market inched up 1.9% q-o-q to KRW2,602.1 trillion (USD2,223.7 billion) at the end of September (**Table 1**).

The marginal growth was lower than the 3.1% q-o-q growth posted in Q2 2020. Growth for the quarter continued to be mainly driven by the government sector, particularly the rise in the stock of central government bonds, while the corporate segment rose at a slower pace. Compared with the same period in 2019, the Republic of Korea's domestic bond market rose 9.8% year-on-year (y-o-y), almost at par with the 9.5% y-o-y increase posted in Q2 2020.

Government bonds. The outstanding size of the Republic of Korea's LCY government bond market rose 3.0% q-o-q to KRW1,069.1 trillion at end-September. The main driver of the growth was the 4.2% q-o-q rise in central government bonds to KRW707.7 trillion. Bonds issued by state-owned entities also posted an increase of 2.3% q-o-q to KRW194.6 trillion. Monetary Stabilization Bonds issued by the Bank of Korea registered a decrease of 1.3% q-o-q to KRW166.7 trillion.

Issuance of government bonds declined in Q3 2020 to KRW99.1 trillion due to there being a higher base after issuance surged in Q2 2020 as the government needed to fund the supplementary budgets and other fiscal measures implemented to lessen the economic impact of the pandemic.

Corporate bonds. The Republic of Korea's LCY corporate bond market posted marginal growth of 1.1% q-o-q in Q3 2020, increasing the corporate bond stock to a size of KRW1,533.0 trillion at the end of September. **Table 2** lists the top 30 LCY corporate bond

Table 1: Size and Composition of the Local Currency Bond Market in the Republic of Korea

	Outstanding Amount (billion)						Growth Rate (%)			
	Q3 2019		Q2 2020		Q3 2020		Q3 2019		Q3 2020	
	KRW	USD	KRW	USD	KRW	USD	q-o-q	y-o-y	q-o-q	y-o-y
Total	2,370,666	1,982	2,553,743	2,123	2,602,081	2,224	1.7	6.6	1.9	9.8
Government	953,854	797	1,038,139	863	1,069,062	914	0.8	2.8	3.0	12.1
Central Government Bonds	607,015	507	679,020	565	707,681	605	1.2	4.8	4.2	16.6
Central Bank Bonds	170,960	143	168,870	140	166,750	143	(0.4)	(2.1)	(1.3)	(2.5)
Others	175,879	147	190,249	158	194,631	166	0.3	0.8	2.3	10.7
Corporate	1,416,812	1,184	1,515,604	1,260	1,533,019	1,310	2.3	9.4	1.1	8.2

( ) = negative, KRW = Korean won, q-o-q = quarter-on-quarter, Q2 = second quarter, Q3 = third quarter, USD = United States dollar, y-o-y = year-on-year.
Notes:
1. Calculated using data from national sources.
2. Bloomberg LP end-of-period local currency–USD rates are used.
3. Growth rates are calculated from local currency base and do not include currency effects.
4. "Others" comprise Korea Development Bank Bonds, National Housing Bonds, and Seoul Metro Bonds.
5. Corporate bonds include equity-linked securities and derivatives-linked securities.
Sources: The Bank of Korea and *EDAILY BondWeb*.

Table 2: Top 30 Issuers of Local Currency Corporate Bonds in the Republic of Korea

	Issuers	Outstanding Amount		State-Owned	Listed on		Type of Industry
		LCY Bonds (KRW billion)	LCY Bonds (USD billion)		KOSPI	KOSDAQ	
1.	Korea Housing Finance Corporation	141,841	121.2	Yes	No	No	Housing Finance
2.	Mirae Asset Daewoo Co.	72,365	61.8	No	Yes	No	Securities
3.	Industrial Bank of Korea	71,380	61.0	Yes	Yes	No	Banking
4.	Korea Investment and Securities	61,858	52.9	No	No	No	Securities
5.	KB Securities	54,091	46.2	No	No	No	Securities
6.	Hana Financial Investment	51,684	44.2	No	No	No	Securities
7.	NH Investment & Securities	41,928	35.8	Yes	Yes	No	Securities
8.	Samsung Securities	33,479	28.6	No	Yes	No	Securities
9.	Korea Electric Power Corporation	28,510	24.4	Yes	Yes	No	Electricity, Energy, and Power
10.	Korea Land & Housing Corporation	28,239	24.1	Yes	No	No	Real Estate
11.	Shinhan Bank	26,712	22.8	No	No	No	Banking
12.	Shinhan Investment Corporation	24,606	21.0	No	No	No	Securities
13.	The Export-Import Bank of Korea	24,025	20.5	Yes	No	No	Banking
14.	Korea Expressway	24,010	20.5	Yes	No	No	Transport Infrastructure
15.	Shinyoung Securities	19,920	17.0	No	Yes	No	Securities
16.	Kookmin Bank	19,614	16.8	No	No	No	Banking
17.	Korea Rail Network Authority	19,100	16.3	Yes	No	No	Transport Infrastructure
18.	Woori Bank	19,070	16.3	Yes	Yes	No	Banking
19.	KEB Hana Bank	18,960	16.2	No	No	No	Banking
20.	NongHyup Bank	18,270	15.6	Yes	No	No	Banking
21.	Hanwha Investment and Securities	16,791	14.3	No	No	No	Securities
22.	Korea SMEs and Startups Agency	16,528	14.1	Yes	No	No	SME Development
23.	Shinhan Card	15,945	13.6	No	No	No	Credit Card
24.	Meritz Securities Co.	15,152	12.9	No	Yes	No	Securities
25.	Hyundai Capital Services	14,325	12.2	No	No	No	Consumer Finance
26.	KB Kookmin Bank Card	14,020	12.0	No	No	No	Consumer Finance
27.	Standard Chartered Bank Korea	13,360	11.4	No	No	No	Banking
28.	Korea Deposit Insurance Corporation	12,720	10.9	Yes	No	No	Insurance
29.	NongHyup	12,430	10.6	Yes	No	No	Banking
30.	Korea Gas Corporation	11,759	10.0	Yes	Yes	No	Gas Utility
	Total Top 30 LCY Corporate Issuers	**942,692**	**805.6**				
	Total LCY Corporate Bonds	**1,533,019**	**1,310.1**				
	Top 30 as % of Total LCY Corporate Bonds	**61.5%**	**61.5%**				

KOSDAQ = Korean Securities Dealers Automated Quotations, KOSPI = Korea Composite Stock Price Index, KRW = Korean won, LCY = local currency, SME = small and medium-sized enterprise, USD = United States dollar.
Notes:
1. Data as of 30 September 2020.
2. State-owned firms are defined as those in which the government has more than a 50% ownership stake.
3. Corporate bonds include equity-linked securities and derivatives-linked securities.
Sources: *AsianBondsOnline* calculations based on Bloomberg LP and *EDAILY BondWeb* data.

issuers in the Republic of Korea at the end of September with their outstanding bonds reaching an aggregate size of KRW942.7 trillion and comprising 61.5% of the total LCY corporate bond market. Financial companies such as banks and securities and investment firms continued to dominate the list. Government-related entity Korea Housing Finance Corporation remained the largest corporate bond issuer in the market with total bonds outstanding valued at KRW141.8 trillion. Financial companies Mirae Asset Daewoo and Industrial Bank of Korea were the next largest bond issuers with total bonds outstanding of KRW72.4 trillion and KRW71.4 trillion, respectively.

The marginal increase in the size of the LCY corporate bond market was due to tepid issuance during Q3 2020, particularly from both special public entities and private companies, while financial debentures saw increased issuance. Market volatility and economic uncertainty continued to have an impact on the decline of corporate bond issuance during the quarter. **Table 3** lists the notable corporate bond issuances in Q3 2020. Financial firms such as KEB Hana Bank, Kookmin Bank, Sinbo Securitization, and Nonghyup Bank had the largest aggregate issuances during the quarter.

Foreign Exchange Stabilization Fund Bonds. On 10 September, the Government of the Republic of Korea issued USD1.4 billion worth of Foreign Exchange Stabilization Fund Bonds. The issuance consisted of EUR700 million worth of zero coupon 5-year euro bonds with a yield of −0.059% and USD625 million worth of 10-year dollar bonds with a yield of 1.198% and a coupon of 1.000%. The issuance is expected to push down yields of sovereign bonds and provide lower-yield guidance for the foreign borrowings of other private Korean entities.

Table 3: Notable Local Currency Corporate Bond Issuances in the Third Quarter of 2020

Corporate Issuers	Coupon Rate (%)	Issued Amount (KRW billion)	Corporate Issuers	Coupon Rate (%)	Issued Amount (KRW billion)
KEB Hana Bank			Sinbo Securitization Specialty		
1-year bond	0.75	500	2-year bond	1.09	188
1-year bond	0.76	390	3-year bond	1.22	507
1-year bond	0.75	250	3-year bond	1.19	411
2-year bond	0.92	250	3-year bond	1.19	211
2-year bond	0.98	220	3-year bond	1.15	210
2-year bond	0.88	200	3-year bond	1.15	147
2-year bond	0.92	200	Nonghyup Bank		
2-year bond	0.92	200	1-year bond	0.90	400
2-year bond	0.88	200	2-year bond	0.99	410
3-year bond	0.92	300	2-year bond	1.03	100
10-year bond	2.14	340	3-year bond	1.12	200
Kookmin Bank			3-year bond	1.01	110
2-year bond	0.75	300	3-year bond	1.07	100
2-year bond	0.90	300	5-year bond	1.33	260
2-year bond	0.57	300	Woori Bank		
2-year bond	0.90	250	1-year bond	–	300
2-year bond	0.91	250	1-year bond	0.91	200
2-year bond	0.79	200	2-year bond	0.93	200
2-year bond	0.79	350	3-year bond	1.01	300
2-year bond	0.93	220	3-year bond	1.02	250
2-year bond	1.02	220	5-year bond	1.32	300
10-year bond	2.05	500	Korea Investment Securities		
			6-year bond	3.30	470
			Shinhan Financial Group		
			29-year bond	3.12	450

– = not applicable, KRW = Korean won.
Source: Based on data from Bloomberg LP.

Investor Profile

Insurance companies and pension funds remained the largest holders of the Republic of Korea's LCY government bonds at the end of June 2020 with a share of 34.2%, almost at par with its share of 34.4% in June 2019 (**Figure 2**). Banks surpassed the general government as the second-largest investor group at the end of Q2 2020. However, both of their respective shares declined from a year earlier, with banks' share falling to 16.7% at the end of Q2 2020 from 17.3% and the general government declining to 16.5% from 17.5%. Meanwhile, the share of other financial institutions rose to 16.0% from 15.1% during the review period. Foreign holdings of LCY

government bonds also increased to 13.0% at the end of June 2020 from 11.9% a year earlier.

Other financial institutions surpassed insurance companies and pension funds as the largest investor group of the Republic of Korea's LCY corporate bonds at the end of June 2020, with its share rising to 37.4% from 35.5% in the same period in 2019 (**Figure 3**). Meanwhile, the share of insurance companies and pension funds declined to 37.2% from 38.0% during the review period. The share of the general government was almost unchanged at 13.5%, while the share of foreign holders remained negligible.

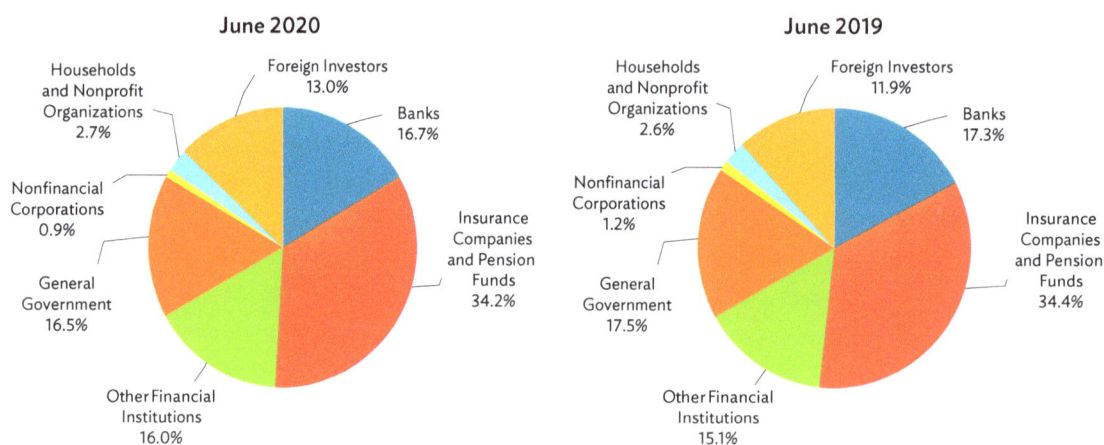

Figure 2: Local Currency Government Bonds Investor Profile

June 2020

Households and Nonprofit Organizations 2.7%
Foreign Investors 13.0%
Banks 16.7%
Nonfinancial Corporations 0.9%
Insurance Companies and Pension Funds 34.2%
General Government 16.5%
Other Financial Institutions 16.0%

June 2019

Households and Nonprofit Organizations 2.6%
Foreign Investors 11.9%
Banks 17.3%
Nonfinancial Corporations 1.2%
Insurance Companies and Pension Funds 34.4%
General Government 17.5%
Other Financial Institutions 15.1%

Source: The Bank of Korea.

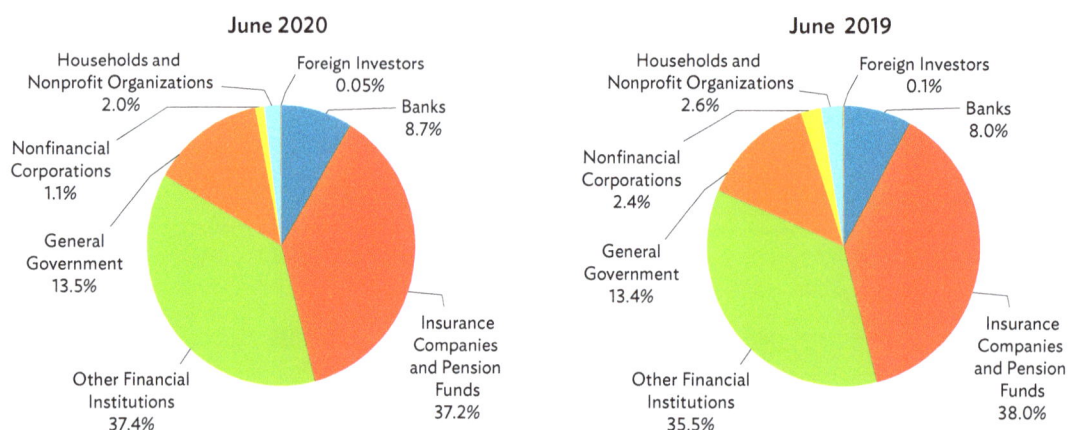

Figure 3: Local Currency Corporate Bonds Investor Profile

June 2020

Households and Nonprofit Organizations 2.0%
Foreign Investors 0.05%
Banks 8.7%
Nonfinancial Corporations 1.1%
General Government 13.5%
Insurance Companies and Pension Funds 37.2%
Other Financial Institutions 37.4%

June 2019

Households and Nonprofit Organizations 2.6%
Foreign Investors 0.1%
Banks 8.0%
Nonfinancial Corporations 2.4%
General Government 13.4%
Insurance Companies and Pension Funds 38.0%
Other Financial Institutions 35.5%

Source: The Bank of Korea.

Figure 4: Net Foreign Investment in Local Currency Bonds in the Republic of Korea

KRW billion

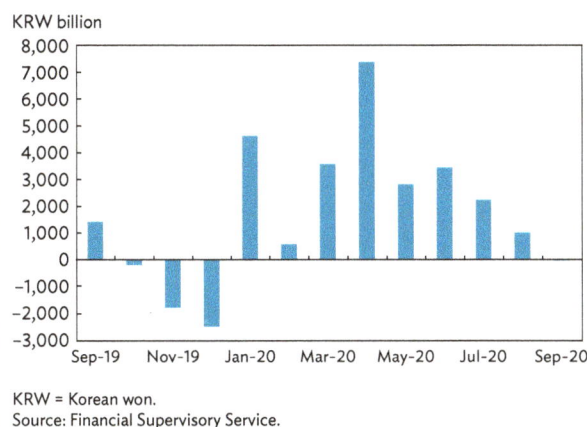

KRW = Korean won.
Source: Financial Supervisory Service.

Foreign investors continued buying the Republic of Korea's LCY bonds in August, albeit at a smaller value of KRW997 billion versus a monthly average of KRW3,521 billion in the first 7 months of the year (**Figure 4**). However, this was reversed as the bond market registered net foreign outflows of KRW31 billion in September, due to profit-taking by foreign investors, particularly for securities with tenors of less than 1 year. Selling in this category surpassed net inflows registered in bonds with mid- to long-term tenors.

Ratings Update

On 6 October, Fitch Ratings affirmed the Republic of Korea's sovereign credit rating at AA– with a stable outlook. The rating agency cited the Republic of Korea's "steady macroeconomic performance, robust external finances, and sufficient fiscal headroom" as the reasons behind the rating affirmation. These, along with other government policies to control the spread of the virus, have helped mitigate the economic impact of the COVID-19 pandemic, especially in comparison with its similarly rated peers. In addition, the rating agency also forecast a 1.1% economic contraction in 2020, based on a gradual recovery in the second half of the year supported by the rebound in exports in recent months. The fiscal deficit for 2020 is also expected to widen to 4.4% of GDP in 2020 given the rise in government debt following financial stimulus to address the economic impact of the virus, but it is still considered modest compared to its peers.

Policy, Institutional, and Regulatory Developments

The National Assembly Passed the Fourth Supplementary Budget

On 22 September, the National Assembly passed the fourth supplementary budget of 2020 worth KRW7.8 trillion. This brings the aggregate amount of all four supplementary budgets to KRW62.2 trillion. The budget is expected to fund additional COVID-19 relief programs to support small businesses and low-income households.

The Republic of Korea Announces New Fiscal Rules

On 5 October, the Government of the Republic of Korea announced new fiscal rules to address the rapid increase in national debt. Although the economy's fiscal soundness and debt ratios are still considered low compared to its similarly rated peers, the government aims to maintain its fiscal sustainability. One rule is to maintain the government-debt-to-GDP ratio below 60% and the consolidated fiscal balance deficit at 3% or less of GDP. Implementation is expected to take effect starting in 2025 after a transition period of 3 years.

The Bank of Korea and the People's Bank of China Renew Currency Swap Agreement

On 22 October, the Bank of Korea and the People's Bank of China signed the renewal of the Korean Won–Chinese Yuan Bilateral Currency Swap Agreement for another 5 years. The swap amount was also increased to KRW70 trillion–CNY400 billion from KRW64 trillion–CNY360 billion.

Malaysia

Yield Movements

Between 31 August and 30 October, Malaysia's local currency (LCY) government bond yield movements were mixed (**Figure 1**). Yields of tenors from 1 month to 6 years declined an average of 10 basis points (bps). The longer-end of the yield curve (from 7 years to 15 years) increased an average of 2 bps, while the 30-year tenor jumped 17 bps. The yield spread between 2-year and 10-year government bonds expanded from 84 bps to 96 bps during the review period.

The decline in yields at the shorter-end of the curve can be attributed to the effect of Bank Negara Malaysia's (BNM) cumulative 125-bps reduction in the overnight policy rate year-to-date through 30 October. Attractive real yields, which are driven by persistent consumer price deflation and high liquidity in the financial system, also contributed to high demand for government securities. Adding to the demand were foreign capital inflows after Malaysian Government Securities (MGS) and Government Investment Issues were given a higher weight in the JP Morgan Government Bond Index–Emerging Market Index in September.

On the other hand, the low demand for long-term securities reflects some investors' flight to safety amid uncertainties caused by the coronavirus disease (COVID-19) pandemic. Excess supply concerns may also be a factor as Malaysia's fiscal deficit is projected to increase following the government's stimulus programs that will be funded through domestic borrowing. In August, Malaysia's Parliament raised the government's debt ceiling to 60% of its gross domestic product from 55% as part of measures to counter the effects of the COVID-19 pandemic.

BNM's monetary policy committee previously reduced its policy rate in July but decided to keep it steady at 1.75% during its latest meeting in September given the committee's cautiously optimistic outlook for the economy. Despite some resurgence in COVID-19 cases, analysts expect BNM to maintain its policy rate during its meeting in November as its accommodative and stimulus packages are deemed sufficient to support the economy during the pandemic.

Malaysia's economy contracted 2.7% year-on-year (y-o-y) in the third quarter (Q3) of 2020, an

Figure 1: Malaysia's Benchmark Yield Curve— Local Currency Government Bonds

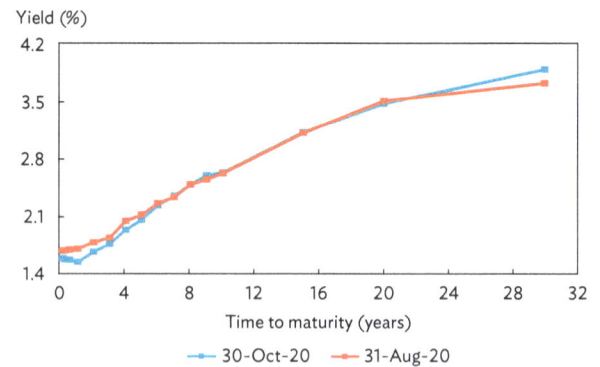

Source: Based on data from Bloomberg LP.

improvement from the contraction of 17.1% y-o-y in the second quarter (Q2) of 2020, as economic activities resumed after the easing of Movement Control Order measures. The sharp decline in Q2 2020 prompted the World Bank in September to downgrade its full-year 2020 economic growth forecast for Malaysia to –4.9% y-o-y from –3.1% y-o-y in June. This was in line with BNM's forecast for growth of between –5.5% y-o-y and –3.5% y-o-y. BNM and the World Bank are cautiously optimistic about the economy's gradual recovery in the second half of 2020 as economic activities resumed in May. Analysts, however, are still wary that recent spikes in COVID-19 cases will greatly affect Malaysia's economic recovery, especially as restrictions may be reintroduced.

Prices of basic goods and services in Malaysia decreased 1.4% y-o-y in September, the same rate of decline recorded in August, after contracting 1.3% y-o-y in July. Consumer prices were pulled down by declines in the cost of transport; housing, water, electricity, gas, and other fuels; and clothing and footwear. BNM expects negative inflation for full-year 2020 due to falling global oil and other commodity prices.

Size and Composition

Malaysia's LCY bond market expanded 1.9% quarter-on-quarter (q-o-q) in Q3 2020 to reach a size of MYR1,583.7 billion (USD381.0 billion), up from MYR1,554.8 billion at the end of Q2 2020 (**Table 1**). The growth corresponds to a 6.1% y-o-y jump from

Table 1: Size and Composition of the Local Currency Bond Market in Malaysia

| | Outstanding Amount (billion) | | | | | | Growth Rate (%) | | | |
| | Q3 2019 | | Q2 2020 | | Q3 2020 | | Q3 2019 | | Q3 2020 | |
	MYR	USD	MYR	USD	MYR	USD	q-o-q	y-o-y	q-o-q	y-o-y
Total	1,493	357	1,555	363	1,584	381	0.3	8.3	1.9	6.1
Government	786	188	829	193	848	204	0.8	8.3	2.3	8.0
Central Government Bonds	749	179	797	186	820	197	0.9	9.9	2.9	9.6
of which: Sukuk	331	79	367	86	377	91	(0.6)	10.1	2.7	13.8
Central Bank Bills	10	2	5	1	4	1	10.9	(34.2)	(20.0)	(60.8)
of which: Sukuk	4	0.8	0	0	0	0	133.3	16.7	–	(100.0)
Sukuk Perumahan Kerajaan	27	6	27	6	24	6	(3.9)	(5.6)	(10.1)	(10.1)
Corporate	707	169	726	169	735	177	(0.2)	8.3	1.3	3.9
of which: Sukuk	559	133	582	136	592	142	0.7	13.2	1.7	6.0

( ) = negative, – = not applicable, MYR = Malaysian ringgit, q-o-q = quarter-on-quarter, Q2 = second quarter, Q3 = third quarter, USD = United States dollar, y-o-y = year-on-year.
Notes:
1. Calculated using data from national sources.
2. Bloomberg LP end-of-period local currency–USD rates are used.
3. Growth rates are calculated from local currency base and do not include currency effects.
4. Sukuk refers to Islamic bonds.
5. Sukuk Perumahan Kerajaan are Islamic bonds issued by the Government of Malaysia to refinance funding for housing loans to government employees and to extend new housing loans.
Sources: Bank Negara Malaysia Fully Automated System for Issuing/Tendering and Bloomberg LP.

MYR1,493.1 billion at the end of Q3 2019. The growth in the LCY bond market in Q3 2020 was supported by expansions in both LCY government and corporate bonds, which accounted for 53.6% and 46.4%, respectively, of the total LCY bonds outstanding at the end of September. Total outstanding sukuk (Islamic bonds) at the end of the review period stood at MYR993.2 billion on growth of 1.7% q-o-q from MYR976.2 billion at the end of the previous quarter, spurred by increased stocks of government and corporate sukuk.

Issuance of LCY bonds in Q3 2020 declined 4.5% q-o-q to MYR90.0 billion from MYR94.2 billion in Q2 2020, driven by decreased government bond issuance.

Government bonds. The LCY government bond market grew 2.3% q-o-q to MYR848.4 billion in Q3 2020, up from MYR829.0 billion in the previous quarter. The growth was due to the 2.9% q-o-q increase in outstanding central government bonds, which comprised 96.7% of total outstanding LCY government bonds. Outstanding central bank bills, which comprised a 0.5% share of total LCY government bonds outstanding at the end of September, contracted 20.0% q-o-q as some bills matured. The outstanding stock of Sukuk Perumahan Kerajaan (2.8% of total outstanding LCY government bonds) declined 10.1% q-o-q from the previous quarter.

LCY government bonds issued in Q3 2020 fell 14.0% q-o-q to MYR51.6 billion from MYR60.0 billion in the previous quarter, as issuance of Treasury bills

declined and no central bank bills were issued during the quarter. The lack of issuance of Bank Negara Monetary Notes may be attributed to the central bank's liquidity enhancement measures. Another move to expand liquidity in the LCY bond market was the increased issuance of MGS from the previous quarter, as MGS switch auctions were conducted in September. The government redeemed some illiquid bonds and replaced them with more liquid benchmark MGS. The high level of MGS issuance may also be attributed to the government's funding needs for its economic programs to battle the COVID-19 pandemic. On the other hand, issuance volume of Government Investment Issues slightly declined from the previous quarter.

Corporate bonds. LCY corporate bonds outstanding expanded 1.3% q-o-q to MYR735.3 billion in Q3 2020 from MYR725.8 billion in Q2 2020. Outstanding corporate sukuk rose 1.7% q-o-q to MYR592.0 billion at the end of September from MYR582.3 billion in the prior quarter.

The top 30 corporate bond issuers in Malaysia accounted for an aggregate MYR445.9 billion of corporate bonds outstanding at the end of Q3 2020, or 60.6% of the total corporate bond market (**Table 2**). Government institution Danainfra Nasional continued to dominate all issuers with outstanding LCY corporate bonds amounting to MYR71.6 billion (9.7% of total LCY corporate bonds outstanding). By industry, finance comprised the largest share (53.1%) of the top 30 issuers with MYR236.9 billion

Table 2: Top 30 Issuers of Local Currency Corporate Bonds in Malaysia

	Issuers	Outstanding Amount		State-Owned	Listed Company	Type of Industry
		LCY Bonds (MYR billion)	LCY Bonds (USD billion)			
1.	Danainfra Nasional	71.6	17.2	Yes	No	Finance
2.	Prasarana	36.0	8.7	Yes	No	Transport, Storage, and Communications
3.	Cagamas	31.2	7.5	Yes	No	Finance
4.	Project Lebuhraya Usahasama	29.4	7.1	No	No	Transport, Storage, and Communications
5.	Urusharta Jamaah	27.6	6.6	Yes	No	Finance
6.	Lembaga Pembiayaan Perumahan Sektor Awam	24.4	5.9	Yes	No	Property and Real Estate
7.	Perbadanan Tabung Pendidikan Tinggi Nasional	21.6	5.2	Yes	No	Finance
8.	Pengurusan Air	18.1	4.4	Yes	No	Energy, Gas, and Water
9.	Khazanah	14.2	3.4	Yes	No	Finance
10.	CIMB Bank	14.1	3.4	Yes	No	Banking
11.	Maybank Islamic	13.0	3.1	No	Yes	Banking
12.	Sarawak Energy	13.0	3.1	Yes	No	Energy, Gas, and Water
13.	Maybank	12.8	3.1	No	Yes	Banking
14.	CIMB Group Holdings	11.3	2.7	Yes	No	Finance
15.	Tenaga Nasional	10.0	2.4	No	Yes	Energy, Gas, and Water
16.	Jimah East Power	9.0	2.2	Yes	No	Energy, Gas, and Water
17.	Danum Capital	8.0	1.9	No	No	Finance
18.	Danga Capital	8.0	1.9	Yes	No	Finance
19.	Public Bank	7.9	1.9	No	No	Banking
20.	GOVCO Holdings	7.2	1.7	Yes	No	Finance
21.	Bank Pembangunan Malaysia	7.2	1.7	Yes	No	Banking
22.	GENM Capital	6.5	1.6	No	No	Finance
23.	YTL Power International	6.1	1.5	No	Yes	Energy, Gas, and Water
24.	Bakun Hydro Power Generation	5.9	1.4	No	No	Energy, Gas, and Water
25.	Telekom Malaysia	5.8	1.4	No	Yes	Telecommunications
26.	Rantau Abang Capital	5.5	1.3	Yes	No	Finance
27.	Turus Pesawat	5.3	1.3	Yes	No	Transport, Storage, and Communications
28.	EDRA Energy	5.1	1.2	No	Yes	Energy, Gas, and Water
29.	Sunway Treasury Sukuk	5.1	1.2	No	No	Finance
30.	1Malaysia Development	5.0	1.2	Yes	No	Finance
	Total Top 30 LCY Corporate Issuers	445.9	107.3			
	Total LCY Corporate Bonds	735.3	176.9			
	Top 30 as % of Total LCY Corporate Bonds	60.6%	60.6%			

LCY = local currency, MYR = Malaysian ringgit, USD = United States dollar.
Notes:
1. Data as of 30 September 2020.
2. State-owned firms are defined as those in which the government has more than a 50% ownership stake.
Source: AsianBondsOnline calculations based on Bank Negara Malaysia Fully Automated System for Issuing/Tendering data.

in outstanding LCY corporate bonds at the end of September.

Issuance of LCY corporate bonds increased 12.1% q-o-q to MYR38.4 billion in Q3 2020 from MYR34.2 billion in Q2 2020. The growth may be attributed to corporations taking advantage of, and investors chasing yields in, a low-interest-rate environment.

Danainfra Nasional issued the most tranches of Islamic medium-term notes (MTNs), issuing six tranches with tenors ranging from 7 years to 30 years (**Table 3**). The issuance was via the state-owned funding vehicle's Islamic MTN program. Government-owned utility company Tenaga Nasional Berhad issued three tranches of Islamic MTNs, with its MYR1.5 billion 20-year tranche recording the highest issuance amount during the quarter. Malaysia Rail Link issued two multitranche bonds. In July, Malaysia Rail Link issued four tranches from its Islamic MTN program to fund its East Coast Rail project. In September, it issued a triple-tranche bond to further fund the same project. Malaysia Rail Link raised a total of MYR2.8 billion from the two issuances.

Table 3: Notable Local Currency Corporate Bond Issuances in the Third Quarter of 2020

Corporate Issuers	Coupon Rate (%)	Issued Amount (MYR million)
Danainfra Nasional		
7-year Islamic MTN	2.66	600
10-year Islamic MTN	2.86	500
15-year Islamic MTN	3.35	500
20-year Islamic MTN	3.72	600
25-year Islamic MTN	3.87	600
30-year Islamic MTN	4.01	1,200
Tenaga Nasional Berhad		
10-year Islamic MTN	2.90	750
15-year Islamic MTN	3.25	750
20-year Islamic MTN	3.55	1,500
Malaysia Rail Link		
10-year Islamic MTN	3.13	895
15-year Islamic MTN	3.58	390
20-year Islamic MTN	3.88	405
25-year Islamic MTN	4.11	310
10-year Islamic MTN	2.87	200
20-year Islamic MTN	3.75	300
25-year Islamic MTN	3.89	300

MTN = medium-term note, MYR = Malaysian ringgit.
Source: Bank Negara Malaysia Bond Info Hub.

Investor Profile

Foreign holdings of LCY government bonds in Q3 2020 jumped to MYR575.2 billion from MYR518.5 billion in Q2 2020, with monthly holdings increasing during the quarter, an extension of the trend of expanded monthly holdings in place since May (**Figure 2**). A total of MYR12.0 billion in net capital inflows were recorded in Q3 2020, with most of the inflows coming in July. The September inflows were driven by increased foreign holdings of MGS after the JP Morgan Government Bond Index–Emerging Market Index gave more weight to Malaysian debt securities. The net inflows in Q2 2020 and Q3 2020 were due to improving global investor sentiment and a sustained nonresident investor base in the Malaysian LCY bond market. However, investors remain cautious as FTSE Russell retained Malaysia on its fixed-income watch list for possible exclusion from its FTSE World Government Bond Index. As a share of LCY government bonds, foreign holdings increased to 23.6% at the end of Q3 2020 from 22.7% at the end of Q2 2020.

At the end of Q2 2020, financial institutions and social security institutions led all investors in LCY government bond holdings with 35.5% and 30.1% of the total, respectively (**Figure 3**). Financial institutions held a larger share at the end of June compared to the same month in 2019, while the share of social security institutions

Figure 2: Foreign Holdings and Capital Flows in the Malaysian Local Currency Government Bond Market

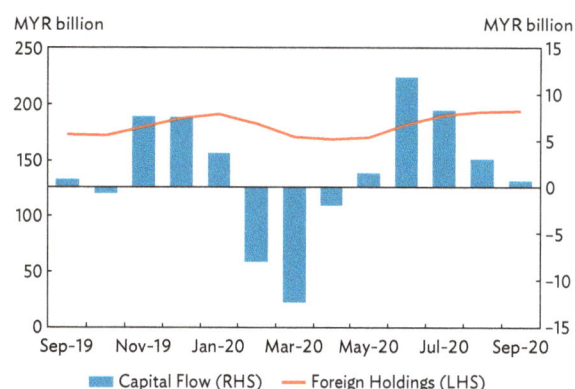

LHS = left-hand side, MYR = Malaysian ringgit, RHS = right-hand side.
Notes:
1. Figures exclude foreign holdings of Bank Negara Malaysia bills.
2. Month-on-month changes in foreign holdings of local currency government bonds were used as a proxy for bond flows.
Source: Bank Negara Malaysia Monthly Statistical Bulletin.

Figure 3: Local Currency Government Bonds Investor Profile

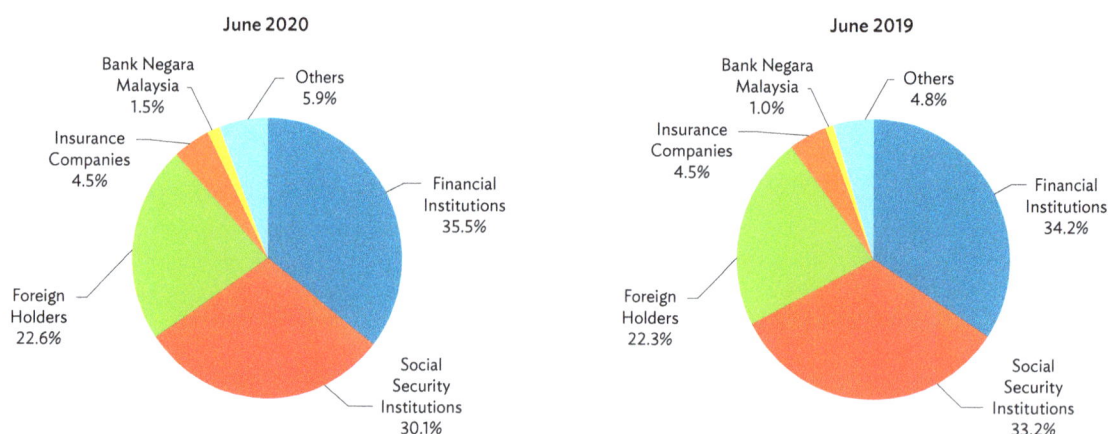

June 2020

- Bank Negara Malaysia 1.5%
- Others 5.9%
- Insurance Companies 4.5%
- Financial Institutions 35.5%
- Foreign Holders 22.6%
- Social Security Institutions 30.1%

June 2019

- Bank Negara Malaysia 1.0%
- Others 4.8%
- Insurance Companies 4.5%
- Financial Institutions 34.2%
- Foreign Holders 22.3%
- Social Security Institutions 33.2%

Note: "Others" include statutory bodies, nominees and trustee companies, and cooperatives and unclassified items.
Source: Bank Negara Malaysia.

dropped. Foreign holders slightly increased their share of total holdings to 22.6% from 22.3% during the review period. The holdings share of insurance companies remained unchanged at 4.5% between Q2 2019 and Q2 2020, while the share of total holdings of BNM increased to 1.5% from 1.0%.

Policy, Institutional, and Regulatory Developments

Japan and Malaysia Sign Bilateral Swap Agreement

On 18 September, the Bank of Japan and BNM signed a bilateral swap agreement allowing the two central banks to swap their Japanese yen and Malaysian ringgit, respectively, for United States dollars. The swap agreement provides up to USD3.0 billion each for Japan and Malaysia. The agreement supports stability in the financial markets of both economies, and strengthens ties and economic cooperation between the two economies.

FTSE Russell Keeps Malaysia in Its FTSE World Government Bond Index

On 24 September, FTSE Russell decided to keep Malaysia in its FTSE World Government Bond Index, but the economy remained on the data provider's FTSE Russell Fixed Income Watch List for possible exclusion. In its September 2020 fixed-income review, FTSE Russell acknowledged BNM's policy reforms to enhance secondary market bond liquidity and improve foreign exchange market structure. FTSE Russell will continue to monitor developments in the Malaysian bond market as BNM's policies take effect and assess whether these regulatory reforms translate into practical improvements for international participants.

Philippines

Yield Movements

The yield curve of local currency (LCY) government bonds in the Philippines steepened between 31 August and 30 October (**Figure 1**). Yields on bonds with 1-month, 3-month, and 2-year maturities dropped on an average of 7 basis points (bps). The remaining tenors all saw increases in their yields. Bond yield for 1-year tenor increased the least at 0.6 bps, while those for 6-month and 3-year to 10-year tenors increased an average of 15 bps. Larger yield increases were seen in 20-year and 25-year maturities at 45 bps and 29 bps, respectively. This steepening led to a widening of the yield spread between 2-year and 10-year tenors during the review period from 69 bps to 89 bps.

The decline in government bond yields at the shorter-end of the curve was due largely to the accommodative monetary policy stance of the Bangko Sentral ng Pilipinas (BSP) and the inflation rate remaining subdued.

The reverse repurchase rate was held steady at 2.25% for the second consecutive time during the BSP's monetary policy meeting on 1 October, citing easing inflation and encouraging signs of domestic economic recovery. Since the start of the year through October 2020, the central bank had slashed 175 bps from the policy rate, placing it to a historically low level. The BSP maintained the view that the pause will allow it to evaluate previous easing measures' effect in the economy. The BSP is expected to reassess its policy actions based on the third quarter (Q3) economic performance which remained sluggish. The slower-than-expected gross domestic product (GDP) growth provides room for a rate cut, while excess liquidity and negative real interest rates will likely restrain the central bank's policy space.

Consumer price inflation picked up to 2.5% y-o-y in October after easing in September (2.3% y-o-y) and August (2.4% y-o-y). The acceleration mainly came on the back of higher prices of heavily-weighted food and non-alcoholic beverages. Inflation rate averaged 2.5% for the first 10 months of the year and is within the government target of 2.0%–4.0% for full-year 2020. With domestic demand remaining weak due to the coronavirus

Figure 1: Philippines' Benchmark Yield Curve—Local Currency Government Bonds

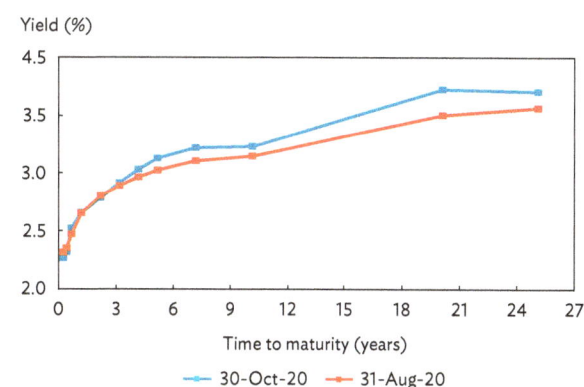

Source: Based on data from Bloomberg LP.

disease (COVID-19) pandemic, the BSP has forecast inflation to average 2.3% in 2020, 2.8% in 2021, and 3.0% in 2022.[8]

High liquidity in the financial system, along with a sustained preference for liquid assets, has also kept bond yields grounded at the shorter-end of the curve. The uncertainty and risks surrounding the pandemic have made investors position their funds in the more liquid portion of the curve as they await fresh developments.

On the other hand, yield increases at the longer-end of the curve stem from expectations that inflation may pick up with the further reopening of the economy and easing of quarantine restrictions that will spur economic activities. Gloomy economic growth forecasts may have also weighed on investor sentiment, leading some to trim their demand for long-term investments to avoid looming risks.

The Philippine economy remained in a recession after recording a GDP contraction of 11.5% y-o-y in Q3 2020; however, it was an improvement from the revised 16.9% y-o-y decline in Q2 2020. The double-digit decline in growth rate can be attributed to the 2-week reimposition of stricter quarantine measures in August in some areas, including the country's economic center of Metro Manila, after daily cases of COVID-19

---

[8] BSP forecast as of October 2020.

had escalated. Only government consumption on the expenditure side and agriculture sector on the income side saw y-o-y increases. The government expects the economy to contract between 4.5% y-o-y and 6.6% y-o-y in 2020, but will review its projections to account for the Q3 2020 figure.

The Philippine peso sustained its strength against the United States (US) dollar despite the recession and the extended community quarantine resulting from the Philippines having the highest number of COVID-19 cases in emerging East Asia.[9] The strength of the peso is generally traced to low domestic demand that reflects low imports and thus weak demand for US dollars. In October, the exchange rate movement was range-bound, prompted by the passage of the 2021 Philippine national budget, continued reopening of the economy, decline in daily COVID-19 cases, easing of some community quarantine restrictions, and ongoing negotiations over a COVID-19 pandemic stimulus package as well as elections in the US. The peso traded at PHP48.41 to the US dollar on 30 October, reflecting a year-to-date gain of 4.6%.

Size and Composition

Total LCY bond outstanding in the Philippines reached PHP8,136.4 billion (USD167.8 billion) at the end of September on growth of 8.8% quarter-on-quarter (q-o-q) and 21.5% y-o-y (**Table 1**). The rate of expansion in

Q3 2020 was faster than in Q2 2020 and was supported by both the government and corporate segments on the back of higher issuance volumes. At the end of Q3 2020, government bonds comprised 79.9% of the LCY bond market, and corporate bonds accounted for the remaining 21.1%.

Government bonds. LCY government bonds outstanding amounted PHP6,503.0 billion at the end of Q3 2020, increasing 10.1% q-o-q. The increase in market size was supported by Treasury bills and, in particular, Treasury bonds. The Bureau of the Treasury (BTr) issued another tranche of Retail Treasury Bonds (RTBs) to raise more funds for the government's pandemic responses. At the same time, the BSP started issuing its own securities as additional instrument for its monetary policy implementation and liquidity management operations, adding to the government's debt.

Government bond issuance in Q3 2020 strongly rebounded on growth of 65.4% q-o-q, following a decline of 6.9% q-o-q in Q2 2020. It totaled PHP1,105.8 billion, lifted by Treasury bonds and the maiden issuances of central bank securities.

Treasury bonds issued in the quarter reached PHP651.3 billion, more than triple the amount issued in Q2 2020. The high debt sales volume was due to the issuance of RTBs in August when the BTr raised a record PHP516.3 billion. The timing has been conducive for

Table 1: Size and Composition of the Local Currency Bond Market in the Philippines

| | Outstanding Amount (billion) | | | | | | Growth Rate (%) | | | |
| | Q3 2019 | | Q2 2020 | | Q3 2020 | | Q3 2019 | | Q3 2020 | |
	PHP	USD	PHP	USD	PHP	USD	q-o-q	y-o-y	q-o-q	y-o-y
Total	6,699	129	7,477	150	8,136	168	(0.1)	15.7	8.8	21.5
Government	5,253	101	5,904	119	6,503	134	(0.7)	14.4	10.1	23.8
Treasury Bills	553	11	797	16	876	18	(15.3)	25.9	10.0	58.5
Treasury Bonds	4,678	90	5,068	102	5,537	114	1.3	13.5	9.3	18.4
Central Bank Securities	0	0	0	0	50	1	–	–	–	–
Others	22	0.4	40	0.8	40	0.8	(0.03)	(35.5)	(0.02)	83.3
Corporate	1,447	28	1,573	32	1,633	34	2.1	20.7	3.8	12.9

( ) = negative, – = not applicable, PHP = Philippine peso, q-o-q = quarter-on-quarter, Q2 = second quarter, Q3 = third quarter, USD = United States dollar, y-o-y = year-on-year.
Notes:
1. Calculated using data from national sources.
2. Bloomberg end-of-period local currency–USD rates are used.
3. Growth rates are calculated from local currency base and do not include currency effects.
4. "Others" comprise bonds issued by government agencies, entities, and corporations for which repayment is guaranteed by the Government of the Philippines. This includes bonds issued by Power Sector Assets and Liabilities Management and the National Food Authority, among others.
5. Peso Global Bonds (PHP-denominated bonds payable in USD) are not included.
Sources: Bloomberg LP and Bureau of the Treasury.

[9] This covers the period from 6 August to 15 October. 2020. COVID-19 in Charts: Where Does PH Stand in ASEAN, World? 16 October. https://www.rappler.com/newsbreak/data-documents/coronavirus-charts-where-philippines-stands-asean-world.

the government to secure a good portion of funds for its spending needs amid the COVID-19 pandemic as interest rates remain low while high liquidity in the market drew in strong demand from investors. The 5-year security is the Treasury's second RTB issuance in 2020, following its PHP310.8 billion sale in February. During the quarter, the BTr rejected bids for 10-year and 20-year Treasury bonds at two auctions subsequent to the RTB sale as investors sought higher yields and, to some extent, the government had already secured sufficient financing.

The BSP issued central bank securities totaling PHP50.0 billion in Q3 2020. The initial offerings were small in volume with short maturities, but they will be adjusted depending on market response as well as the market liquidity forecast.

Issuance of Treasury bills, on the other hand, amounted to PHP488.6 billion on a decline of 17.2% q-o-q in contrast to the double-digit growth posted in Q2 2020. The drop in debt sales was traced to lower offer volumes during the quarter. The BTr also rejected bids for 365-day Treasury bills in one of the auctions as investors demanded higher rates.

The BTr deferred its plan to issue samurai and panda bonds in 2020 as funds raised domestically were enough to cover the government's financing requirements. At the onset of the COVID-19 pandemic, the BTr considered tapping debt markets in the People's Republic of China and Japan to raise funds. However, the government's PHP540 billion advance credit from the BSP allowed the BTr to shelf this plan. Instead, the BTr will issue a second tranche of *Premyo* bonds to retail investors in November.[9]

Corporate bonds. The LCY corporate bond market rebounded in Q3 2020 to expand 3.8% q-o-q after contracting 0.4% q-o-q in Q2 2020. Corporate bonds outstanding reached PHP1,633.3 billion at the end of Q3 2020 on the back of more bond issuances during the quarter as the economy gradually reopened.

The banking sector remained the largest segment of the LCY corporate bond market in Q3 2020. The sector's share increased to 41.7% at the end of September from 37.9% at the end of September 2019 as banks upped their issuance volume over the past year (**Figure 2**). Properties and utilities companies hold the second and third spots, respectively, comprising 23.8% and 14.5% of the market; however, their shares were lower compared with September 2019. The holding firms, transport, and telecommunications sector saw lower shares in September 2020 versus a year earlier, while the share of "others" was slightly up.

The top 30 corporate issuers have an aggregate debt outstanding of PHP1,451.3 billion at the end of September or 88.9% of the total corporate bond market (**Table 2**). The banking sector comprised the largest share at 43.8%, which was equivalent to PHP649.9 billion. This was

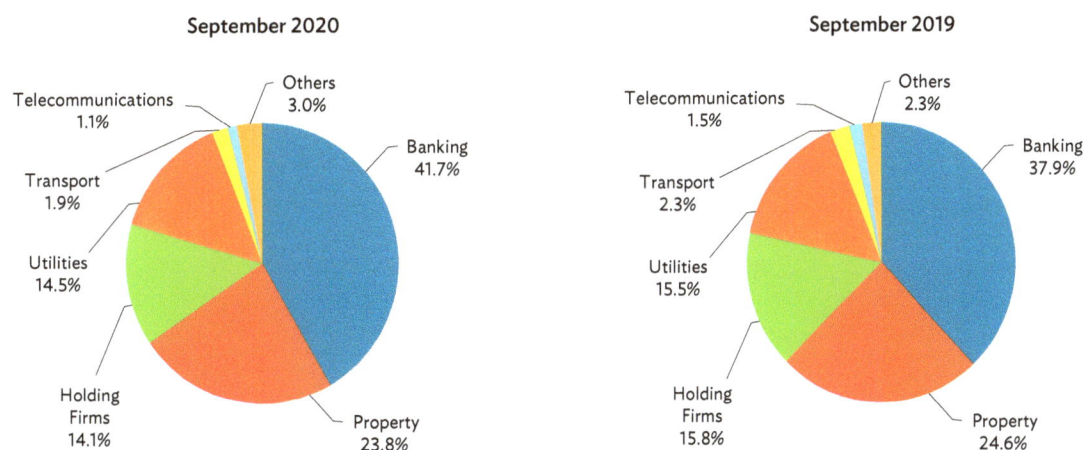

Figure 2: Local Currency Corporate Bonds Outstanding by Sector

Source: Based on data from Bloomberg LP.

---

[10] *Premyo* bonds act as an investment and a ticket to win cash and noncash prizes for retail investors.

Table 2: Top 30 Issuers of Local Currency Corporate Bonds in the Philippines

	Issuers	Outstanding Amount		State-Owned	Listed Company	Type of Industry
		LCY Bonds (PHP billion)	LCY Bonds (USD billion)			
1.	Metropolitan Bank	130.8	2.7	No	Yes	Banking
2.	Ayala Land	121.2	2.5	No	Yes	Property
3.	BDO Unibank	117.4	2.4	No	Yes	Banking
4.	SM Prime Holdings	103.6	2.1	No	Yes	Holding Firms
5.	Bank of the Philippine Islands	86.1	1.8	No	Yes	Banking
6.	SMC Global Power	80.0	1.6	No	No	Electricity, Energy, and Power
7.	Security Bank	66.3	1.4	No	Yes	Banking
8.	San Miguel	60.0	1.2	No	Yes	Holding Firms
9.	China Bank	56.2	1.2	No	Yes	Banking
10.	Rizal Commercial Banking Corporation	55.3	1.1	No	Yes	Banking
11.	Philippine National Bank	52.2	1.1	No	Yes	Banking
12.	SM Investments	48.3	1.0	No	Yes	Holding Firms
13.	Vista Land	43.6	0.9	No	Yes	Property
14.	Petron	42.9	0.9	No	Yes	Electricity, Energy, and Power
15.	Ayala Corporation	40.0	0.8	No	Yes	Holding Firms
16.	Aboitiz Power	40.0	0.8	No	Yes	Electricity, Energy, and Power
17.	Aboitiz Equity Ventures	37.0	0.8	No	Yes	Holding Firms
18.	Maynilad	32.5	0.7	No	No	Water
19.	Union Bank of the Philippines	26.6	0.5	No	Yes	Banking
20.	Philippine Savings Bank	25.4	0.5	No	Yes	Banking
21.	Robinsons Land	25.2	0.5	No	Yes	Property
22.	Manila Electric Company	23.0	0.5	No	Yes	Electricity, Energy, and Power
23.	Filinvest Land	22.0	0.5	No	Yes	Property
24.	San Miguel Brewery	22.0	0.5	No	No	Brewery
25.	East West Banking	17.7	0.4	No	Yes	Banking
26.	Robinsons Bank	16.0	0.3	No	No	Banking
27.	GT Capital	15.1	0.3	No	Yes	Holding Firms
28.	Doubledragon	15.0	0.3	No	Yes	Property
29.	PLDT	15.0	0.3	No	Yes	Telecommunications
30.	San Miguel Food and Beverage	15.0	0.3	No	Yes	Food and Beverage
	Total Top 30 LCY Corporate Issuers	**1,451.3**	**29.9**			
	Total LCY Corporate Bonds	**1,633.3**	**33.7**			
	Top 30 as % of Total LCY Corporate Bonds	**88.9%**	**88.9%**			

LCY = local currency, PHP = Philippine peso, USD = United States dollar.
Notes:
1. Data as of 30 September 2020.
2. State-owned firms are defined as those in which the government has more than a 50% ownership stake.
Source: *AsianBondsOnline* calculations based on Bloomberg LP data.

followed by holdings firms and property firms with shares of 20.5% (PHP304.0 billion) and 15.3% (PHP227.0 billion), respectively. The corporate issuers are Metropolitan Bank, Ayala Land, BDO Unibank, and SM Prime Holdings with bonds outstanding of over PHP100 billion each.

Bond issuance activities from the corporate sector picked up in Q3 2020 to PHP126.3 billion from PHP27.6 billion in the previous quarter. As the economy gradually reopened, even amid continued uncertainty from the COVID-19 pandemic, firms returned to tap the capital market to fund their business operations and recovery plans. The timing is favorable as firms can take advantage of the low-interest-rate environment and abundant liquidity in the market.

Notable debt issuances in Q3 2020 were predominantly from the banking sector with the purpose largely to support their lending activities. BDO Unibank had the largest bond issuance during the quarter with a PHP36.0 billion 2-year bond (**Table 3**). Another notable bond issuance was the Bank of the Philippine Islands' landmark COVID-19 response bond, which raised PHP21.5 billion. It was the Philippines' first bond issued as a direct response to the COVID-19 pandemic. The proceeds will be used to support lending activities to eligible micro, small, and medium-sized enterprises to sustain or restart their operations amid financial difficulties caused by the pandemic.

Table 3: Notable Local Currency Corporate Bond Issuances in the Third Quarter of 2020

Corporate Issuers	Coupon Rate (%)	Issued Amount (PHP billion)
BDO Unibank		
2-year bond	3.13	36.00
Bank of the Philippine Islands		
2-year bond	3.05	21.50
Rizal Commercial Banking Corporation		
2-year bond	3.25	16.62
Security Bank		
2-year bond	3.13	13.50
Robinsons Land		
3-year bond	3.68	12.76

PHP = Philippine peso.
Source: Based on data from Bloomberg LP.

Investor Profile

Contractual savings and tax-exempt institutions and banks and investment houses had nearly the same share of LCY government bond holdings as one another at the end of September, which reflected a change in the investor landscape from a year earlier (**Figure 3**). Contractual savings and tax-exempt institutions' market shares rose significantly to 36.7% from 23.9% in September 2019. During the same period, banks and investment houses market share dropped to 36.2% from 42.6% a year earlier. BTr-managed funds had the third-largest market share with 9.6%, outpacing the "others"

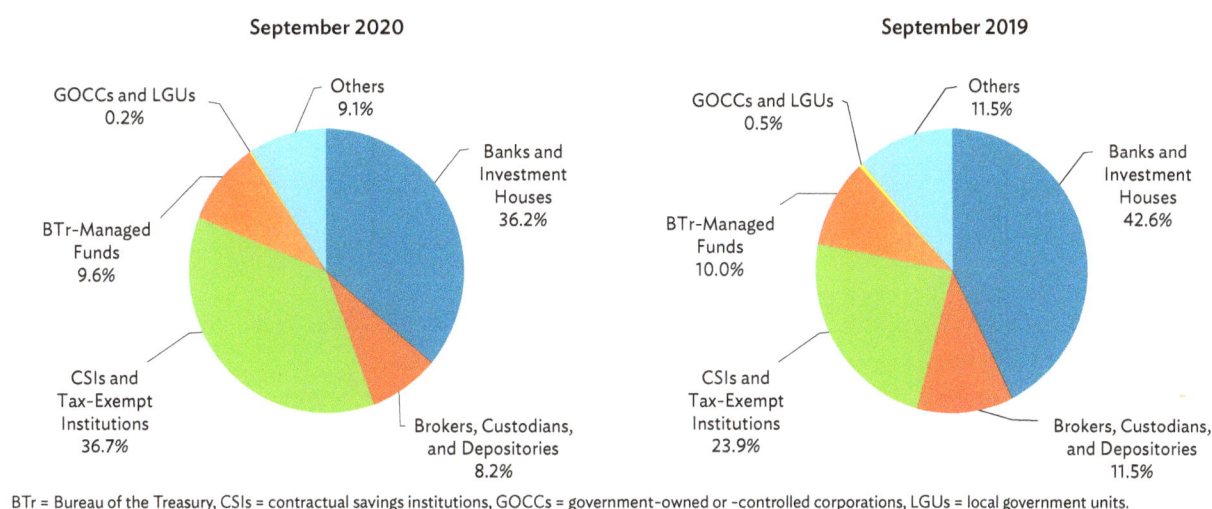

Figure 3: Local Currency Government Bonds Investor Profile

September 2020

GOCCs and LGUs 0.2%
Others 9.1%
Banks and Investment Houses 36.2%
BTr-Managed Funds 9.6%
CSIs and Tax-Exempt Institutions 36.7%
Brokers, Custodians, and Depositories 8.2%

September 2019

GOCCs and LGUs 0.5%
Others 11.5%
Banks and Investment Houses 42.6%
BTr-Managed Funds 10.0%
CSIs and Tax-Exempt Institutions 23.9%
Brokers, Custodians, and Depositories 11.5%

BTr = Bureau of the Treasury, CSIs = contractual savings institutions, GOCCs = government-owned or -controlled corporations, LGUs = local government units.
Source: Bureau of the Treasury.

investor group and brokers, custodians, and depositories with 9.1% and 8.2% shares, respectively. Government-owned or -controlled corporations and local government units remained the smallest investor group with only a 0.2% market share.

Policy, Institutional, and Regulatory Developments

Bangko Sentral ng Pilipinas Issues Central Bank Securities

The BSP started issuing BSP securities on 18 September as an additional instrument to manage liquidity in the financial system. According to the BSP, this initiative will help the central bank shift to more market-based monetary operations and support the implementation of monetary policy under the interest rate corridor framework. The addition of BSP securities to the supply of risk-free financial instruments in the banking system could help in the development of the LCY bond market. The BSP securities will be one of the monetary policy tools

to mop up excess liquidity. Initial offerings will be small in volume and have shorter tenors but will eventually be scaled up and have longer maturities. The issuance of the securities is allowed under the New Central Bank Act that was signed in February 2019.

Bangko Sentral ng Pilipinas Approves Provisional Advance to the Government of the Philippines

On 1 October, the BSP approved the Government of the Philippines' request for a provisional advance of PHP540.0 billion to be used for budget deficit financing amid the COVID-19 pandemic. This came after the BTr fully settled the previous PHP300.0 billion repurchase agreement on 29 September. The fresh funds will be settled on or before 29 December and will have zero interest. The new tranche is pursuant to Section 89 of the New Central Bank Act as amended in the Bayanihan II Act, which allows the government to avail of provisional advances from the central bank of up to PHP846.0 billion. Market participants expect the new funds to lift some burden from the government to increase borrowing.

Singapore

Yield Movements

Between 31 August and 30 October, Singapore's local currency (LCY) government bond yields declined for most tenors (**Figure 1**). The shorter-end of the yield curve (from 3 months to 1 year) declined an average of 1 basis point (bp). Yields of longer-term tenors (from 5 years to 30 years) recorded larger declines, decreasing an average of 20 bps. The yield spread between 2-year and 10-year government bonds contracted from 77 bps to 56 bps during the review period.

The yield curve for Singapore's LCY government bonds shifted downward during the review period because of the impact of the monetary policy of Monetary Authority of Singapore (MAS). At the end of March, MAS decided to reduce the slope of its exchange rate policy and lower the midpoint of its policy band. These measures weakened the exchange rate and arrested deflation, supporting Singapore's export-oriented economy amid the coronavirus disease (COVID-19) pandemic. Singapore's nonoil domestic exports have been expanding monthly since June, with August exports recording 7.7% year-on-year (y-o-y) growth.

In October, MAS kept its monetary policy unchanged. The appreciation rate of the Singapore dollar nominal effective exchange rate remained at zero, and the center of the policy band was left unchanged. MAS expects the economy to continue improving in the last quarter of 2020, albeit at a weak pace. The sluggish growth is expected to continue until 2021 amid limited improvements in domestic services and cross-border travel. The central bank also factored in receding deflation risks in its monetary policy decision. The decision was in line with most analysts' expectations and the view that economic recovery would also be supported by more fiscal stimulus.

Based on advance estimates, Singapore's economy contracted 7.0% y-o-y in the third quarter (Q3) of 2020, moderating from the contraction of 13.3% y-o-y in the second quarter (Q2) of 2020. On a quarter-on-quarter (q-o-q) seasonally adjusted basis, Singapore's gross domestic product expanded 7.9% y-o-y as output in manufacturing, construction, and services picked up from

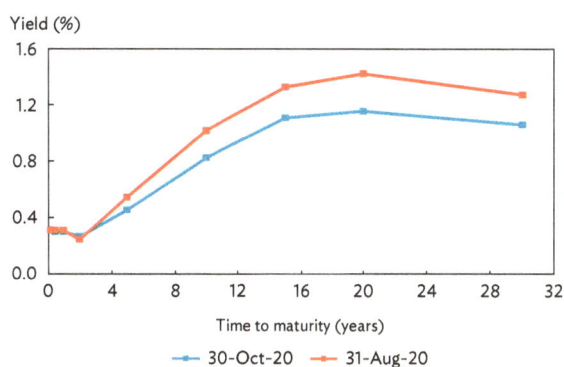

Figure 1: Singapore's Benchmark Yield Curve—Local Currency Government Bonds

Source: Based on data from Bloomberg LP.

the preceding quarter due to the phased reopening of the economy that allowed domestic economic activities to resume. Policy stimulus also started taking effect, contributing to the rebound. The Ministry of Trade and Industry forecasts Singapore's economic growth to fall between –7.0% y-o-y and –5.0% y-o-y for full-year 2020. In June, Singapore exited from Circuit Breaker measures—measures limiting the population's movement inside the city-state to prevent the spread of COVID-19—and transitioned to a planned reopening of the economy in three phases. Singapore is currently in Phase 2 in which more activities are permitted if infection rates remain stable and manageable. As cases remain low and testing and tracing scale up, Singapore may see a transition to Phase 3 by the end of 2020.

Consumer price inflation in Singapore was flat in September after falling 0.4% y-o-y in both August and July. The overall steady prices of basic goods and services was driven by smaller price declines for services, electricity, and gas, and private transport. Core inflation, which excludes the cost of accommodations and private transport, was –0.1% y-o-y, compared with –0.3% y-o-y recorded in August. Domestically, inflationary pressures are expected to remain subdued. MAS projects inflation for full-year 2020 to fall between –0.5% and 0.0%.

As the COVID-19 pandemic continues to affect the world economy, authorities in Singapore are ensuring continued support to employees and businesses by extending the duration of various relief measures. Expected to save hundreds of thousands of jobs, the government's wage subsidy was extended to May 2021. Subsidies for employee trainings in various sectors were extended to June 2021. The government's program ensuring that businesses have access to loans has been extended to September 2021. The extension of relief measures prevented Singapore's economic growth from dipping further.

Size and Composition

Singapore's LCY bond market expanded 1.8% q-o-q in Q3 2020 to reach SGD489.5 billion (USD358.5 billion) at the end of September, up from SGD480.6 billion at the end of June (**Table 1**). On an annual basis, growth slowed to 9.8% y-o-y in Q3 2020 from 11.9% y-o-y a year earlier. The expansion in the LCY bond market was supported by growth in both government and corporate bonds, which accounted for 63.7% and 36.3%, respectively, of total LCY bonds outstanding at the end of Q3 2020.

Issuance of LCY bonds in Q3 2020 increased 6.8% q-o-q to SGD201.7 billion from SGD188.8 billion in Q2 2020, driven by rising government bond issuance. This was slightly offset by a drop in the issuance of corporate bonds.

Government bonds. The LCY government bond market grew 2.0% q-o-q to SGD311.7 billion in Q3 2020 from SGD305.7 billion in the previous quarter, spurred by the new MAS floating-rate notes. On an annual basis, outstanding Singapore Government Securities (SGS) bills

and bonds, which comprised 61.4% of total outstanding LCY government bonds at the end of September, jumped 17.7% y-o-y. Since July 2019, 6-month SGS bills have gradually replaced 24-week MAS bills in order to meet the demand for short-term SGD-denominated securities as SGS bills are more accessible to a wider range of investors.

LCY government bond issuance in Q3 2020 rose 7.5% q-o-q. The growth was due to an increase in MAS bills spurred by issuances of 6-month floating-rate notes meant to promote the use of the Singapore Overnight Rate Average as a benchmark in Singapore's financial market.

Corporate bonds. LCY corporate bonds outstanding increased 1.6% q-o-q in Q3 2020 to reach SGD177.8 billion at the end of September, up from SGD174.9 billion at the end of June, buoyed by the increase in outstanding corporate bonds in the real estate and finance industries.

The top 30 LCY corporate bond issuers in Singapore accounted for combined outstanding bonds of SGD88.0 billion, or 49.5% of the total LCY corporate bond market, at the end of Q3 2020 (**Table 2**). The government-owned Housing & Development Board continued to be the largest issuer with outstanding LCY corporate bonds amounting to SGD26.0 billion (14.6% of total LCY corporate bonds outstanding). By industry type, real estate companies continued to comprise the largest share (43.4%) among the top 30 issuers of LCY corporate bonds with SGD38.2 billion of aggregate LCY corporate bonds outstanding at the end of Q3 2020.

Table 1: Size and Composition of the Local Currency Bond Market in Singapore

	Outstanding Amount (billion)						Growth Rate (%)			
	Q3 2019		Q2 2020		Q3 2020		Q3 2019		Q3 2020	
	SGD	USD	SGD	USD	SGD	USD	q-o-q	y-o-y	q-o-q	y-o-y
Total	446	322	481	345	489	358	4.9	11.9	1.8	9.8
Government	277	200	306	219	312	228	5.6	15.0	2.0	12.5
SGS Bills and Bonds	163	118	195	140	191	140	25.8	33.0	(1.7)	17.7
MAS Bills	114	83	111	80	120	88	(14.0)	(3.5)	8.4	5.2
Corporate	169	122	175	126	178	130	3.8	7.2	1.6	5.4

( ) = negative, MAS = Monetary Authority of Singapore, q-o-q = quarter-on-quarter, Q2 = second quarter, Q3 = third quarter, SGD = Singapore dollar, SGS = Singapore Government Securities, USD = United States dollar, y-o-y = year-on-year.
Notes:
1. Government bonds are calculated using data from national sources. Corporate bonds are based on *AsianBondsOnline* estimates.
2. SGS bills and bonds do not include the special issue of SGS held by the Singapore Central Provident Fund.
3. Bloomberg LP end-of-period local currency–USD rates are used.
4. Growth rates are calculated from local currency base and do not include currency effects.
Sources: Bloomberg LP, Monetary Authority of Singapore, and Singapore Government Securities.

Table 2: Top 30 Issuers of Local Currency Corporate Bonds in Singapore

	Issuers	Outstanding Amount		State-Owned	Listed Company	Type of Industry
		LCY Bonds (SGD billion)	LCY Bonds (USD billion)			
1.	Housing & Development Board	26.0	19.0	Yes	No	Real Estate
2.	Land Transport Authority	9.5	6.9	Yes	No	Transportation
3.	Singapore Airlines	7.4	5.4	Yes	Yes	Transportation
4.	Frasers Property	4.0	3.0	No	Yes	Real Estate
5.	United Overseas Bank	3.3	2.4	No	Yes	Banking
6.	Capitaland Treasury	3.1	2.3	No	No	Finance
7.	Mapletree Treasury Services	2.7	2.0	No	No	Finance
8.	Keppel Corporation	2.7	1.9	No	Yes	Diversified
9.	Temasek Financial	2.6	1.9	Yes	No	Finance
10.	DBS Group Holdings	2.5	1.9	No	Yes	Banking
11.	Sembcorp Financial Services	2.1	1.5	No	No	Engineering
12.	City Developments Limited	1.7	1.3	No	Yes	Real Estate
13.	Oversea-Chinese Banking Corporation	1.7	1.2	No	Yes	Banking
14.	Ascendas REIT	1.6	1.2	No	Yes	Finance
15.	NTUC Income	1.4	1.0	No	No	Finance
16.	CMT MTN	1.4	1.0	No	No	Finance
17.	Shangri-La Hotel	1.4	1.0	No	Yes	Real Estate
18.	Olam International	1.3	1.0	No	Yes	Consumer Goods
19.	Public Utilities Board	1.3	1.0	Yes	No	Utilities
20.	GLL IHT	1.2	0.9	No	No	Real Estate
21.	Capitaland	1.2	0.9	Yes	Yes	Real Estate
22.	Singapore Technologies Telemedia	1.2	0.9	Yes	No	Utilities
23.	Suntec REIT	1.0	0.8	No	Yes	Real Estate
24.	Singapore Press Holdings	1.0	0.7	No	Yes	Communications
25.	Hyflux	0.9	0.7	No	Yes	Utilities
26.	Mapletree Commercial Trust	0.9	0.7	No	Yes	Real Estate
27.	DBS Bank	0.8	0.6	No	Yes	Banking
28.	SMRT Capital	0.8	0.6	No	No	Transportation
29.	Sembcorp Industries	0.8	0.6	No	Yes	Shipbuilding
30.	Wing Tai Holdings	0.8	0.6	No	Yes	Real Estate
	Total Top 30 LCY Corporate Issuers	**88.0**	**64.5**			
	Total LCY Corporate Bonds	**177.8**	**130.2**			
	Top 30 as % of Total LCY Corporate Bonds	**49.5%**	**49.5%**			

LCY = local currency, MTN = medium-term note, REIT = real estate investment trust, SGD = Singapore dollar, USD = United States dollar.
Notes:
1. Data as of 30 September 2020.
2. State-owned firms are defined as those in which the government has more than a 50% ownership stake.
Source: *AsianBondsOnline* calculations based on Bloomberg LP data.

In Q3 2020, issuance of LCY corporate bonds declined to SGD5.1 billion, a contraction of 16.1% q-o-q from SGD6.0 billion in the previous quarter, due to a large base effect. The high level of issuance in Q2 2020 compensated for the limited issuance in the first quarter of 2020 as companies were affected by the COVID-19 pandemic. Q3 2020 issuance was in line with typical issuance levels seen in 2019.

Insurance cooperative NTUC Income issued the single-largest LCY corporate bond in Q3 2020, an SGD800.0 million 30-year callable bond with coupon rate of 3.10% (**Table 3**). Several companies issued callable perpetual bonds during the quarter, three of which were real estate investment trust (REIT) companies. Most

Table 3: Notable Local Currency Corporate Bond Issuances in the Third Quarter of 2020

Corporate Issuers	Coupon Rate (%)	Issued Amount (SGD million)
NTUC Income		
30-year bond	3.10	800.0
Singapore Technologies Telemedia		
Perpetual bond	4.10	375.0
Keppel Real Estate Investment Trust		
Perpetual bond	3.15	300.0
Ascendas Real Estate Investment Trust		
Perpetual bond	3.00	300.0
Oversea-Chinese Banking Corporation		
Perpetual bond	3.00	200.0
AIMS APAC Real Estate Investment Trust		
Perpetual bond	5.65	125.0
Banyan Tree Holdings		
2-year bond	7.50	50.4

SGD = Singapore dollar.
Source: Bloomberg LP.

notable among the perpetual bonds was Ascendas REIT, as it became the first nonfinancial green perpetual bond. At 3.00%, it also achieved the lowest yield for a perpetual bond issued by a corporation outside the banking sector. On the other hand, the effect of the COVID-19 pandemic on credit spreads was felt by AIMS APAC, REIT as it had to price its perpetual bond at a high rate of 5.65% in August. The 2-year convertible bond issued by Banyan Tree Holdings had the highest coupon rate during the review period at 7.50%.

Policy, Institutional, and Regulatory Developments

Monetary Authority of Singapore Expands Access to Liquidity Facilities

On 3 September, MAS announced various measures to enhance financial institutions' access to Singapore dollar and United States (US) dollar funding. On 28 September, a Singapore Dollar Term Facility was launched to provide financial institutions flexible options in terms of SGD-denominated borrowing at longer tenors. The facility, which compliments the overnight MAS Standing Facility, offers SGD-denominated funds with 1-month and 3-month tenors. The new facility makes available more options for collateral composed of cash and other marketable securities in various currencies. For domestic systemically important banks, residential property loans may be pledged as collateral with the Singapore Dollar Term Facility. MAS also enhanced the US Dollar Facility, established in March, which allows banks to borrow US dollars by pledging SGD-denominated collateral. Similar to the Singapore Dollar Term Facility guidelines, options for collateral for the US Dollar Facility were also expanded.

Thailand

Yield Movements

Movements in Thailand's local currency (LCY) government bond yield curve were mixed between 31 August and 30 October (**Figure 1**). Bonds with maturities of 2 years or below gained 3 basis points (bps) on average, while the 3-year tenor held steady, and the 4-year tenor jumped 10 bps. Meanwhile, yields fell an average of 6 bps for bonds with maturities of 5 years or longer, with the 20-year tenor showing the steepest drop at 16 bps. Yields dropped an average of 3 bps across all tenors. The spread between the 2-year and 10-year tenors narrowed from 89 bps to 78 bps during the review period.

The rise in yields at the shorter-end of the curve reflected weakened appetite for Thai sovereign bonds amid the recession brought by the coronavirus disease (COVID-19) and rising political uncertainty. Expectations of a gradual recovery helped boost yields for tenors with maturities of 5 years or more.

Thailand's gross domestic product dropped 6.4% year-on-year (y-o-y) in the third quarter (Q3) of 2020 after declining 12.1% y-o-y in the second quarter. Economic contraction narrowed in the third quarter as easing of business lockdowns and expansion of government relief efforts boosted consumption and domestic tourism. The National Economic and Social Development Council revised its full-year 2020 gross domestic product growth forecast to –6.0% from the earlier projection of 7.3%–7.8% decline, while predicting 2021 growth to be within a range of 3.5% to 4.5%.

Consumer prices fell 0.7% y-o-y in September, marking 7 straight months of deflation. Falling energy prices, particularly retail gasoline and electric bills, as well as depressed demand due to COVID-19, drove deflationary pressures.

Thailand's benchmark interest rate remained at a record low as the Bank of Thailand (BOT) decided to leave it unchanged at 0.5% in September. The BOT previously cut the policy rate by 25 bps in May. Since the beginning of the year, the BOT has reduced the benchmark rate by a total of 75 bps in response to the COVID-19 pandemic.

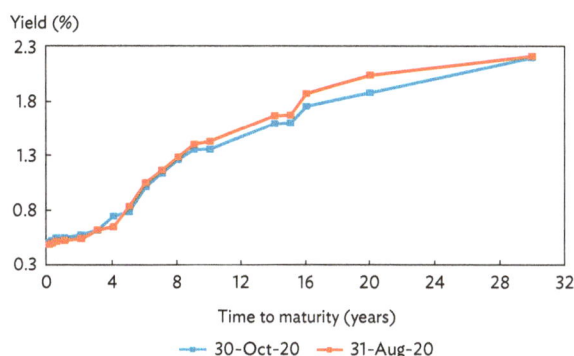

Figure 1: Thailand's Benchmark Yield Curve— Local Currency Government Bonds

Sources: Based on data from Bloomberg LP and Thai Bond Market Association.

Among emerging East Asian currencies, the Thai baht is among those that has depreciated the most against the United States dollar thus far in 2020. Between 1 January and 30 October, the Thai baht depreciated 3.3% against the dollar.

Rising political risks, as antigovernment protests gain momentum, pose additional threat to Thailand's economic recovery amid the global pandemic.

Size and Composition

Thailand's LCY bonds outstanding amounted to THB14,018.4 billion (USD443.7 billion) at the end of September on growth of 4.2% quarter-on-quarter (q-o-q) and 8.3% y-o-y (**Table 1**). Growth in Q3 2020 accelerated from 2.1% q-o-q and 3.2% y-o-y in Q2 2020, driven by strong growth in the government bond segment as the government continued to issue debt to finance relief measures to boost the economy amid the COVID-19 pandemic. Government bonds dominate Thailand's LCY bond market, accounting for a 73.2% share at the end of September, up from 72.4% at the end of June.

Government bonds. The size of the LCY government bond market amounted to THB10,260.4 billion at the end of September, with growth increasing to 5.4% q-o-q in Q3 2020 from 4.1% q-o-q in Q2 2020. Growth

Table 1: Size and Composition of the Local Currency Bond Market in Thailand

	Outstanding Amount (billion)						Growth Rate (%)			
	Q3 2019		Q2 2020		Q3 2020		Q3 2019		Q3 2020	
	THB	USD	THB	USD	THB	USD	q-o-q	y-o-y	q-o-q	y-o-y
Total	12,946	423	13,449	435	14,018	444	(0.7)	6.6	4.2	8.3
Government	9,220	301	9,732	315	10,260	325	(1.1)	6.0	5.4	11.3
Government Bonds and Treasury Bills	4,827	158	5,306	172	5,735	182	1.5	4.6	8.1	18.8
Central Bank Bonds	3,636	119	3,633	118	3,702	117	(3.6)	9.4	1.9	1.8
State-Owned Enterprise and Other Bonds	757	25	793	26	823	26	(4.5)	(0.6)	3.9	8.7
Corporate	3,726	122	3,716	120	3,758	119	0.2	8.3	1.1	0.9

( ) = negative, q-o-q = quarter-on-quarter, Q2 = second quarter, Q3 = third quarter, THB = Thai baht, USD = United States dollar, y-o-y = year-on-year.
Notes:
1. Calculated using data from national sources.
2. Bloomberg LP end-of-period local currency–USD rates are used.
3. Growth rates are calculated from local currency base and do not include currency effects.
Source: Bank of Thailand.

in outstanding government bonds and Treasury bills drove much of the gain, rising 8.1% q-o-q to reach THB5,735.1 billion at the end of September. BOT bonds outstanding stood at THB3,702.0 billion at the end of September, with growth moderating to 1.9% q-o-q in Q3 2020 from 4.0% q-o-q in the prior quarter. State-owned enterprise and other bonds reached THB823.3 billion at the end of September, as growth more than doubled to 3.9% q-o-q in Q3 2020 from 1.4% q-o-q in Q2 2020. On an annual basis, growth in Thailand's government bond segment accelerated to 11.3% y-o-y in Q3 2020 from 4.4% y-o-y in the previous quarter.

Total LCY bond issuance from the government amounted to THB2,624.9 billion in Q3 2020. Growth in total government bond issuance jumped to 20.2% q-o-q in Q3 2020 from 7.5% q-o-q in Q2 2020, driven by strong issuance from all government bond segments. Growth in issuance of government bonds and Treasury bills moderated to 62.7% q-o-q in Q3 2020 from 117.7% q-o-q in Q2 2020, as the government continued to issue debt to finance economic relief measures, albeit at a weaker pace than in the prior quarter. Issuance of BOT bonds expanded 11.2% q-o-q in Q3 2020, reversing the 0.4% q-o-q decline in the previous quarter. Issuance of state-owned enterprise bonds rose 124.0% q-o-q in Q3 2020, rebounding from a 38.5% q-o-q drop in Q2 2020. On a y-o-y basis, issuance of government bonds increased 32.7% in Q3 2020, a reversal of the 5.8% decline posted in the previous quarter.

Corporate bonds. Outstanding corporate bonds totaled THB3,758.1 billion at the end of September on growth of 1.1% q-o-q and 0.9% y-o-y. Growth in Q3 2020 showed

modest recovery from the 2.6% q-o-q and 0.03% y-o-y contractions in Q2 2020. Corporate bond issuance recovered strongly in Q3 2020, rising 27.4% q-o-q after contracting 23.7% q-o-q in Q2 2020, as the easing of lockdown measures revived business confidence.

The LCY bonds outstanding of the top 30 corporate issuers amounted to THB2,186.5 billion at the end of September, representing 58.2% of the total corporate bond market (**Table 2**). Food and beverage firms dominated the list, with an outstanding bond stock amounting to THB432.9 billion. Firms in commerce, banking, and communications industries were the next largest issuers, with bonds totaling THB305.8 billion, THB258.8 billion, and THB257.6 billion, respectively. The majority of the top 30 issuers were listed on the Thai Stock Exchange, while only four were state-owned. Due to a large issuance during the quarter, CP ALL became the top issuer in the market in Q3 2020, with a total outstanding bond stock amounting to THB183.9 billion. Siam Cement and Thai Beverage had the next largest total bond stocks at THB175.0 billion and THB170.3 billion, respectively.

In Q3 2020, PTT and CP ALL were the two largest issuers, with corporate debt issuance of THB35.0 billion and THB25.0 billion, respectively (**Table 3**). PTT raised funds from seven issuances of bonds with tenors ranging from 2 years to 25 years and carrying coupons ranging from 1.21% to 3.74%. CP ALL issued bonds with tenors ranging from 2.5 years to 15.0 years and carrying coupons ranging from 1.9% to 3.9%. True Corp was the third-largest issuer during the quarter, with issuances amounting to THB23.4 billion from bonds with

Table 2: Top 30 Issuers of Local Currency Corporate Bonds in Thailand

	Issuers	Outstanding Amount		State-Owned	Listed Company	Type of Industry
		LCY Bonds (THB billion)	LCY Bonds (USD billion)			
1.	CP ALL	183.9	5.8	No	Yes	Commerce
2.	Siam Cement	175.0	5.5	Yes	Yes	Construction Materials
3.	Thai Beverage	170.3	5.4	No	No	Food and Beverage
4.	Bank of Ayudhya	133.8	4.2	No	Yes	Banking
5.	Berli Jucker	121.9	3.9	No	Yes	Commerce
6.	Charoen Pokphand Foods	116.4	3.7	No	Yes	Food and Beverage
7.	PTT	114.6	3.6	Yes	Yes	Energy and Utilities
8.	True Move H Universal Communication	112.2	3.6	No	No	Communications
9.	True Corp	106.4	3.4	No	No	Communications
10.	CPF Thailand	76.0	2.4	No	No	Food and Beverage
11.	Toyota Leasing Thailand	71.9	2.3	No	No	Finance and Securities
12.	Minor International	62.0	2.0	No	Yes	Hospitality and Leisure
13.	Indorama Ventures	61.4	1.9	No	Yes	Petrochemicals and Chemicals
14.	PTT Global Chemical	51.7	1.6	No	Yes	Petrochemicals and Chemicals
15.	Krungthai Card	45.6	1.4	Yes	Yes	Banking
16.	Global Power Synergy	45.0	1.4	No	Yes	Energy and Utilities
17.	Bangkok Commercial Asset Management	44.2	1.4	No	Yes	Finance and Securities
18.	Krung Thai Bank	44.0	1.4	Yes	Yes	Banking
19.	Banpu	43.6	1.4	No	Yes	Energy and Utilities
20.	Bangkok Expressway & Metro	41.2	1.3	No	Yes	Transportation and Logistics
21.	TPI Polene	39.3	1.2	No	Yes	Property and Construction
22.	dtac TriNet	39.0	1.2	No	Yes	Communications
23.	CH Karnchang	37.9	1.2	No	Yes	Property and Construction
24.	Land & Houses	37.6	1.2	No	Yes	Property and Construction
25.	Mitr Phol Sugar	37.1	1.2	No	No	Food and Beverage
26.	Muangthai Capital	36.8	1.2	No	Yes	Finance and Securities
27.	Bangchak	36.0	1.1	No	Yes	Energy and Utilities
28.	TMB Bank	35.4	1.1	No	Yes	Banking
29.	Sansiri	33.3	1.1	No	Yes	Property and Construction
30.	Thai Union Group	33.1	1.0	No	Yes	Food and Beverage
	Total Top 30 LCY Corporate Issuers	**2,186.5**	**69.2**			
	Total LCY Corporate Bonds	**3,758.1**	**118.9**			
	Top 30 as % of Total LCY Corporate Bonds	**58.2%**	**58.2%**			

LCY = local currency, THB = Thai baht, USD = United States dollar.
Notes:
1. Data as of 30 September 2020.
2. State-owned firms are defined as those in which the government has more than a 50% ownership stake.
Source: *AsianBondsOnline* calculations based on Bloomberg LP data.

Table 3: Notable Local Currency Corporate Bond Issuances in the Third Quarter of 2020

Corporate Issuers	Coupon Rate (%)	Issued Amount (THB billion)	Corporate Issuers	Coupon Rate (%)	Issued Amount (THB billion)
PTT			True Corp		
2-year bond	1.21	2.0	1.8-year bond	3.00	5.9
3-year bond	2.25	2.0	3-year bond	3.50	6.4
5-year bond	2.05	3.0	4.5-year bond	4.15	4.0
7-year bond	2.85	13.0	5.5-year bond	4.40	7.1
10-year bond	2.84	2.0	CPF Thailand		
15-year bond	3.20	6.0	4.5-year bond	3.15	13.4
25-year bond	3.74	7.0	7-year bond	3.35	2.4
CP ALL			10-year bond	3.55	0.8
2.5-year bond	1.90	6.0	12-year bond	3.80	0.9
4.8-year bond	3.00	13.2	15-year bond	4.11	2.5
9.6-year bond	3.40	2.4	Ananda		
15-year bond	3.90	3.5	Perpetual bond	0.00	1.0

THB = Thai baht.
Source: Bloomberg LP.

tenors ranging from 1.8 years to 5.5 years and carrying coupons ranging from 3.0% to 4.4%. CPF Thailand was the next largest issuer, with multitranche issuances ranging from 4.5 years to 15 years and amounting to THB20.0 billion. Another notable issuance during the quarter was property developer Ananda's zero-coupon perpetual bond.

Central government bonds. The combined shares of the four largest holders of government bonds in Thailand dropped slightly to 89.5% at the end of September 2020 from 91.0% a year earlier (**Figure 2**). Financial

corporations continued to hold the largest share of government bonds, although their share inched down to 39.9% at the end of September from 40.8% in September 2019. The share of other depository corporations rose to 19.2% from 17.2% a year earlier. The central government's share dipped to 16.4% from 16.9% between September 2019 and September 2020. During the same period, nonresidents' share of government bonds dropped to 14.0% from 16.1% amid outflows driven by weakening investor confidence, as Thailand's economy suffered from the adverse impact of COVID-19.

Figure 2: Local Currency Government Bonds Investor Profile

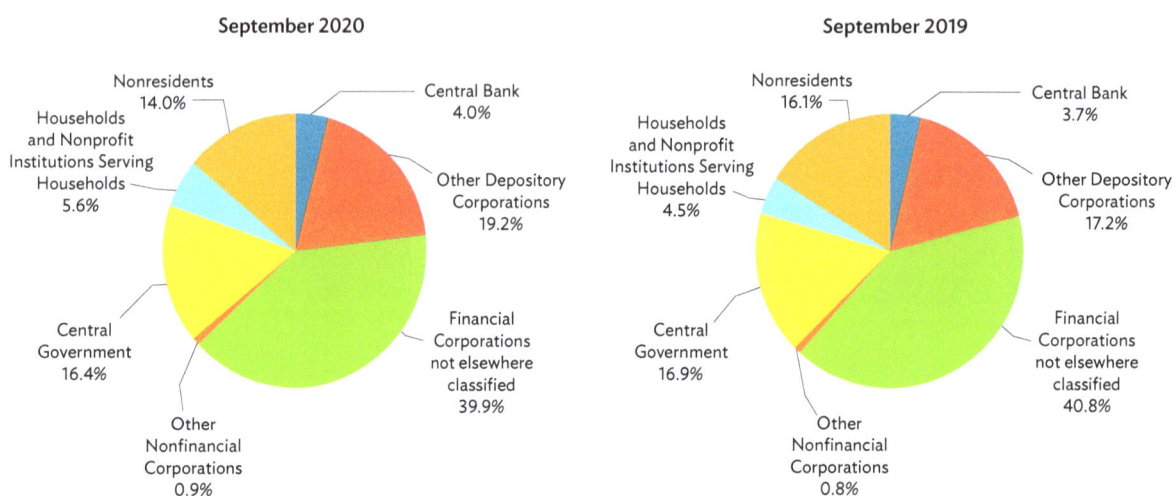

September 2020

Nonresidents 14.0%
Households and Nonprofit Institutions Serving Households 5.6%
Central Bank 4.0%
Other Depository Corporations 19.2%
Central Government 16.4%
Financial Corporations not elsewhere classified 39.9%
Other Nonfinancial Corporations 0.9%

September 2019

Nonresidents 16.1%
Households and Nonprofit Institutions Serving Households 4.5%
Central Bank 3.7%
Other Depository Corporations 17.2%
Central Government 16.9%
Financial Corporations not elsewhere classified 40.8%
Other Nonfinancial Corporations 0.8%

Notes:
1. Government bonds include Treasury bills and bonds.
2. Local government not presented in the chart due to its relatively small shares of 0.00002% in September 2019 and 0.00003% in September 2020.
Source: Bank of Thailand.

Figure 3: Local Currency Central Bank Securities Investor Profile

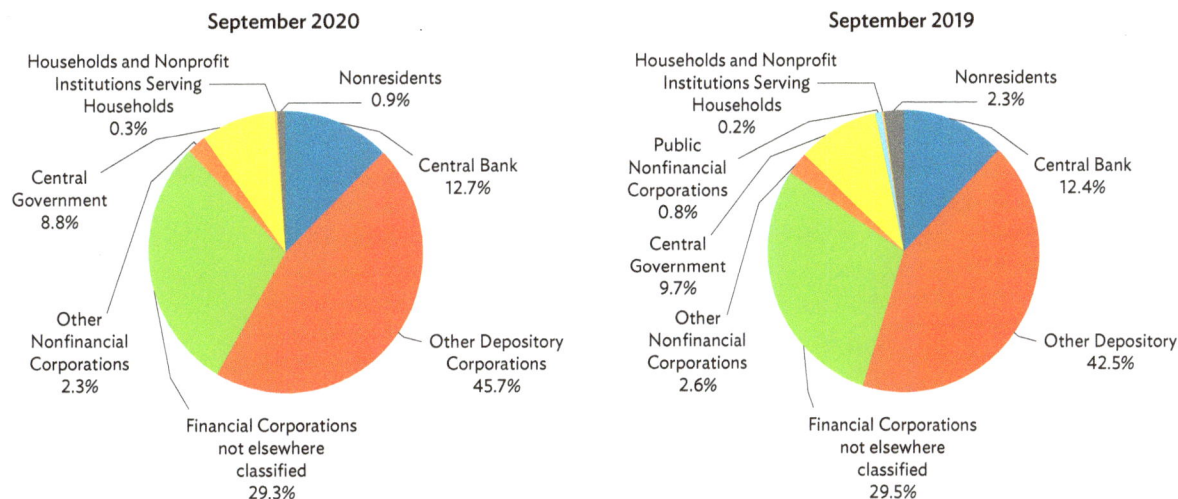

September 2020

- Households and Nonprofit Institutions Serving Households 0.3%
- Nonresidents 0.9%
- Central Bank 12.7%
- Central Government 8.8%
- Other Nonfinancial Corporations 2.3%
- Other Depository Corporations 45.7%
- Financial Corporations not elsewhere classified 29.3%

September 2019

- Households and Nonprofit Institutions Serving Households 0.2%
- Nonresidents 2.3%
- Public Nonfinancial Corporations 0.8%
- Central Bank 12.4%
- Central Government 9.7%
- Other Nonfinancial Corporations 2.6%
- Other Depository 42.5%
- Financial Corporations not elsewhere classified 29.5%

Source: Bank of Thailand.

Central bank bonds. The combined shares of the top four holders of BOT bonds rose to 96.5% in September from 94.1% in September 2019 (**Figure 3**). Other depository corporations held the largest share of BOT bonds at 45.7%, up from 42.5% a year earlier. The share of financial corporations inched down to 29.3% from 29.5% in the previous year. During the same period, the BOT's holdings rose to 12.7% from 12.4%, while central government holdings dropped to 8.8% from 9.7%. Nonresidents held a marginal amount of BOT bonds at the end of September 2020 at 0.9%, down from 2.3% a year earlier.

Figure 4: Foreign Investor Net Trading of Local Currency Bonds in Thailand

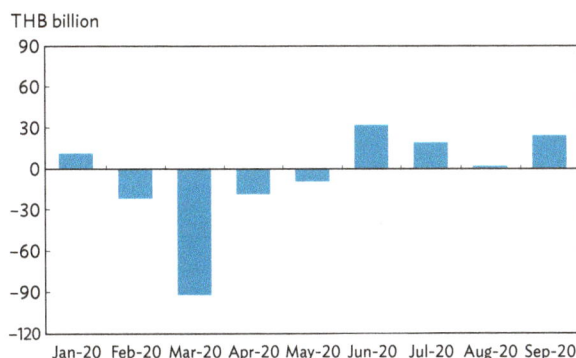

THB billion

THB = Thai baht.
Source: Thai Bond Market Association.

Foreign investors in Thailand's LCY bond market recorded net inflows of THB45.1 billion in Q3 2020, up from THB4.6 billion in Q2 2020 (**Figure 4**). The bond market saw net foreign fund outflows amounting to THB101.8 billion in the first quarter of 2020 amid the COVID-19 outbreak. The easing of lockdown measures and the government's stimulus packages provided a boost to investor confidence, resulting in net foreign inflows in June through September.

Policy, Institutional, and Regulatory Developments

Thailand Issues First Sustainable Government Bonds

In August, the Public Debt Management Office issued Thailand's first sustainable government bonds. The issuance was divided in two tranches. The first tranche, amounting to THB10.0 billion, will be used to finance green infrastructure, the Mass Rail Transit's Orange (East) Project. The second tranche, amounting to THB20.0 billion, will be used to finance measures to combat the adverse effects of COVID-19, including public health measures, support for small- and medium-sized enterprises, and local public infrastructure development with social and environmental benefits.

Securities and Exchange Commission and Thai Bond Market Association Launch Environment, Social, and Governance Bond Hub

On 21 October, the Securities and Exchange Commission and the Thai Bond Market Association jointly launched an environment, social, and governance (ESG) information platform to support investors and issuers of ESG bonds by making information publicly available. The ESG bond information hub was created by the Thai Bond Market Association from a platform developed by Luxembourg Green Exchange.

Viet Nam

Yield Movements

The yields of local currency (LCY) government securities in Viet Nam fell across the length of the curve between 31 August and 30 October (**Figure 1**). Yields on bonds with 1-year and 2-year maturities dropped 14 basis points (bps) and 10 bps, respectively, while yields on bonds with tenors from 3 years to 15 years had larger declines ranging from 31 bps to 50 bps, with 7-year bonds having the largest drop. The yield spread between the 2-year and 10-year tenors narrowed from 240 bps to 217 bps during the review period.

As elsewhere in the region, a low-interest-rate environment and abundant liquidity in the financial system, as a result of the State Bank of Vietnam's (SBV) accommodative monetary policy stance, and easing inflation drove the downward movement of the yield curve. Good volume participation was observed in bond auctions as investors continued to pick government bonds as a safe investment. Smaller yield declines for bonds with shorter maturities reflected investor interest in this portion of the curve, given the uncertainties brought about by the coronavirus disease (COVID-19) pandemic.

The SBV reduced the refinancing interest rate by 50 bps to 4.00%, effective 1 October, to sustain the domestic economic recovery. It was the third time in 2020 that the central bank had lowered the benchmark interest rate, resulting in a total rate cut of 200 bps, as part of its effort to prop up the economy amid the COVID-19 pandemic.

Weak inflationary pressures remained to keep yields floored. Consumer price inflation sustained its downtrend in October to 2.5% year-on-year (y-o-y) from 3.0% y-o-y in September, despite aggressive monetary easing by the SBV. Transport largely pulled down the inflation rate as prices declined 13.5% y-o-y. Meanwhile, the price of food and catering services increased 9.5% y-o-y. Inflation for the first 10 months of the year averaged 3.7% y-o-y, and the General Statistics Office of Viet Nam expects it to remain within the government's target of below 4.0% y-o-y for full-year 2020.

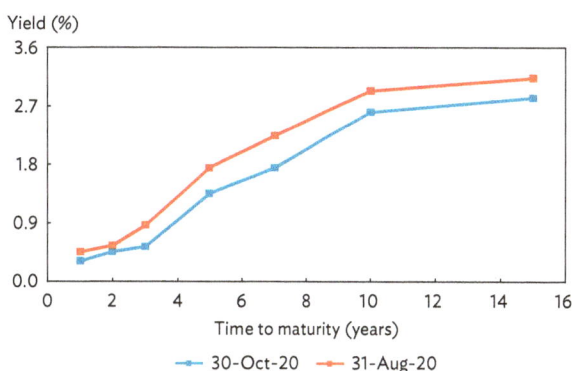

Figure 1: Viet Nam's Benchmark Yield Curve— Local Currency Government Bonds

Source: Based on data from Bloomberg LP.

Viet Nam's economic expansion gained momentum in the third quarter (Q3) of 2020 on growth of 2.6% y-o-y, up from revised growth of 0.4% y-o-y in the second quarter (Q2); however, it is the slowest pace of Q3 growth recorded since 2011. The growth was largely supported by the gradual resumption of business operations as the COVID-19 pandemic, including its partial resurgence during the quarter, was successfully contained.

The Vietnamese dong's exchange rate was stable from 1 July through 30 October, with movement in the range of VND23,165 to VND23,206 to USD1. The stability of the dong was supported by the weakness of the United States dollar and the economy's high trade surplus, which allowed the SBV to build its foreign exchange reserves and manage the exchange rate.

Size and Composition

Viet Nam's LCY bond market grew 11.6% quarter-on-quarter (q-o-q) in Q3 2020, recovering strongly from a decline of 1.4% q-o-q in the preceding quarter (**Table 1**). Total bonds outstanding registered VND1,514.3 trillion (USD65.3 billion) at the end of September, supported by the government and corporate bond market segments, which both expanded during the quarter. On an annual basis, growth in LCY bonds outstanding accelerated to 17.0% y-o-y from 9.8% y-o-y in Q2 2020. The LCY bond market comprised 83.8% government bonds and 16.2% corporate bonds at the end of September.

Table 1: Size and Composition of the Local Currency Bond Market in Viet Nam

	Outstanding Amount (billion)						Growth Rate (%)			
	Q3 2019		Q2 2020		Q3 2020		Q3 2019		Q3 2020	
	VND	USD	VND	USD	VND	USD	q-o-q	y-o-y	q-o-q	y-o-y
Total	1,293,992	56	1,356,398	58	1,514,275	65	4.7	3.1	11.6	17.0
Government	1,186,748	51	1,162,754	50	1,268,599	55	5.2	2.9	9.1	6.9
Treasury Bonds	955,061	41	1,019,096	44	1,128,861	49	2.5	6.5	10.8	18.2
Central Bank Bills	71,997	3	0	0	0	0	118.2	(4.0)	–	(100.0)
Government-Guaranteed and Municipal Bonds	159,690	7	143,658	6	139,738	6	(1.7)	(11.9)	(2.7)	(12.5)
Corporate	107,244	5	193,644	8	245,677	11	(0.7)	5.1	26.9	129.1

( ) = negative, – = not applicable, q-o-q = quarter-on-quarter, Q2 = second quarter, Q3 = third quarter, USD = United States dollar, VND = Vietnamese dong, y-o-y = year-on-year.
Notes:
1. Bloomberg LP end-of-period local currency–USD rates are used.
2. Growth rates are calculated from local currency base and do not include currency effects.
Sources: Bloomberg LP and Vietnam Bond Market Association.

Government bonds. The size of the government bond market grew 9.1% q-o-q in Q3 2020 to VND1,268.6 trillion, after declining 7.8% q-o-q in Q2 2020. The expansion was driven by Treasury bonds, which grew 10.8% q-o-q, or double the growth rate in Q2 2020, on the back of increased issuance from the State Treasury. There were no outstanding central bank bills at the end of Q3 2020 as the SBV continued to support liquidity in the market. Government-guaranteed and municipal bonds outstanding posted a decline in Q3 2020, albeit at a slower pace of 2.7% q-o-q compared with 6.1% q-o-q in Q2 2020. On an annual basis, total government debt outstanding grew 6.9% y-o-y in Q3 2020.

Issuance of government bonds in Q3 2020 totaled VND116.9 trillion, more than doubling the amount issued in Q2 2020. The State Treasury had a higher bond offering volume as it continued to raise funds for the government's COVID-19 pandemic response. Auctions were met favorably by investors as safe assets like government bonds remained attractive amid lingering uncertainty.

Corporate bonds. Corporate bonds outstanding continued to increase in Q3 2020, reaching VND245.7 trillion, on growth of 26.9% q-o-q and 129.1% y-o-y. While the corporate bond market grew, issuance activity in Q3 2020 was rather meek. Debt sales by corporates amounted to VND67 trillion, down from VND83 billion in Q2 2020. The decline is attributed to the government's Decree No. 81/2020/ND-CP, which

raises the standards for corporate bond issuance in the market. The bulk of the issuance was seen in August as firms took advantage of the time before the regulation came into effect on 1 September. In September, debt sales from the corporate sector dropped sharply by about 70% from August.

The combined bonds outstanding of the top 30 issuers in the corporate market amounted to VND189.4 trillion, or 77.1% of the total debt stock in the corporate segment (**Table 2**). Nearly half of the outstanding bonds, totaling VND93.7 trillion, were from the banking sector, followed by property firms with VND47.5 trillion, or 25.1% of the total. The Bank for Investment and Development of Vietnam, Vinhomes, Masan Group, Vietnam International Commercial Joint Stock Bank, and Ho Chi Minh City Development Joint Stock Commercial Bank had the largest amounts of bonds outstanding with over VND10 trillion each.

Banking and property firms remained the largest issuers in Q3 2020, as their combined debt sales comprised almost 75% of the total corporate issuances during the quarter. Notable issuances listed in **Table 3** were largely from banks and comprised of medium-term tenors. HSBC's (Viet Nam) VND600 billion issuance was the first debt sale of a foreign commercial bank in the local market. Proceeds will be used in the bank's operations and as a channel to diversify its funding sources to accelerate its business growth in Viet Nam.

Table 2: Top 30 Issuers of Local Currency Corporate Bonds in Viet Nam

	Issuers	Outstanding Amount		State-Owned	Listed Company	Type of Industry
		LCY Bonds (VND billion)	LCY Bonds (USD billion)			
1.	Bank for Investment and Development of Vietnam	20,350	0.88	Yes	Yes	Banking
2.	Vinhomes	16,390	0.71	Yes	Yes	Property
3.	Masan Group	13,500	0.58	Yes	Yes	Diversified Operations
4.	Vietnam International Commercial Joint Stock Bank	10,503	0.45	Yes	Yes	Banking
5.	Ho Chi Minh City Development Joint Stock Commercial Bank	10,248	0.44	Yes	Yes	Banking
6.	Vietnam Prosperity Joint Stock Commercial Bank	9,150	0.39	Yes	Yes	Banking
7.	Lien Viet Post Joint Stock Commercial Bank	9,100	0.39	Yes	Yes	Banking
8.	Vietnam Joint Stock Commercial Bank for Industry and Trade	8,850	0.38	Yes	Yes	Banking
9.	Asia Commercial Joint Stock Bank	8,300	0.36	Yes	Yes	Banking
10.	Saigon Glory Company Limited	8,000	0.35	No	No	Property
11.	Sovico Group Joint Stock Company	7,550	0.33	Yes	Yes	Diversified Operations
12.	Vingroup	7,000	0.30	Yes	Yes	Property
13.	Vinpearl	6,000	0.26	No	No	Hotel Operator
14.	Ho Chi Minh City Infrastructure Investment Joint Stock Company	4,690	0.20	Yes	Yes	Construction
15.	Bac A Commercial Joint Stock Bank	4,640	0.20	Yes	Yes	Banking
16.	Nui Phao Mining and Processing Co., Ltd.	4,310	0.19	No	No	Mining
17.	NoVa Real Estate Investment Corporation JSC	4,207	0.18	Yes	Yes	Property
18.	Orient Commercial Joint Stock Bank	3,635	0.16	No	No	Banking
19.	Sun Ha Long Co., Ltd.	3,500	0.15	No	No	Property
20.	Vietnam Technological and Commercial Joint Stock Bank	3,000	0.13	No	No	Banking
21.	Vietnam Maritime Commercial Joint Stock Bank	2,999	0.13	Yes	Yes	Banking
22	TNL Investment and Leasing Joint Stock Company	2,926	0.13	No	No	Property
23.	Tien Phong Commercial Joint Stock Bank	2,911	0.13	Yes	Yes	Banking
24.	Phu Long Real Estate Joint Stock Company	2,800	0.12	No	No	Property
25.	Binh Hai Golf Investment and Development Joint Stock Company	2,745	0.12	No	No	Leisure
26.	Phu My Hung Corporation	2,640	0.11	No	No	Property
27.	Masan Resources	2,500	0.11	No	No	Manufacturing
28.	Hoan My Medical	2,330	0.10	No	No	Healthcare Services
29.	Refrigeration Electrical	2,318	0.10	Yes	Yes	Manufacturing
30.	Vincommerce General Trading Service Joint Stock Company	2,300	0.10	No	No	Retail Trading
	Total Top 30 LCY Corporate Issuers	**189,391**	**8.17**			
	Total LCY Corporate Bonds	**245,677**	**10.60**			
	Top 30 as % of Total LCY Corporate Bonds	**77.1%**	**77.1%**			

LCY = local currency, USD = United States dollar, VND = Vietnamese dong.
Notes:
1. Data as of 30 September 2020.
2. State-owned firms are defined as those in which the government has more than a 50% ownership stake.
Sources: *AsianBondsOnline* calculations based on Bloomberg LP and Vietnam Bond Market Association data.

Table 3: Notable Local Currency Corporate Bond Issuances in the Third Quarter of 2020

Corporate Issuers	Coupon Rate (%)	Issued Amount (VND billion)	Corporate Issuers	Coupon Rate (%)	Issued Amount (VND billion)
HSBC (Viet Nam) Bank Limited			Saigon Glory Company Limited		
3-year bond	5.80	600	3-year bond	Floating	1,000
Vietnam International Commercial Joint Stock Bank			5-year bond	–	1,000
3-year bond	–	1,500	5-year bond	–	1,000
3-year bond	–	1,500	5-year bond	–	1,000
3-year bond	–	1,400	5-year bond	–	1,000
3-year bond	–	1,000	5-year bond	–	1,000
Lien Viet Post Joint Stock Commercial Bank			Bank for Investment and Development of Vietnam		
3-year bond	5.80	1,000	7-year bond	–	1,500
3-year bond	5.80	1,000			
3-year bond	5.80	1,000			
3-year bond	–	1,000			

– = not available, VND = Vietnamese dong.
Sources: Bloomberg LP and Vietnam Bond Market Association.

Investor Profile

Banks were the major holders of LCY government bonds at the end of September, accounting for 44.8% of total government debt (**Figure 2**). This share was 0.8 percentage points higher than in September 2019. Pension funds were the second-largest holders with a 43.9% share, up from 43.1% a year earlier. The shares

of the remaining investor groups saw marginal declines between September 2019 and September 2020. Foreign investors held only 0.6% of government securities at the end of September 2020, which was the smallest foreign holdings share among all emerging East Asian economies. Mutual funds had the smallest holdings share in Viet Nam's LCY government bond market at the end of September at 0.01%, down from 0.14% a year earlier.

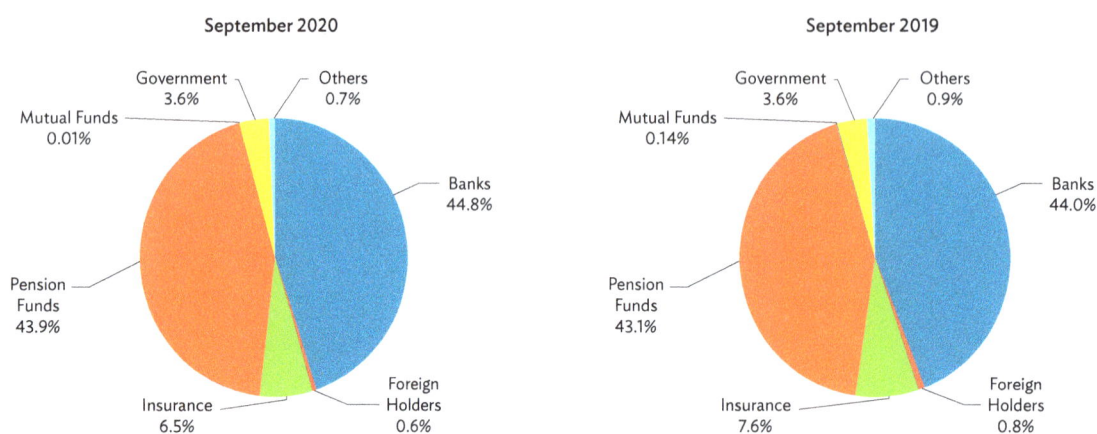

Figure 2: Local Currency Government Bonds Investor Profile

September 2020

Government 3.6%
Others 0.7%
Mutual Funds 0.01%
Banks 44.8%
Pension Funds 43.9%
Insurance 6.5%
Foreign Holders 0.6%

September 2019

Government 3.6%
Others 0.9%
Mutual Funds 0.14%
Banks 44.0%
Pension Funds 43.1%
Insurance 7.6%
Foreign Holders 0.8%

Source: Viet Nam Ministry of Finance.

Policy, Institutional, and Regulatory Developments

Ministry of Finance Issues Guidance on Bond Issuance Information Disclosure

On 14 August, the Ministry of Finance issued Circular No. 77/2020/TT-BTC to provide guidance on its existing decrees, Decree No. 81/2020/ND-CP and Decree No. 163/2018/ND-CP, on the provision of bond issuance information in the domestic market. In particular, the circular guides the (i) information disclosure regime of bond issuers; (ii) information disclosure on the corporate bond website; and (iii) reporting regime of the stock exchange, corporate bond issuance consulting organizations, and bond depository organizations.[11]

---

[11] The Ministry of Finance guides the issuance of corporate bonds. See https://english.luatvietnam.vn/circular-no-77-2020-tt-btc-dated-august-14-2020-of-the-ministry-of-finance-on-guiding-a-number-of-provisions-of-the-governments-decree-no-81-2020-189347-Doc1.html.

www.ingramcontent.com/pod-product-compliance
Lightning Source LLC
Chambersburg PA
CBHW042035220326
41599CB00045BA/7471